T H E N

WILLIAM GOLDING

THE NOVELS OF

WILLIAM GOLDING

Second Edition

S. J. BOYD

Lecturer in English
University of St Andrews

HARVESTER
WHEATSHEAF

New York London Toronto Sydney Tokyo Singapore

First published 1988 by
The Harvester Press Ltd
This second edition published 1990 by
Harvester Wheatsheaf
66 Wood Lane End, Hemel Hempstead
Hertfordshire HP2 4RG
A division of
Simon & Schuster International Group

© S. J. Boyd, 1988, 1990

Typeset in 11/12 pt Sabon
by Inforum Typesetting, Portsmouth

Printed and bound in Great Britain by
Billing and Sons Limited, Worcester

British Library Cataloguing in Publication Data

Boyd, Stephen, *1957–*
  The novels of William Golding.
  2nd ed
  I. Title
  823.914

ISBN 0–7450–0825–9

1 2 3 4 5 94 93 92 91 90

For Susie

·CONTENTS·

Preface to the First Edition   ix
Preface to the Second Edition   xii
Acknowledgements   xiii
A Note on the Texts   xiv

Chapter 1   The Nature of the Beast: *Lord of the Flies*   1

Chapter 2   Innocence and Experience: *The Inheritors*   24

Chapter 3   The Dark Centre: *Pincher Martin*   46

Chapter 4   Responsibilities: *Free Fall*   63

Chapter 5   Divine Tragi-Comedy: *The Spire*   83

Chapter 6   The Flat Earth Society: *The Pyramid*   106

Chapter 7   Chiaroscuro: *Darkness Visible*   125

Chapter 8   Dark Tropics: *Rites of Passage*   154

Chapter 9   Saltwater Soap: *Close Quarters* and
                    Fire Down Below   178

Chapter 10   Eschatological: *The Paper Men*   199

Notes   215
Bibliography   222
Index   227

·PREFACE·TO·THE·
·FIRST·EDITION·

The origins of this book lie in my experience of reading *Darkness Visible* and *Rites of Passage*. A novelist whom I had been inclined to think a spent force appeared reborn in two works of extraordinary power and fascination. It seemed an event worthy of critical attention and I wanted to write out my own thoughts and feelings about the novels, also to explore and perhaps resolve my own puzzlement at certain aspects of them. The book grew from there and the chapters on those novels remain, to some extent, the heart of the matter. I re-read the earlier novels with renewed enthusiasm, however, and decided to start work on a full-length study of Golding's fiction.

This book is aimed at any reader of the novels of William Golding. I offer my interpretations of these novels in the hope that they will prove interesting, stimulating and perhaps illuminating to anyone who reads Golding, whether for pleasure or under compulsion. These essays present those things which I thought it necessary or worthwhile to say about Golding's fiction. The novels ask us to think about certain moral, social and religious issues: my interpretations inevitably reflect my own views on these matters. I make no apology for this, since I believe that critics are perpetually moralists and that it is best to be honest and acknowledge this. I have no doubt that some readers will disagree with the interpretations offered here, perhaps find some of them bizarre or outrageous. So be it. If these readers return to the works of Golding fired up with determination to show how misguided I am, I shall be very pleased.

I was determined to go my own way in this book, to write
what I thought and felt, to be myself creative. To this end I
treated the existing critical literature on Golding in a rather
cavalier fashion. I read those works which were widely available and some others, but my reading was by no means
exhaustive. In defence of this I can say only that I wanted to
avoid clogging the flow of my own writing with a crippling
awareness of everything everyone else has said: this approach
was for me a psychological necessity. I can only hope that the
originality of this book comes from the fact that it is *my*
reading of Golding and that its justification is found in its
chapters and not in its preface or bibliography. With regard
to the critics cited in my bibliography my method was to try
to ignore what they had said when I was setting down my
own thoughts and then return to them with a view to insert-
ing some kind of acknowledgement where there were obvious
overlaps. I hope that I have treated everyone fairly, but two
cases require special mention here. The expositions of Golding's plots, structures and themes offered in Mark Kinkead-
Weekes and Ian Gregor's *William Golding: A Critical Study*
are so compelling that it was difficult to avoid covering the
same sort of ground at times. I can only crave their indulgence and hope that I have succeeded in getting out from
under their admirable study. While I was in the process of
writing, Don Crompton's work *A View from the Spire* was
published. This admirable book, which concentrates on the
later Golding novels, does have significant overlaps with my
own work and I have endeavoured to acknowledge these.
There are significant differences also.

The organisation of the book is straightforward. Each novel,
with the exception of the two novels which complete the *Rites
of Passage* trilogy, is given its own chapter and each chapter
constitutes a self-contained essay which could be read to some
purpose in isolation from the rest of the book. That is not to
say that the individual chapters are unconnected by themes
which run throughout the book: they are so connected, but
this will become clear in the reading of the chapters themselves
and does not require further discussion here.

My thanks are due to the Department of English at St
Andrews for financial help in the preparation of this book; to

my colleagues Michael Alexander and Neil Rhodes, who read chapters and commented in ways both helpful and encouraging, who have been, indeed, friends in need in all sorts of ways; to my typist Mrs Angel Black, whose patience with my endless delaying and tinkering was much appreciated, as was her skill; to my editors at Harvester, especially Sue Roe, for similar patience and forbearance. My greatest debt of thanks is paid in the dedication: my wife kept me going through a thousand crises of confidence in my ability to write. Without her faith and love this book would not exist. I hope that it is worthy of its subject and of her.

S.J. Boyd
Crail, Fife

·PREFACE·TO·THE· ·SECOND·EDITION·

I have added to the original text a chapter dealing with Golding's most recent novels, *Close Quarters* and *Fire Down Below*, which bring to a conclusion the *Rites of Passage* trilogy.

I should like to thank Sylvia Halley for her help in preparing the typescript and my editor at Harvester Wheatsheaf, Jackie Jones, for her encouragement, help and kindness.

S.J.B.
December, 1989

·ACKNOWLEDGEMENTS·

The author gratefully acknowledges permission to reprint extracts from the works of William Golding.

Reprinted by permission of Faber and Faber Ltd.:

Excerpts from *Darkness Visible, The Inheritors, The Paper Men, The Pyramid, Close Quarters, Free Fall, The Hot Gates, Lord of the Flies, A Moving Target, Pincher Martin, Rites of Passage, The Spire* and *Fire Down Below* by William Golding. Excerpt from *North* by Seamus Heaney.

Reprinted by permission of Farrar, Straus and Giroux, Inc.:

Excerpts from *Close Quarters* by William Golding. Copyright © 1987 by William Golding. Excerpts from *Darkness Visible* by William Golding. Copyright © 1982 by William Golding. Excerpts from *The Paper Men* by William Golding. Copyright © 1984 by William Golding. Excerpts from *Rites of Passage* by William Golding. Copyright © 1980 by William Golding. Excerpts from *A Moving Target* by William Golding. Copyright © 1982 by William Golding.

Reprinted by permission of Harcourt Brace Jovanovich, Inc.:

Excerpts from *Free Fall, The Hot Gates, The Inheritors, Pincher Martin, The Pyramid, The Spire*, copyright 1955, 1956, 1959, 1964, 1965, 1966, 1967 by William Golding: renewed 1984 by William Gerald Golding.

Reprinted by permission of The Putnam Publishing Group:

Excerpts from *Lord of the Flies* by William Gerald Golding. Copyright © 1954 by William Gerald Golding.

·A·NOTE·ON·THE·TEXTS·

Page-references in the text to the works of William Golding are to the Faber editions, generally the popular and widely available paperback editions. Titles are abbreviated according to the following scheme.

LF	*Lord of the Flies* (1958 edition)
IH	*The Inheritors* (1961 edition)
PH	*Pincher Martin* (1956 edition)
FF	*Free Fall* (1961 edition)
SP	*The Spire* (1965 edition)
PY	*The Pyramid* (1969 edition)
SG	*The Scorpion God* (1973 edition)
DV	*Darkness Visible* (1979 edition)
RP	*Rites of Passage* (1980 edition)
PM	*The Paper Men* (1984 edition)
CQ	*Close Quarters* (1987 edition)
FDB	*Fire Down Below* (1989 edition)
HG	*The Hot Gates* (1965 edition)
MT	*A Moving Target* (1982 edition)

· 1 ·

THE NATURE OF THE BEAST
·LORD OF THE FLIES (1954)·

And Jesus called a little child unto him, and set him in the midst
of them,
And said, Verily I say unto you, Except ye be converted,
and become as little children, ye shall not enter the kingdom of
heaven.

St Matthew 18. 2–3

As flies to wanton boys, are we to th' Gods;
They kill us for their sport.

King Lear

Lord of the Flies has become almost compulsory reading for
those enduring the painful process of growing up. One has
the impression that *everyone* has studied and been impressed
by this novel in the latter part of schooldays. It is not
difficult to give reasons for this popularity: its protagonists
are schoolboys, drawn with a remarkable awareness of the
realities of the playground world, its unhappy theme 'the
end of innocence' (LF p. 223). The loss of innocence for
which Ralph weeps at the novel's close is not, however,
a matter of transformation from childish goodness to adolescent depravity, is not a growing into wickedness. It is
rather the coming of an awareness of darkness, of the evil in
man's heart that was present in the children all along. To
acknowledge the presence of this darkness in one's own
heart is a necessary but devastating condition of growing
up, of becoming fully and yet flawedly human.

Golding's concern is to present us with a vision of human
nature and also of the nature of the world which we inhabit

through the experiences of a group of children cast away on a desert island. The two quotations above represent polar opposites of optimism and pessimism with regard to the nature of children (which we might take to be representative of essential or pristine human nature) and the nature of the universe in which we live. In the words of Jesus in St Matthew childhood is presented as a state of innocent goodness, a state which may be regarded as the kingdom of heaven on earth. As adults, fallen from this happy state, we may well hanker after a return to it and the possibility of such a conversion is held out to us in this passage by Jesus. There is room for optimism about human nature then, and there is considerable cause for optimism about the nature of our universe, for the speaker has traditionally been regarded as the creator and loving ruler of the universe, come down to earth to suffer and die so that we might be redeemed or rescued from our wickedness and restored to the original purity and happiness we see in children and remember, or think we remember, as our experience of childhood.

The tragic universe of *King Lear* is at its darkest in Gloucester's terrible words: we live in a cruel world which can only be governed by malevolent demons whose delight is to torture us; if we wish to see an image of these dark gods or devils we need look no further than children or our own childhood, need only examine 'the ghastly and ferocious play of children' (FF p. 150), where we see how little devils torture and kill insects for fun, playing god with flies. From within and without we are beset by evil, 'All dark and comfortless'.[1] *King Lear* is not everywhere so hopeless in outlook but it does seem to force us to accept that nature provides no evidence of beneficent paternal care for us and that in our human nature there is a terrifying propensity towards wanton cruelty which is evident even in children.

It scarcely needs to be said that the picture of childhood, of human nature, and of the nature of things, which emerges from *Lord of the Flies* is closer to that expressed by Gloucester than that in the passage from St Matthew, though in Golding's novel and in Shakespeare's play, as we shall see, some redeeming features are suggested which have much to do with the life of Jesus. The bleakness of the novel's vision has been eloquently encapsulated by Golding himself in a sentence which recalls the despair of Lear in its bludgeoning repetitions: 'The theme of *Lord of the Flies* is grief, sheer grief, grief, grief, grief' (MT p. 163). The grief which Golding expresses and powerfully elicits in the novel is grief at man's very nature and the nature of his world, grief that the boys, and we too, are 'suffering from the terrible disease of being human' (HG p. 87). Shakespeare's tragedy and Golding's novel both present us with a fearless and savage close-up of human nature, a stripping-down of man to what essentially he is. The effect is appalling and humiliating: we are, in Golding's words, a species that 'produces evil as a bee produces honey' (HG p. 87). As naturally as the humble insect produces sweetness, we produce the wickedness and violence which sour our lives. In *King Lear* the burgeoning evil of Lear's daughters and Cornwall finds extravagant expression in the blinding of Gloucester: in *Lord of the Flies* Jack and his gang with comparable callousness steal Piggy's glasses: '"That's them," said Piggy. "They blinded me. See? That's Jack Merridew."' (p. 187). Piggy has been blinded and his complaint indicates that this action of blinding was an expression of the essential nature of Jack Merridew and friends. The blinded Piggy has been granted insight. The darkness of Gloucester's experience leads to his despairing suicide attempt at the Dover cliff. He is, however, saved from death and despair by the loving care of his son: his heart, we are told, 'Twixt two extremes of passion, joy and grief,/Burst smilingly.'[2] Piggy too is led to the rocks at the island's tip—'"Is it safe? Ain't there a cliff? I can hear the sea."' (p. 193)[3]—but for him there is to be no comforting or consolation. The deathsman Roger wantonly knocks him over the cliff and his head bursts messily: 'His head opened and stuff came out and turned red' (p. 200). Piggy's experiences seem to recall those of Gloucester, but his end is more terrible. The crass prose that records his end matches the callousness of Cornwall in transforming Gloucester's eye to 'vile jelly',[4] which is exactly what Roger has done to Piggy's brain.

The evil of Cornwall and Roger transforms humanity into

vileness. The compulsive viciousness of Roger might well provoke us to adapt Lear's exclamation concerning Cornwall's accomplice Regan: 'let them anatomise *Roger*; See what breeds about *his* heart.'[5] Roger's evil is inexplicable, in part because he is a shadowy character about whose background we know almost nothing, but Golding is determined, as was Shakespeare in *King Lear*, that we should confront the Roger or Regan within us, '"the reason why it's no go"' (LF p. 158). He has himself spoken of this characteristic determination to anatomise 'the darkness of man's heart' (LF p. 223):

> What man *is*, whatever man is under the eye of heaven, that I burn to know and that—I do not say this lightly—I would endure knowing. The themes closest to my purpose, to my imagination have stemmed from that preoccupation, have been of such a sort that they might move me a little nearer that knowledge. They have been themes of man at an extremity, man tested like a building material, taken into the laboratory and used to destruction; man isolated, man obsessed, man drowning in a literal sea or in the sea of his own ignorance. (MT p. 199)

In *King Lear* the trial by ordeal of human nature takes place on the inhospitable landscapes of a storm-blasted Dark Age Britain; the laboratory in which Golding's schoolboys are used to destruction is the apparently more idyllic world of a tropical island. As we shall see, there are many islands, both real and metaphorical, in Golding's fiction: in *The Inheritors* the new people (i.e. we humans) are first discovered on an island and it is characteristic of them that they are isolated from each other in a way that the Neanderthal people are not; in *Pincher Martin* the central figure finds himself utterly alone and forgotten on a mere rock in the ocean; to Jocelyn in *The Spire* the great ship of the cathedral seems to offer insulation against the evils of the dangerous sea of the world; Wilfred Barclay in *The Paper Men*, despite his credit-card-given ability to travel anywhere at anytime, is isolated from his fellow man and from his own past by his alcoholism and his spiritual crisis occurs on one of the Lipari islands. Isolation is everywhere.

In confining the boys to a small island in *Lord of the Flies* Golding is using a long-established literary method of examining human nature and human polity in microcosm, as in Shakespeare's *The Tempest* or Thomas More's *Utopia*, in Defoe's *Robinson Crusoe* or Swift's *Gulliver's Travels*. These books provide a literary background to the boys' adventures on their island. In such works we find a tendency to present human nature at an extreme: in More's utopian fantasy and in Aldous Huxley's *Island* we see human nature and society at their best. In his introduction to the former Paul Turner remarks:

> The old-fashioned method of getting to Utopia is to be wrecked on an island, preferably in the South Seas, and Huxley's last essay in the genre [*Island*] is to this extent traditional. So is William Golding's *Lord of the Flies* ..., which may, I think, be considered a rather individual form of Dystopia.[6]

The South-Sea island setting suggests everyone's fantasy of lotus-eating escape or refuge from troubles and cares. But for Golding this is the sheerest fantasy: there is no escape from the agony of being human, no possibility of erecting utopian political systems where all will go well. Man's inescapable depravity makes sure 'it's no go' on Golding's island just as it does on the various islands visited by Gulliver in Swift's excoriating examination of the realities of the human condition.

Robinson Crusoe belongs in part to the world of sheer escapist boys' adventure stories which also contribute to the literary background of *Lord of the Flies*. The castaway boys themselves are reminded of *Treasure Island, Swallows and Amazons* and Ballantyne's *The Coral Island*: prompted by the mention of these works, Ralph assures them: ' "It's a good island. Until the grown-ups come to fetch us we'll have fun" ' (p. 38). The boys imagine that they can have fun not only in swimming and hunting but in imposing decent, civilised English values upon their island, as Ralph, Jack and Peterkin Gay had done on Ballantyne's island and as Robinson Crusoe had done by converting his island to an English gentleman's country estate. But their efforts in this direction are a dismal failure. Things fall apart, or 'break up' in Ralph's phrase (p. 89), into atavism, savagery and bloodshed.[7] The boys regress to what might be called a state of nature, but the experience of this is not of an earthly paradise but a hell on earth.

Golding is determined to disabuse us not only of naive optimism about the nature of children but also of the sort of faith in the goodness of all things natural described by Aldous Huxley in his essay 'Wordsworth in the Tropics':

> In the neighbourhood of latitude fifty north, and for the last hundred years or thereabouts, it has been an axiom that Nature is divine and morally uplifting ... To commune with the fields and waters, the woodlands and the hills, is to commune, according to our modern and northern ideas, with the visible manifestations of the 'Wisdom and Spirit of the Universe'.[8]

Such an optimistically Romantic view of the beneficence of the natural world is not confirmed by the visit of Golding's northern boys to the tropics. Golding has remarked of Huxley: 'I owe his writings much myself, I've had much enjoyment and some profit from them—in particular, release from a certain starry-eyed optimism' (MT p. 181). Huxley proposes in 'Wordsworth in the Tropics' that a visit to the tropics would cure any Wordsworthian of his faith in nature. The tropical island of Golding's novel, which seems to the boys paradisial in its unspoilt wildness, proves to be an inferno, a sort of pressure-cooker heated by a vertical sun which aims blows at the boys' heads in its violent intensity, which fires 'down invisible arrows' (p. 67) like an angry or malevolent god. It is just as Huxley describes: 'Nature, under a vertical sun, and nourished by the equatorial rains, is not at all like that chaste, mild deity who presides over ... the prettiness, the cosy sublimities of the Lake District.'[9] Prettiness and cosiness are important elements in Ralph's memories of natural wildness back in England, but Ralph's experience of nature is hopelessly limited and naively comfortable: 'But the remembered cottage on the moors (where "wildness" was ponies, or the snowy moor seen through a window past a copper-kettle ...) is utterly out of reach and unreal; a flimsy dream.'[10] The reality of nature in the tropics is profoundly sinister and threatening. From their experience of this natural environment the boys derive a sort of religion, but their theology is a demonology, their lord or god is a devil. In this they merely conform to the ways of indigenous jungle-dwellers as described by Huxley: 'The sparse inhabitants of the equatorial forest are all believers in devils.'[11]

The boys' physical surroundings are terrifying and encourage in them a belief in a malevolent god; the boys' own physical condition also is not improved by their stay on the island. Their return to a state of nature, insofar as it implies a lack of toilet facilities and wholesome food, has a very unpleasant effect on them. The 'littluns' in particular quickly become 'filthily dirty' and are affected by 'a sort of chronic diarrhoea' (p. 64). One of Ralph's problems as chief is that the boys fail to abide by the rule that only one clutch of tide-washed rocks should be used as a lavatory: 'Now people seem to use anywhere. Even near the shelters and the platform' (p. 87). Man seems to be a natural producer of filth as well as evil, and the one is a symbol of the other. Of this aspect of the boys' plight Leighton Hodson writes: 'the odour of decay pervades life from the diarrhoea of the littluns ... to Jack hunting the pigs by following their steaming droppings; the association of the Beast, evil, excrement, and blood is both overpowering and purposeful.'[12] This physical degeneration is matched by an upsurge of cruelty, bloodlust and violent rapacity as the Beast, which they take to be a spirit or monster outside of themselves, rises up within them and takes over their lives. Overwhelmed by the horrors that have entered their lives, littluns will isolate themselves to wail, gibber and howl at the misery of their condition. Were Lemuel Gulliver to land on the island, he would instantly recognise that he had returned to a land inhabited by Yahoos.

In Book Four of *Gulliver's Travels* the hero lands on an island dominated by the Houyhnhnms, a nation of intelligent horses whose name signifies '*the perfection of nature*'[13] and whose generally very admirable way of life is lived in accordance with nature or, more precisely, with reason, which they take to be the supreme gift of nature. The peacefulness, cleanliness and reasonableness of their lives make their society an ideal towards which we humans might well wish to aspire. The humanoids of the island, however, have no such aspirations for they are, as Gulliver is mortified to discover, a disgusting race of passionate, violent, irrational, greedy and lustful creatures: these are the Yahoos. Their appearance and presence are rendered particularly offensive by 'their strange disposition to nastiness and dirt'.[14] They wallow in their filth, symbolising their propensity towards evil and the dark, perverse psychological forces which make them incapable of behaving reasonably or organising and maintaining a rational society. Swift thus gives us a painfully simple sketch of the human condition: we aspire to reasonableness and would like to construct and live in rational societies, but the nature of the beast within us, the innate propensity towards violence, cruelty and selfish and self-destructive wickedness, makes such optimistic schemes incapable of realisation. Swift rubs our noses mercilessly in our own filth. John S. Whitley has suggested that 'the Hebrew word "Beelzebub", though it means literally "Lord of flies", might be rendered in English as "lord of dung", that substance around which flies gather'.[15]

The Yahoo-nature inevitably brings about misery. It is not surprising that even the insensitive, brute Yahoo is driven at times 'to retire into a corner, to lie down and howl, and groan' like the half-demented littluns on Golding's island.[16] The transformation from schoolboys to Yahoos forces upon us the bitter truth of *Gulliver's Travels*, that we are creatures whose nature renders us incapable of maintaining rational, equable and peaceful societies such as that of the Houyhnhnms. Ralph and Piggy attempt to create such a society on the island. Piggy in particular has great faith in Houyhnhnm-like values, believing in government by persuasion, deciding issues by debate, above all in reason itself. For Piggy the world is reasonable: at one point he seems amusingly reminiscent of René Descartes: 'I been in bed so much I done some thinking' (p. 102). But Piggy's rationalism is as inadequate as his grammar. His reason cannot control the boys, his belief that science can explain everything makes him unable to comprehend the reality of the Beast, his democracy crumbles before the onslaught of the atavistic Jack, intuitively adept at using the Beast for his own ends. Piggy may be the brains of the outfit but the Beast in Roger, by smashing his skull, makes those brains useless. Piggy's body is quickly swallowed by the sea, which in the chapter 'Beast from Water' was suggested as a possible dwelling-place of the Beast. When Ralph first inspects the spot where Piggy dies, the sea's motion is described by the narrator as 'like the breathing of some stupendous creature', 'the sleeping leviathan' (p. 115). The sea is an insuperable obstacle to the boys' escape and one is tempted to detect a reference to Thomas Hobbes' *Leviathan*, wherein the life of man in a state of nature is characterised as being just as Yahoo-like as the boys discover it to be. It is, in Hobbes' famous phrase, 'solitary, poor, nasty, brutish, and short'.[17] *Lord of the Flies* insists that this is a truth, a grim reality, from which there is no escaping.[18]

The boys' return to nature, then, is not an idyll but a nightmare. It is tempting to see their misadventures as a regression from the Houyhnhnm-like values of our civilisation into the caveman world of the Yahoos. This is Piggy's view of the matter: if only they would behave like grown-ups all would be well; if only a ship carrying grown-ups would spot them they would be saved. This is a comforting view of the book since it seems to put us grown-ups on the side of the angels and endorse the view that our civilisation is rational, peaceful and even salvific. To take such a view is, however, to fall into what Golding suggests is one of the most dangerous of errors: to attempt to deny that the Beast is in us and to limit its existence or operancy to some other time, place, or group of people. Such a reading of the book is untenable. Piggy's faith in grown-ups is shown to be sadly misplaced. Here, displaying typical common sense and faith in the known laws of science, he tries to reassure Ralph: '"The trouble is: Are there ghosts, Piggy? Or beasts?" "Course there aren't." "Why not?" "'Cos things wouldn't make sense. Houses an' streets, an'—TV—they wouldn't work."' (p. 101). But the horrible truth is that man's organised civilisation and sophisticated systems of communication have failed to work, have been destroyed or have broken down in the nightmare of nuclear war.

Civilised values *are* endorsed by the novel—it is heartbreaking to see how friendship and fair-play are replaced by hostility and tyranny—but our actual civilisations are condemned as barbaric and monstrously destructive. Ralph and Jack, chiefs of rival gangs or tribes on the island, are 'two continents of experience and feeling, unable to communicate' (p. 60). They are thus an image of the tragic state of world politics in the mid-twentieth century and of the seemingly eternal need of civilisations to find rivals with whom to quarrel, the perennial argy-bargy of history which Joyce in *Finnegans Wake* sums up as 'wills gen wonts'.[19] When the Lord of the Flies himself, the focus of evil in the book, condescends to speak, it is with the voice of a schoolmaster, whose duty it is to instil the values of our civilisation into developing children. That these values are, to say the least, defective is made very clear by an outburst from Piggy just before his fatal fall: ' "Which is better—to be a pack of painted niggers like you are, or to be sensible like Ralph is?" ' (p. 199). Piggy *in extremis* lets slip that being 'sensible' may well involve adhering to tribal values and loyalties, regarding whomever is judged to be alien with contempt or loathing and treating them accordingly. But then Piggy knows what it is to be an alien, because he is made an outsider in part by his being physically unattractive but also as a function of that prominent feature of English civilisation, the class system.

Golding's later novels, especially *The Pyramid* and *Rites of Passage*, make abundantly clear his deep bitterness at and hatred of the evils of class. But even in this first novel, even on a desert island, this Golding obsession is in evidence. The novelist Ian McEwan has written of his adolescent reading of *Lord of the Flies*: 'As far as I was concerned, Golding's island was a thinly disguised boarding school.'[20] At one point the narrator seems to claim that class is of no importance in the alienation and persecution of Piggy: 'There had grown up tacitly among the biguns the opinion that Piggy was an outsider, not only by accent, which did not matter, but by fat, and ass-mar, and specs, and a certain disinclination for manual labour' (p. 70). But the narrator implicitly admits that accent, a mark of class, *is* an alienating factor ['not only'] and actually mocks, in passing, Piggy's way of speaking. The view that class does not matter in Piggy's misfortunes is scarcely borne out by events. From the very outset Piggy is isolated, stranded on an island within the island, by being lower-class. On the book's first page Ralph's 'automatic gesture' of pulling up his socks makes 'the jungle seem for a moment like the Home Counties' (p. 7) and unfortunately Piggy just does not fit into the middle-class ambience implied thereby. Ralph is a good-natured boy, but in this initial scene he seems very reluctant to accept the friendship of the one companion he has so far found on the desert island: ' "What's your name?" "Ralph." The fat boy waited to be asked his name in turn but this proffer of acquaintance was not made' (p. 9). One has the uncomfortable feeling throughout this scene that Ralph has been conditioned to be unfriendly towards boys who talk like Piggy. Ralph is not slow to inform Piggy that his father is officer-class, but in response to the crucial question ' "What's your father?" ' Piggy can produce only the poignant reply: ' "My dad's dead," he said quickly, "and my mum—" ' (p. 14). The unseemly haste with which Piggy announces that his father is dead suggests a reluctance to reveal his place in life and the blank after the mention of his mum speaks unhappy volumes. Piggy has failed to produce satisfactory credentials. It is at least partly for this reason that Piggy is doomed to become 'the centre of social derision so that everyone felt cheerful and normal' (p. 164). Life seems cheery and normal provided there are the likes of Piggy around to be looked down on and derided.

Piggy's main persecutor is Jack, who from the first evinces contempt and hatred for Piggy, whom he seems to regard as an upstart. Jack's education appears to have instilled in him the belief that it is his right to give commands, to rule: ' "I ought to be chief," said Jack with simple arrogance, "because I'm chapter chorister and head boy" ' (p. 23). His privileged choir-school background has no doubt taught him much about the necessity of hierarchies, including the notion that head boy from such a school ought to be top man anywhere. Whitley comments: 'This assumption of leadership, bred by being part of a civilised élite, is maintained when he becomes a member of a primitive élite. The perfect prefect becomes the perfect savage.'[21] It would be difficult to imagine anything more suggestive of innocence than a group of cathedral choristers, but we first see the choir as 'something dark' in the haze, as 'the darkness' (p. 20): the choir is from the outset associated with evil. A cathedral choir connotes also a certain English middle-class cosiness, a social world 'assured of certain certainties'. Here is Jack at his most 'sensible', declaring some important certainties: '"... We've got to have rules and obey them. After all, we're not savages. We're English; and the English are best at everything"' (p. 47). Golding has written that such cosy English chauvinism was something he particularly wished to attack in Lord of the Flies:

> One of our faults is to believe that evil is somewhere else and inherent in another nation. My book was to say: you think that now the war is over and an evil thing destroyed, you are safe because you are naturally kind and decent. (HG p. 89).

The English error is to objectify and externalise the Devil, as the boys do, and this self-congratulatory attitude is dangerous because it allows the Devil to go to work, evils to be perpetrated, under cover of the belief that English people are good, decent and fair-minded. The classic jingoistic expression of such an attitude might be: 'Come off it! This is England! Something like that couldn't happen in England!' Whoever adopts such an attitude blinds himself to the evils which do exist in English life, prominent among which is the class system. Golding tries to expose the truth about this evil by translating it from England to a desert island: Jack's hatred of and violence towards Piggy is the raw naked truth about English social organisation. Classist attitudes not only ensure that under the motto of fair play a very unfair deal is given to most members of a society, they also bring about the reification of people. Thus a person may be treated not on the merits of his complex make-up as an individual but merely in accordance with his being recognised as a component of a mass class-group. The final blow dealt to Piggy transforms the extraordinary and miraculous complexity and beauty of his brain, the seat of consciousness and what makes him the particular and unique person he is, into mere 'stuff'.

The treatment meted out to Piggy makes the view that the boys' story is one of simple regression and degeneration a very difficult one to hold. But such a view is completely undermined by the adventitious arrival of the naval officer at the close. Every reader of the novel must have felt profoundly relieved when Ralph stumbles upon this white-clad saviour. All will be well now that the authority and values of civilisation have returned in the figure of this man, who might indeed almost be Ralph's father come to rescue them all. Critics have long recognised, however, that this warrior who stops the boys' war is anything but snowy-white morally. Virginia Tiger sums the matter up thus:

> There is no essential difference between the island world and the adult one and it is the burden of the fable's structure ... to make it clear that the children's experiment on the island has its constant counterpart in the world outside.[22]

The officer is a warrior, a killer, and he is right to regard the boys' war as mere 'Fun and games', because compared to the massive death-dealing of the nuclear war in which he is involved it is very small-scale indeed. But the officer is nonetheless dismayed that a group of British boys should have degenerated into savages, should have failed 'to put up a better show than that'. Show, the keeping-up of a good appearance, is what this ultra-English officer is all about. The white uniform, the gold buttons, the 'trim cruiser' of the closing sentence are all signs of the officer's belief in orderliness, cleanliness, and of his and his nation's belief in their moral rectitude. The officer's first, and apparently kindly, thought about Ralph is that he 'needed a bath, a hair-cut, a nose-wipe and a good deal of ointment' (pp. 221–3). An advocate, no doubt, of the stiff upper lip, he is embarrassed by Ralph's heartbroken tears. The officer is no saviour at all. He is doubly guilty: of being a warrior on behalf of one of the world's two tribes and of sanitising the killing, the vast butchery, involved in such conflicts, of cleaning and dressing it up so that it seems sane and sensible. He is able to masquerade as a peacemaker, a bringer of light to the savages. He dislikes the blood and filth of the boys, he is embarrassed by Ralph's open display of emotion, but the blood and filth are the true symbols of war or warriors and Ralph's grief is an absolutely human and appropriate reaction to the revelations of the island.

The officer comes ashore like Lemuel Gulliver to discover a pack of Yahoos. Like Gulliver, he finds them distasteful. But Gulliver gradually comes to see that supposedly civilised humans are worse than Yahoos because they have all the filth and vices of the Yahoos, though they hide these under clothes and a clothing of pride in their own supposed moral rectitude, and have abused what reason they have by employing it in the invention of new ways in which to express their viciousness. It is a uniform-wearing Yahoo that has come to rescue the boys: there is even more reason than Ralph thinks to weep for 'the darkness of man's heart'. The phrase describes succinctly enough the central concern of Swift's writing but asks us specifically to think of Conrad. The overall picture of man's nature which emerges from *Lord of the Flies* is indeed similar to the one we find in *Heart of Darkness*. A return to the state of nature, an escape into primitivism such as that attempted by Conrad's Kurtz, leads only to the unleashing of brutality, greed for power, and sadism in the most naked and brutal forms, to the horror of orgiastic and murderous midnight dances and human heads stuck on poles. But the forces of civilisation, clad in shiny white to proclaim their moral excellence, are mere whited sepulchres, every bit as guilty as Kurtz and lacking even the honesty of open savagery. Both books offer this grim view of the human condition: there is no rescue, no way out, and the ending of *Lord of the Flies* is anything but happy. To regard it as such would be to ignore the prophetic voice of Simon.

In *The Coral Island* Ballantyne's three young adventurers had the names Ralph, Jack and Peterkin Gay. In Golding's novel we find a Ralph and a Jack but two boys seem to share the derivation of their names from the third member of Ballantyne's jolly-sounding trio: Piggy's name is an approximate and unpleasant contraction of Peterkin Gay, but the name Simon, we know from the Bible, was the original name of St Peter, so Simon has a claim too. Simon and Piggy are, indeed, alike in sharing a role in *Lord of the Flies*, the role of outsider, scapegoat and victim of murder. Though the two are alike in this way, however, they are otherwise very different from one another and represent, indeed, two mighty opposites, two warring ways of looking at the world, which occur again and again in Golding's fiction. Faith in science and rationality, with a marked disbelief in anything supernatural, is characteristic of Piggy. Simon, by contrast, is intuitive, introspective, other-worldly; his central insight is gained in a vision or trance; Simon represents and has access to a dimension of experience it is proper to call religious. Piggy cannot understand Simon and thinks him mad.

This conflict between the contrasting world-views of science or ratiocination and religious or visionary experience, between worldly commonsense and other-worldly mysticism, is dramatised time and again by Golding: in the figures of Nick Shales and Rowena Pringle in *Free Fall*, in Roger Mason and Jocelin in *The Spire* and in Edmund Talbot and Robert James Colley in *Rites of Passage*. This conflict is clearly of great importance to Golding and it would be true to say that, though he is at pains to be fair to and make a strong case for the scientific or worldly side, his sympathies ultimately lie with the Simons, Jocelins and Colleys. In an essay on education he writes: 'it cannot be said often enough or loudly enough that "Science" is not the most important thing' (HG p. 129). This too has a Swiftian air to it. In Book Three of *Gulliver's Travels* Swift demonstrates powerfully that the analytical intellect, alone and unaided by any higher insight, cannot even begin to offer solutions to the problems of being human. Golding has expressed admiration for Copernicus, whom he characterises as a man devoted to the quest for scientific truth but who nonetheless bears the signs of an inclination towards mysticism.[23] In *Lord of the Flies* Golding's bias in this matter is perhaps most clearly seen in the differing degrees of respect accorded to Piggy and Simon by the narrative in their deaths. Leighton Hodson describes this succinctly:

> Golding manages to deepen his meaning of what the boys' attitudes represent by providing them, in their common ends, with descriptions that correspond to the limited practical intelligence in the case of Piggy—dry in tone—and the intuitive depth of understanding in the case of Simon—eloquent and transfiguring.[24]

The limitations of Piggy's practical intelligence are, indeed, particularly highlighted by comparison with Simon. Piggy's clever and sensible schemes fail to bring about the rescue the boys desperately need; his rational approach is unable to sway the mass of boys in debate or preserve order among them; above all, he rejects Simon's suggestion that the Beast is a reality within the boys themselves. Piggy rightly condemns the notion that there is an external Beast that lives in the forest or the sea, but under great pressure comes to believe that Jack is the Beast or Devil, failing to see that this too is an externalisation, an avoidance of his own guilt. Piggy's scientific views dictate that there is no Devil in the world, but if he must allow that there is evil he is determined to 'believe that evil is somewhere else' and in someone else. He is himself, however, involved in the murder of Simon, for all his predictable attempts to exculpate himself and explain the killing away as an accident.

Simon is murdered by the boys when he emerges from the forest into the frenzy of their dance, supposedly a charm against the Beast. Their defence against an imagined external Beast allows the beast within them to gain absolute control and transform them into murderers. Simon had come to tell them that the creature on the mountain they thought to be the Beast was merely the horribly damaged body of a pilot, evidence of the effects of the beast within us in the world of warring adults. Simon had come to bring them confirmation of the truth that he had proposed earlier and for which he had been shouted down and derided, the dark truth that the Beast is within them, each and every one of them. The reception he is given proves his point once and for all. The truth which Simon offers is a grim one, but Simon himself is not at all a grim or dark figure. He is affectionate, gentle and kind, helping the littluns to find good fruit, for example, but also a loner, a 'queer' boy who isolates himself in a forest glade reminiscent of a church and goes into reveries. It is small wonder that the other boys regard this youthful mystic as mad or 'batty', a fool. We must take Simon a great deal more seriously. The traditional role of the prophet is to awaken men to the truth of their own sinfulness: this Simon does, and he also succeeds in fulfilling the popular view of the prophet's task by foretelling the future. He tells Ralph that he will get home safely and his voice comes back to Ralph just before he is in fact rescued. The boys are living in the dangerous error of believing that the Beast is an evil creature at the mountain-top, so Simon the prophet goes to the mountain to discover the truth. On his way he finds a forest glade desecrated by a sow's head on a stick, a gift for the Beast. Simon falls into a fit, or hallucination, or vision, in which the Lord of the Flies, the Devil, speaks to him through the foul mouthpiece of the head and tells him that he is '"part of you"'. He warns Simon to go back and fall into line or the boys will 'do' him (pp. 157–9). Simon defies the threat, climbs the mountain, finds the parachutist and descends to the beach to be slaughtered.

Amidst the bloody chaos of the storm and the demonic dance we are told that 'Simon was crying out something about a dead man on a hill' (p. 168) as he is being assaulted. He refers of course to the parachutist, but we must hear also a suggestion of the death of Christ on Calvary and realise that, in killing the true prophet who had come down to reveal to them their real nature, their sinfulness, and thus set them on the road towards saving themselves, the boys are re-enacting the crucifixion of Jesus Christ. Simon's life and death are an imitation of Christ. In ascending the mountain and returning to the boys, despite the warnings of the Lord of the Flies about what will happen to him, he takes up and shares the Cross like his namesake from Cyrene: '"Simon. He helps"', as Ralph earlier remarks (p. 59). His self-sacrifice does not, however, achieve an instant conversion of the boys to goodness. Nor did Christ's with regard to mankind as a whole. Piggy blames him for bringing his death on himself: '"Coming in the dark—he had no business crawling like that out of the dark. He was batty. He asked for it"' (p. 173). He walked right into his own death, so he must have been mad, a fool, a Simple Simon.

To suggest that a person or character is a fool would normally undermine any confidence we might have that the person or character concerned had wisdom to offer us. Here this is not the case. Simon imitates the folly of that supreme fool Christ, who allowed himself to be crucified and whose teachings must seem foolish to the worldly-wise. Christ the holy fool is admirably described by Erasmus in the *Praise of Folly*:

> Christ too, though he is the wisdom of the Father, was made something of a fool himself in order to help the folly of mankind, when he assumed the nature of man and was seen in man's form ... Nor did he wish them to be redeemed in any other way save by the folly of the cross and through his simple, ignorant apostles, to whom he unfailingly preached folly.[25]

To those in darkness, to those under the sway of the Lord of This World who is the Lord of the Flies, the wisdom of Christ must indeed appear utter folly. Simon is the first of Golding's holy fools, characters who in many respects are holy or Christ-like and yet, almost by that very token, are ill-fitted for survival in the world of fallen man: two clear examples, whom we shall examine later, are Nathaniel in *Pincher Martin* and Matty in *Darkness Visible*. The holy or prophetic fool dares to challenge the cosy but delusive beliefs of the majority and so must be laughed at, dismissed, driven out or slaughtered by that majority.

The message or wisdom which Simon offers—that the Beast is in us, that we must acknowledge the 'thing of darkness' as our own—is disturbing and negative. He does not appear to bring the good news of redemption or salvation. But his life and death offer some hope in the book's pervasive gloom inasmuch that among all the boys, so to say, at least one good man has been found, one person who is capable of imitating Christ's redemptive example. At the mountain top he is able to free the dead pilot, according to Golding a symbol of the nightmare of human history (HG p. 90), and allow him to fly off, just as Christ, from an orthodox point of view, changed the nature of history by freeing man from the bondage of sin, offering the *possibility* of escape from the endless backsliding and tribulations of human and personal history. There is, furthermore, the 'eloquent and transfiguring' description of the sea's disposal of Simon's body. Simon is carried 'towards the open sea' by the tide, attended by 'strange, moonbeam-bodied creatures with fiery eyes' who weave a halo of brightness around his head (pp. 169–70). These beautiful and seemingly magical little entities we have seen before in broad daylight:

> There were creatures that lived in this last fling of the sea, tiny transparencies that came questing in with the water over the hot, dry sand ... Perhaps food had appeared where the last incursion there had been none; bird droppings, insects perhaps, any of the strewn detritus of landward life. Like a myriad of tiny teeth in a saw, the transparencies came scavenging on the beach. (p. 66)

But there is no beauty or magic or mystery. The creatures are simply the lowest point in the ugly world of living nature, vile scavengers as coldly destructive as sawteeth. It is Simon's self-sacrifice that transforms them to beauty, goes some way towards redeeming the world of nature and re-establishing its beauty and harmony.

What light there is in the book does, indeed, seem to be concentrated around Simon. There are, however, certain other aspects of the novel which may be seem as mitigating the generally excoriating treatment of human nature. 'I am by nature an optimist' Golding has remarked 'but a defective logic—or a logic which I sometimes hope desperately is defective—makes a pessimist of me' (HG p. 126). Though this is rather a dark utterance, it does make explicit that tension between optimism and pessimism, between hope and despair, which is characteristic of Golding's fiction. Indeed, from *The Spire* onwards it seems appropriate to characterise his fiction as broadly tragi-comic. Though comedy is a grotesquely inappropriate term to apply to

Lord of the Flies, the outlook of the novel is not entirely pessimistic.

There is first the essential decency of Ralph, 'the fair boy' whose eyes proclaim 'no devil' and who tries to keep the other boys' eyes on the values of civilisation, tries 'to keep a clean flag of flame flying' (pp. 8, 11, 45). Though the book suggests that we should be sceptical about such an ocular proclamation and about 'Rally round the flag, boys!' sentiments, there is no doubt that Ralph does strive earnestly and sincerely to be fair and decent. There is also the goodness, the sheer vitality, of the twins Samneric, Ralph's most loyal supporters. Not only are they kind, loyal and generous, but their apparent blending into one another makes them seem representative of average everyday man, the 'man on the Clapham omnibus'. Moreover, we sympathise strongly with this group and abominate Jack and Roger. It seems that we can at least say of ourselves that we would *like to be* decent, fair and good. Our sympathy or even identification with Ralph is also very effective in intensifying the 'thriller' aspect of the novel: in the final chapter we have the very unpleasant feeling that *we* are being hunted by Jack and Roger. How we fear and loathe their extravagant and insatiable evil! There is some comfort to be taken in this, but we must remember that Ralph and Samneric, those models of decency, were involved in the murder of Simon and, like another decent man caught up in evil, they try to wash the innocent martyr's blood from their hands by their denial that they were present at the killing. Further, Samneric are coerced into joining Jack's tribe and in Ralph's final interview with them they have become, for all the kindness towards Ralph which they cannot quite fight down, guardians of a régime where all rules have disappeared except the rule of sadism. Samneric, like other ordinary men before them, have been transformed into concentration camp guards, porters at the Gate of Hell. Ralph's conversation with them at the Castle Rock is perhaps the most heartrending section of the entire book and there is every reason why that should be so.

Just as we sympathise with the nature of Ralph, Samneric and, indeed, even Piggy, so too we are attracted to the democratic system they create. The gentle, exhortatory paternalism of Ralph and Piggy seems both fair and sensible as a way of organising government. It is manifestly preferable to Jack's absolutist tyranny. Again our hearts seem to be in roughly the right place. And yet Jack's system has greater attraction for the boys, who desert Ralph's tribe in droves. In fairness to Jack it must be said that in certain important respects his reign of terror is a more effective form of government than Ralph's. He gives the boys meat and he is able to keep them in order, to put a stop to quarrels, fragmentation and even sheer laziness in a way which Ralph was not: '"See? They do what I want"' (p. 198), he pointedly remarks to Ralph, who has just become a one-man tribe. Once again the Leviathan raises its head: Hobbes' pessimistic view is that human fractiousness requires to be quelled and governed by an absolute monarch. *Lord of the Flies* could never be said to advocate Jack's monarchy however, since though in some ways it clearly 'works' it also panders to and is an expression of the worst aspects of human nature; greed, cruelty and lust. Like a vicious Roman emperor he provides food and entertainment for his mob, entertainment taking the form of beating littluns, murderous ritual dances, and the obscene and rapacious violence of the hunt: 'The sow collapsed under them and they were heavy and fulfilled upon her' (p. 149). Jack intuitively knows all about the lowest and vilest elements in our nature and how to exploit them:

> Simon became inarticulate in his effort to express mankind's essential illness. Inspiration came to him.
> "What's the dirtiest thing there is?"
> As an answer Jack dropped into the uncomprehending silence that followed it the crude expressive syllable. Release was like an orgasm ... The hunters were screaming with delight. (p. 97)

Obscenity can be delightful: that is a symptom of our essential illness.

Jack may be successful in satisfying in the short-term certain basic and base human cravings, but his system offers no hope of rescue. Behaviour such as Jack indulges in and encourages seems to preclude redemption or salvation, even if salvation is no more than the imitation of Christ in *this* world which we see in Simon, whom Jack and his minions kill. The symbol of his terrible régime is the stick sharpened at both ends, the support of the totem Lord of the Flies, a weapon which seems to suggest that its killing-power may rebound against the user. It is a symbol which reminds us of the self-defeating nature of the weaponry deployed for nuclear war by those who build fortresses and bunkers against imagined external threats and evils in the world outside the island. The spear is sharpened by Roger and, for all that has been said about Jack's ability to command obedience, it is not difficult to imagine this sinister figure returning Jack's violent means to power upon him and completing his bloody and Macbeth-like career by sticking *his* head on a pole.

At the close the naval officer arrives to find the island paradise lost and burning, the scene 'with dreadful faces thronged and fiery arms'.[27] Coming from his warship, he is a veritable *deus ex machina* descending from the 'above' of the adult world to set things right and rescue the erring children. Despite the sinister associations of the naval officer, might he not still be seen as the caring and omnipotent God who finally intervenes in man's world to stop the course of the bloody history of fallen man and restore peace forever? Such a view would offer a glimmer of religious light at the end of the tunnel. Such a reading is perhaps allowable, but there is evidence in the novel which counts against it and which ought not to be ignored. There seems to be no haven for the boys to be rescued *to*. We are told much earlier that 'Roger's arm was conditioned by a civilisation that knew nothing of him and was in ruins' (p. 67). When the boys first spot a passing ship on the horizon the narrative speaks of 'the smoke of home' beckoning to them (p. 73), a touching phrase since it suggests both the homeliness the boys long for and the smoking ruins that are all that remain of home. Having been terrified by the dead parachutist that seems to be the Beast, Ralph complains that the 'thing squats by the fire as though it didn't want us to be rescued' (p. 138), and the corpse is, indeed, a sign that the civilisation which might rescue them has been destroyed by war. The naval officer has played a part in that war. Perhaps there is no comfort in seeing him as an image of God, because the image is of a flawed and irresponsible god, perhaps like the forgetful or lazy creator of the island's reef: 'The coral was scribbled in the sea as though a giant had bent down to reproduce the shape of the island in a flowing, chalk line but tired before he had finished' (p. 31). The creator's signature does not inspire confidence in his character and evidences from nature generally, as we have seen, from the 'enmity' of the sun, that traditional symbol of the Godhead, downwards, are not such as to encourage faith in absolute beneficence (pp. 13–15). The weight of evidence would seem to indicate that any creator must be a cruel selfish wielder of power, that the gods are indeed as Gloucester described them, swatting men like flies with an ease the naval officer might well envy or might even match, a source of no comfort or hope. What desperate hope the book offers is simply the example of Simon, the acknow- ledgement of our guilt, of the 'thing of darkness' within us, and the overcoming of this guilt and darkness in generous, if unsuccessful, self-sacrifice for the sake of others. Simon, like Cordelia, allows a little room for hope, but the book's abiding impression remains like that of *King Lear*: 'grief, sheer grief, grief, grief, grief'.

·2·

INNOCENCE AND EXPERIENCE
·THE INHERITORS (1955)·

Blessed are the meek: for they shall inherit the earth.
St Matthew 5.5

We, life's pride and cared-for crown,
Have lost that cheer and charm of earth's past prime:
Our make and making break, are breaking, down
To man's last dust, drain fast towards man's first slime.
G.M. Hopkins, 'The Sea and the Skylark'

In these words from the Sermon on the Mount Jesus offers
an apocalyptic vision of the triumph of innocence on earth.
If such a splendid state of affairs is to be achieved, a very
radical change in the way of the world will have to take
place, for experience teaches us that it is generally the self-
seeking, the aggressive, the ambitious and the ruthless who
gain and hold earthly power and property. Hopkins, with
the voice of experience, describes an apocalypse which is
less inspiring but more probable: the values of the late-
Victorian world, with the emphasis on manufacture and
making money, create a war-like society in which there are
only those who make it and those who are broken in the
process, a society whose brutality and turmoil are powerfully conveyed to us in the buckling of Hopkins' syntax. The
world may appear to be making progress by 'getting and
spending' but the reality is a regression from Christian
values to the law of the jungle, to the ruthless and greedy
thirst for domination which lifted man out of the slime and
gave him possession of the world and power over all other
creatures.

The Inheritors deals with a moment of pre-history at which a group of primitive men, our ancestors, makes progress and gains ground by ruthlessly exterminating the remnants of a race of humanoids, their (and our) cousins and rivals, the Neanderthal Men. In the epigraph to the novel Golding quotes H. G. Wells, who describes the Neanderthals as ugly and vicious monsters and quotes an authority to suggest that they 'may be the germ of the ogre in folklore'. To Golding such a view is another example of refusing to see that the ogre or devil is in us, the tragic mistake of the boys in *Lord of the Flies*.

> And when I re-read it as an adult I came across his picture of Neanderthal man, our immediate predecessors, as being those gross brutal creatures who were possibly the basis of the mythological bad man, whatever he may be, the ogre. I thought to myself that this is just absurd. What we're doing is external-izing our own inside.[1]

The Inheritors offers an alternative view of pre-history in which the meek and gentle Neanderthals, the innocents, are slaughtered by our ancestors, who possess the monstrous and brutal qualities of ruthlessness and self-interest which will enable them to survive and progress. The price of such 'progress' is, indeed, terrible. These aspirant humans may give us the world as an inheritance, but we inherit also the regrettable qualities which made 'getting on' possible.

The novel's overall vision is reminiscent of Blake's *Songs of Innocence and Experience*, where the loving and generous eyes of innocence see love and generous care everywhere in the world, create an earthly paradise, and where this very predisposition renders the innocent easy prey to the cynical, selfish and exploitative world of experience. In no poem is this aspect of Blake's vision better encapsulated than 'The Clod and the Pebble': '"Love seeketh not Itself to please,/ Nor for itself hath any care,/But for another gives its ease,/ And builds a Heaven in Hell's despair."'[2] So sings a 'Clod of Clay', expressing a conception of love at its highest, the love of which St Paul speaks so movingly.[3] But such a view of the nature of love is severely limited and dangerously naive. A clod is an idiot or simpleton and this particular innocent's fate is to be 'trampled' underfoot. The voice of experience regarding love is that of a pebble, evidently a hard-headed survivor: '"Love seeketh only Self to please,/To bind another to Its delight,/Joys in another's loss of ease,/ And builds a Hell in Heaven's despite."' This is a bitter and cynical view of love, but it must be conceded that human love does sometimes have these characteristics, an instance being the savage and greedy lovemaking of Tuami and Vivani observed by the innocent and incredulous Neanderthal man Lok in *The Inheritors* (pp. 174–7). Lok's loving nature is like the clod's and like the clod he is doomed to be trampled.

The novel begins in innocence, in the innocent perception of the world that is peculiar to 'the people', the Neanderthal tribe. The opening paragraph is all laughter and joyous play; as in *Lord of the Flies* figures emerge from a forest and these figures are again child-like, though their play does not have the sinister undertones of Ralph's enacted machine-gunning of Piggy. The people are in a number of ways like children: when Lok eats of the dead doe, an act for which he feels guilty since the people respect and wish to avoid harming anything that lives, he makes excuses and tells little fibs to himself and the world in general in an amusingly child-like way (p. 56). But the childlikeness of the people is without the propensity towards evil so evident in the human children of Golding's first novel. In the novel's opening pages we may well suspect that we are observing the childhood of our own race, but unfortunately this is far from being the case. When our own ancestors are encountered, they turn out to be anything but innocent: they are unhappy, quarrelsome, wracked by fears, and murderous. Lok, who knows no evil, completely fails to understand the darkness of the human heart. Here the new people fire a lethal arrow at him: 'He looked towards the island, saw the bushes move, then one of the twigs came twirling across the river and vanished beyond him in the forest. He had a confused idea that someone was trying to give him a present' (p. 111). This is a touching innocence such as human childhood could scarcely match. Lok fails to recognise aggression because he has none in him and the lack of that quality makes him vulnerable, in fact makes him doomed.

The flight of the arrow, which Lok failed to understand, is also difficult for us to understand because of Golding's highly stylised description. The style represents Golding's ambitious attempt to narrate the story from the point of view of the people. The style invites us to become one with the people, who know no evil and are more or less incapable of reasoning, enables us to glimpse the world through the eyes of innocence. The people may be very poor thinkers, but their senses are wonderfully acute and alive to their environment. They veritably think with their eyes and fingertips, with their noses and the myriad sensitive antennae of their hair. Their world consists of a dazzling input of sense impressions organised and sorted, if at all, not by reason but by the picture-making faculty of imagination. Golding's prose seeks to render their world with maximum fidelity and that makes the narrative at times very difficult to follow since the world of innocence is one that we have lost. The difficulty we experience with the style is a measure of our fallenness.

The prose style is not, however, merely a difficulty but a marvellous imaginative achievement. As we become weathered to it, as we unlearn the linguistic sophistication and abstraction which draw a veil between us and the world, we come to appreciate its remarkable sensitivity and felicity. The effect, in part, is suggested by Golding's own description of the prose of Gavin Maxwell: 'His prose ... is ... a fit vehicle for the individual nature of his seeing. Details are held and focused close to the eye in a way which is at once poetic and childlike—or perhaps the one because the other' (HG p. 104). The individual, innocent and child-like nature of the people's seeing makes them poetic, or, rather, Golding's efforts to capture the nature of that seeing allow the poet in him to come to the fore. Leighton Hodson writes of Golding that 'His writing ... aspires naturally to the condition of poetry'[4] and Golding has himself confessed to frustrated aspirations in that direction: 'You might say I write prose because I can't write poetry'[5] The stylistic *tour de force* of *The Inheritors* establishes him as a poet among novelists.

Lok thinks and feels through his whole body, from the top of his low brow to the toes of his 'clever' feet (p. 11): an emotional experience for Lok has a physical reality which conveys it to us with a concreteness and force which we associate with poetry. What we would regard as metaphor is for Lok a literal fact, the sheer raw material of experience. Here, investigating the trail of one of the new people (the 'other', the inexplicable alien), he feels for the first time a sense of being alienated from his own people:

> He was cut off and no longer one of the people; as though his communion with the other had changed him he was different from them and they could not see him. He had no words to formulate these thoughts but he felt his difference and invisibility as a cold wind that blew on his skin. (p. 78)

Golding finds the words that Lok cannot to embody the strangeness and intensity of his experience of the world. The language, though difficult for us because of its strangeness, is essentially simple and non-abstract (though 'communion' and 'formulate' above are clearly too advanced for Lok: our language *cannot* be absolutely faithful to Lok's experience just as we can never become what Lok is) and Golding is able to exploit this simplicity to convey or express experiences, especially emotional, with great directness and force, as in this poignant description of Fa's reaction to the disappearance of Ha: 'Astonished, Lok watched the water run out of her eyes. It lingered at the rim of her eye-hollows, then fell in great drops on her mouth and the new one' (p. 69). This reflects the child-like intensity of focus of the people but it is also as unselfconscious, as open, simple and intense as the grief it describes. In general, the primitive nature of the subject matter allows Golding to employ a primitivism of style that is refreshingly and unabashedly imbued with what one might call the poetry of nature, as when Lok's chilling unease about the new people temporarily evaporates: 'The feeling inside him had sunk away and disappeared like the frost when the sun finds it on a flat rock' (p. 163). That may be naive poetry, but Golding has a very good excuse for its naivety and for anyone acquainted with the self-consciousness and emotional indirectness or vapidity of so much twentieth-century poetry the experience of reading it is like a breath of fresh air.

Breaths of fresh air are, indeed, a subject of considerable interest to the people: Lok is an expert on the subject and his experience and knowledge of fresh air is highly complex, as he demonstrates in an attempt to identify a faint scent:

> He blew out air through his nose suddenly, then breathed in. Delicately he sampled this air, drawing a stream into his nostrils and allowing it to remain there till his blood had warmed it and the scent was accessible. He performed miracles of perception in the cavern of his nose. (p. 50)

The life of thought is alien to Lok, but how enviably intense for him is the life of sensations! The 'cavern of his nose' reminds us of his simian appearance and his troglodytic nature but its suggestion of cellarages reinforces the general impression that Lok is like a connoisseur of wines drawing out all the subtleties in the bouquet of some draught of vintage. The sensations of such sensitive noses and palates are notoriously difficult to put into words and Lok's 'miracles of perception', we are asked to believe, surpass anything that a human might achieve. The challenge Golding has set himself is to create miracles of description to match these intense and acute perceptions of the world. His skill and his successes are remarkable, as here where he makes meaningful to us Lok's olfactory world by reference to the visual: 'He flared his nostrils and immediately was rewarded with a whole mixture of smells, for the mist from the fall magnified any smell incredibly, as rain will deepen and distinguish the colours of a field of flowers' (p. 25). The illustration, appealing in itself, helps us towards sharing Lok's world by appealing to our experience. At other times we are required to make the effort ourselves to establish exactly what is going on from a prose steeped in the people's way of experiencing. Thus, when Lok and Fa converse in the icy gully their words echo and reverberate; they perceive this but have no *conception* of the nature of an echo, so the prose records not simply that there was an echo but their poetic apprehension of the effect in terms from their past perceptions: 'Their words had flown away from them like a flock of birds that circled and multiplied mysteriously' (p. 81).

This remarkable periphrasis for 'had echoed' derives much of its beauty from the acuteness of its observation of the living world. That the world is living, that it is animated by a life in which the people share, is the overwhelming impression given by the book's poetic, highly metaphorical prose, as Mark Kinkead-Weekes and Ian Gregor have observed.

> There is a peculiar colouring in the style; they see anthropo-morphically, investing their whole environment with humanity. The river sleeps or is awake, trees have ears, the island is a huge thigh, shin and foot, logs go away, everything is alive.[6]

But the people invest their environment not with humanity but with people-ness: it is in *Lord of the Flies* that we find a world invested with humanity and nature there, for the most part, is sinister, threatening, inimical. The world of the people is, on the face of it, much less idyllic than an island in the sun. It is a cold, hard and hungry place, where there are evil yellow hyenas and where it is sometimes necessary to tear the guts from a dead deer in order to survive. This is no Garden of Eden, yet the vision of the people transforms this harsh world to beauty and wonder, a true earthly paradise. Golding's prose shows us that the people instinct-ively 'see into the life of things',[7] are aware of 'the one Life within us and abroad'.[8] The phrases are from Wordsworth and Coleridge and describe that sense of the *livingness* of things for which their poetry characteristically strives. This sense involves a feeling of belonging, of being at home in and a part of the life of nature, a feeling that is a blessed relief from the habitual isolation and alienation from nature of modern man, and also a greatly heightened sensi-tivity to the minute particulars of the natural world. It is just such a dissolving of self into a greater whole and heightened sensitivity that the people experience in the overhang:

> One of the deep silences fell on them, that seemed so much more natural than speech, a timeless silence in which there were at first many minds in the overhang; and then perhaps no mind at all. So fully discounted was the roar of the water that the soft touch of the wind on the rocks became audible. Their ears as if endowed with separate life sorted the tangle of tiny sounds and accepted them, the sound of breathing, the sound of wet clay flaking and ashes falling in. (p. 34)

Such experience is restorative of the spiritual well-being of the people, their sense of belonging in the world of mother Oa, the life-giving female deity they venerate.

Golding's prose everywhere conveys the people's attunement to the livingness of things, their closeness to Oa and the beauty and wonder of her world. For Wordsworth and Coleridge (and, indeed, for their fellow Romantic poets, Blake, Shelley and Keats) such a felicitous state was alien to modern, civilised man, who had for the most part become, in the struggle to 'get on' and 'make good', blind to the sheer beauty of the world. Blake expresses the matter with admirable succinctness: 'The tree which moves some to tears of joy is in the Eyes of others only a Green thing that stands in the way.'[9] The living beauty of the tree is transformed to a mere dead object that seems to stand against man. The task and gift of the poet was to rouse man from this alienation, to restore his awareness of the glories all around: the classic formulation of the Romantic poets' aims in this regard is given by Coleridge in describing Wordsworth's intentions in *Lyrical Ballads*:

> ... to excite a feeling analogous to the supernatural, by awakening the mind's attention from the lethargy of custom, and directing it to the loveliness and the wonders of the world before us; an inexhaustible treasure, but for which, in consequence of the film of familiarity and selfish solicitude we have eyes, yet see not, ears that hear not, and hearts that neither feel nor understand.[10]

The art of *The Inheritors* belongs to this poetic tradition of re-awakening our faculty of wonder and showing us the world anew. Golding has remarked of his art in general: 'I don't simply describe something. I lead the reader round to discovering it anew'[11] And, still more generally and grandly: 'My epitaph must be "He wondered"' (MT p. 199).

The tradition, though without its pretensions to religious or spiritual awakening, seems still to be alive in contemporary poetry in the form of the so-called 'Martian Poets' or 'metaphor men', whose aim is to defamiliarise our world by presenting it through the prismatic medium of bold and often improbable metaphors. Thus, in the seminal poem 'A Martian Sends a Postcard Home', Craig Raine describes certain aspects of the world from the unfamiliar point of view of a visiting Martian: 'Mist is when the sky is tired of flight/and rests its soft machine on ground'.[12] This 'Martian' technique of defamiliarising seems to be anticipated in *The Inheritors*: 'They could see the shining river where it lay in the gap through the mountains and the vast stretches of fallen sky where the mountains dammed back the lake' (p. 47). 'Fallen sky' (presumably snow, but possibly mist) is beautiful and defamiliarising in itself, but also makes a contribution to the larger-scale pattern of the novel. It is a prolepsis, for the sky is, indeed, going to fall in on the people's heads when they make disastrous contact with our ancestors. Overall, Golding's style does seem to offer the sort of quasi-religious experience aimed at by the Romantics and this is in marked contrast to the mannered insignificance of the poetry of Raine and other contemporary 'Martians'. A certain twentieth-century pessimism can be seen, however, in the fact that the people are emphatically *not* our ancestors. When with the death of Lok the style adjusts itself to the nature of the new people, the vitality and strange beauty vanish, to be replaced by an idiom that is 'emptied, collapsed' like the new people themselves, expressing their experience of the world, which is depressingly familiar to us: 'The world with the boat moving so slowly at the centre was dark amid the light, was untidy, hopeless, dirty' (p. 225). Unfortunately, it is not difficult to recognise our ancestry.

The prose which embodies the new people has, however, gained a great deal in clarity. It is the style of a people who can think and reason with infinitely greater clarity than can the superseded people. It has also a certain cold detachment about it and, though the new people are inclined to frenzied emotion at times, as such it aptly expresses the detachment and distance of the new people from 'the life of things'. Their world is not a marvellous network of aliveness of which they are a part, but a series of obstacles to be overcome in their struggle to get on, to make good, to survive, to advance. Lok and his people are no more than a 'thing in the way' and so must be ruthlessly destroyed. The new people are, to that extent, worldly wise: clearly they are going to conquer the earth and we are going to inherit that conquest. The most poignant stylistic effect in the novel is achieved when Lok's death is described in the new, cold, detached prose: we have experienced the loving and lovable nature of Lok from the inside, as it were; but now he is simply 'the creature' (p. 220), an alien half-ape at a great distance from us, fumbling around to little purpose in the obscurity before lying down to die as the dawn of man breaks.

The people have a marked tendency to lie down and die. They are not equipped by nature for survival in this rough world. Ted Hughes calls them 'saintly defectives'.[13] Beside the smart, go-ahead new people they are not merely innocents but fools. They are much less intelligent than their rivals in terms of practical reason and their generous and trusting nature makes them easy prey, almost willing victims. As in Blake's *Songs of Innocence*, the innocent vision is an admirable thing in itself but makes the innocent extremely vulnerable to exploitation or aggression on the part of those whose nature is not free from evil. Ha runs to greet or embrace those who kill him. Perhaps it is appropriate to think of certain Polynesian tribes eagerly welcoming the civilised white men whose arrival spells doom for the culture of their islands, stretching back in innocent sameness through many generations. The people are fools in just this way; their good nature makes them defenceless. The biggest fool among them is the book's central character, Lok.

Lok is quite explicitly a fool. When first we see him he is clowning around and his role in the tribe is that of buffoon. He makes the others laugh and they are appreciative of that gift. As the novel progresses it becomes clear that his intelligence is far inferior to that of Fa, who shows some ability to reason and to think creatively, to progress mentally. He is slower to learn than Fa, his innocence harder to penetrate. That innocence is protected by sleep from witnessing the death of Liku and thus he fails to appreciate the outrage and horror which the enormities of the new people inspire in Fa. He continues to feel a deadly attraction towards them and to regard them with pity. His feeling for his enemies amounts almost to love. It is the attitude of the supreme fool.

Lok, like Simon before him, is a holy fool and a Christ-figure. He is the only male of the people to penetrate the mysteries of the matriarchal Oa-religion and he is left at his death with the corpse of the religion in the form of Liku's doll, the 'little Oa'. The cult of Oa requires respect for all the living creatures she created and stands in stark contrast to the religion of the new people in which a cruel god demands blood-sacrifices in order to be placated. Lok and Fa observe such a sacrifice from a 'dead tree', a phrase suggestive of the tree upon which the willing and innocent victim Christ was sacrificed. The resemblances to Christ are not confined solely to Lok but extend to others of the people: the fall is the cause of Fa's death on another dead tree; Liku is eaten as part of a religious rite of the new people. The innocent nature of the people is Christ-like, but it is Lok who is most clearly identified with that meek and willing victim who took the sins and sorrows of man upon himself. Here, left alone, he feels he has become the leader, the whole people, and that he has a wise new head that knows sad new truths:

> The new head knew that certain things were gone and done with like a wave of the sea. It knew that the misery must be embraced painfully as a man might hug thorns to him and it sought to comprehend the new people from whom all changes came. (p. 194)

Lok is willing to take the crown of thorns upon himself. He fails, however, to comprehend the new people and they seem equally incapable of understanding him or his kind.

The new people do not give themselves much of a chance to become acquainted with the nature of Lok or his people. They are aliens, thus a threat, thus evil, thus 'forest devils' (p. 224). They project their own darkness, their sins and sorrows, their own propensity towards evil, out onto 'the darkness under the trees' (p. 231), an unwise manoeuvre as we have seen in *Lord of the Flies*. These 'devils' must be destroyed or placated. The new people, terrified by the nocturnal raid of Lok and Fa which intended no harm to them, leave gifts for the devils and ultimately are prepared to sacrifice to them the child Tanakil. Lok and Fa have no desire for such blood-sacrifices. They set free the child and run towards the new people, bringing proof of their innocence. But the new people, in no state to understand, recover their own and repel them, fatally injuring Fa, who drifts back over the fall, and condemning Lok to a death of lonely agony. It is the end of the people. Their Christ-like qualities unfit them for survival in a world of Darwinian survival of the fittest. They are triumphantly innocent: they cannot get past the Fall. But this innocence makes them natural victims. They come with Tanakil offering freedom, but the new people are taking no risks. The new people are concerned merely to defend their own interest and get on in the world; in order to do so they are prepared to reject and crucify Christ. That would seem to be the high cost of gaining the whole world.

The new people gain the world by disinheriting the meek. They dispossess the people, wrench the land from them. Their whole attitude to the world and, indeed, to each other is inimical, violent and alienated. We discover them encamped on an island, guarding themselves with a natural moat against the world outside. Lok describes them later as 'a people of the fall' (p. 195) and so indeed they are, but their fallen state, their lack of innocence, makes them also island people, cursed with a bunker or laager mentality, cut off by mistrust, fear and aggression from nature and from one another. Among the new people *each* man is an island.

The new people have lost that sense of belonging in a living world of Mother Nature (Oa) and of belonging one to another in the extended self of the people. Lok tries to comfort Nil about Ha's disappearance with the 'other': '"They have changed words or shared a picture. Ha will tell us and will go after him." He looked round at them. "People understand each other." The people considered this and shook their heads in agreement' (pp. 71–2). But Lok's reassuring assertions are undermined by heavy irony. The people shake their heads to indicate agreement: our ancestors will not understand that. Nor will it be possible to exchange words, for the language of the new people is different to Lok's. Still less will they be able to 'share a picture' for the new people have not the people's gift of sharing ideas or images with one another, a mark of their extraordinary closeness, intimacy and unity. The minds of the people are open one to another, their consciousness is at times communal: they *understand* each other. The minds of the new people are closed to each other (just as their senses have lost the vital receptivity, the Oa-consciousness one might say, that the people possess) and they are distrustful and wary of one another. '"It is bad to be alone. It is very bad to be alone"' (p. 196), Lok remarks after his temporary loss of Fa: with the new people we see just how bad it can be.

The isolation of the new people breeds fear and aggression in them. Their attitude to nature is belligerent; they are hunters, repeatedly associated with wolves. Their personal relationships are still more violent and fraught. Lok and Fa observe the illicit love-making of Tuami and Vivani, but this is no communion of selves, rather an expression of violence and voracity: 'Their fierce and wolflike battle was ended. They had fought it seemed against each other, consumed each other rather than lain together so that there was blood on the woman's face and the man's shoulder' (p. 176). This attempt at overcoming the pain and loneliness of isolated selfhood seems to be at best a partial and temporary success, vitiated by its brutality and sordidness. The new people as a whole fare no better in their desperate attempts to escape themselves and put to sleep the pain of being human. They have already discovered the perennial escapist tactic of getting drunk, but this is no solution; indeed, as Lok and Fa discover when they are recovering from the effects of the firewater, it is self-defeating, serving only to increase pain and anxiety: 'The honey had not killed the misery but put it to sleep for a while so that now it was refreshed' (p. 208). Their ultimate recourse is a quasi-cannibal ritual or orgy in which the child of the people, Liku, is eaten. This too seems a failure to the new people, since the forest devils descend upon them in the night. These attempts are doomed and self-defeating because they *express* the new people's violence. Their teeth are like wolves', they are driven to consume and engorge the world around them and each other. But such voracity does not bring the spiritual peace they lack: it simply exacerbates their alienation. The novel ends with the new people alone on the waters of a vast lake with darkness all around. Tuami is painfully alone among his people, alone with scorpion thoughts of betrayal and murder.

It is instructive to compare this, the end of chapter twelve, with the close of the sixth chapter, describing Lok and Fa, the remnant of the people by their extinguished hearth:

> Then they were holding on to each other, breast against breast ... The two pressed themselves against each other, they clung, searching for a centre, they fell, still clinging face to face. The fire of their bodies lit, and they strained towards it. (p. 131)

The new people have put out the fire of their community, exposing them to the terrors of darkness and cold, but Lok and Fa have still a togetherness that can warm them and ease their pains and fears. The new people's technical ingenuity enables them to make bigger fires for themselves, but this serves to show their increased fear of the darkness. Their bonfires cannot keep the darkness at bay, because the threat, the evil, is not in the forest outside their encampment, not in the innocents they imagine to be devils, but in their own human natures, in the loneliness and darkness of their own hearts.

The new people are island people, but also people of the fall. When we encounter them they are already fallen, already lacking the innocence of the people, but their experiences at the fall in the river serve to increase their alienation, their *angst*-ridden attitude to the world. Both peoples are struggling up the stream of history, but Lok's people are unable to get past the fall. They are stuck, or locked, in innocence. The novel's first sentence describes Lok in terms of limitation: 'Lok was running as fast as he could.' Their determination to move upstream is also limited. They have struggled up simply to go down again: their movement is seasonal. Like all migratory tribes they see life as essentially unchanging. '"To-day is like yesterday and to-morrow"' (p. 46). In evolutionary terms they are just marking time. Survival, however, requires progress and in order to make progress the fall must be passed. The new people are examples of how to progress and survive. What is required is not simply an improvement in thinking and technology but the emergence and application of ruthless-ness and violence. The respect which Lok's people have for life prevents them from becoming hunters. They live by gathering, by finding whatever is lying around or comes to hand. That is a very risky way of life and means that they will always be controlled by chance and their environment. They cannot gain mastery over nature or shape their own destiny. The new people are already making great strides in this direction. The river, for example, through their ingenuity has been transformed from a fearful barrier to a highway. Though physical weaklings they are also mighty hunters, both because they have invented weaponry and because they have the ruthlessness to use its destructiveness against innocent creatures. They are predators, conquistadors, their life feeds on death. Thus their skin is 'the colour of the big fungi', their drink smells sour 'like the decay of autumn' and Marlan their magician-chief at his secret meal sounds to Lok 'busy at his meat as a beetle in dead wood' (pp 138, 160, 165). They are going to make good.

Making good involves doing evil. The predatory instincts of the new people tell them that it's destroy or be destroyed. Anything or anyone they meet is an enemy, is prey. This is a good recipe for survival and progress, for world-domination even, and the new people are impelled, driven towards that end: 'It was as though something that Lok could not see were supporting them, holding up their heads, thrusting them slowly and irresistably forward' (pp. 143–4). It seems to Lok that one of their number is almost being pulled up by the hair: 'The bone-face in the front of the log had a pine-tree of hair that stood straight up so that his head, already too long, was drawn out as though something were pulling it upwards without mercy' (p. 138). This drive towards progress is merciless both to those in thrall to it and to anyone who stands in the way. In less savage and less lively times Henry Williams, in *The Pyramid*, will be similarly thrust upwards in his pursuit of success, his ascent of the social pyramid, by 'the god without mercy' (PY p. 159). Such single-minded determination brings success but yields also a world in which the gods seem merciless or cruel, a world of ceaseless struggle, violence, fear and insecurity, a hell inhabited by devils. Lok's view of the new people by their fire makes them seem diabolic to us: 'The new people sat on the ground between Lok and the light and no two heads were the same shape. They were pulled out sideways into horns, or spired like a pine tree or were round and huge' (p. 128). The new people feel threatened by devils, but it is they who behave like demons. Their monstrousness makes Fa think that Oa could not have given birth to them and, certainly, the new people could not conceive of Oa and the vision of the world she stands for. The new people turn what might be paradise into an inferno. Their selfish pursuit of self-advancement at others' expense 'builds a hell in heaven's despite'.

The world of the new people is essentially *our* world. We are their inheritors. The new people will go to any lengths, pay any price—including consigning their child to the devil—in order to get on, to gain control of the world. We have control of the world, but the price paid by our ancestors for our position was very high, so high that our triumph seems both empty and precarious. Its emptiness has perhaps been sufficiently outlined in the new people's alienation and fear. Its precariousness derives from their fractiousness and greed combined with their inventiveness. In order to gain ascendancy over other creatures and control of the environment it was necessary for our ancestors to invent weapons and use them aggressively on prey and potential rivals. But the tendency to identify others as rivals and the violence were inevitably also directed towards other humans. The new people are already a splinter-group and the seeds of further violent division are clearly present. That aggression and paranoia combined with weapons of extraordinary power, the products of almost incredible ingenuity, have produced a situation today where at any minute we can destroy ourselves and our world completely. Though it deals with pre-history, *The Inheritors* shares with *Lord of the Flies* a post-nuclear colouring. The new people are associated by both Fa and Lok with a holocaust: '"They are like a fire in the forest."'; '"Now is like when the fire flew away and ate up the trees"' (pp. 197–8). The war-like tendencies of Jack's tribe succeeded in destroying their island world by fire. As Arthur C. Clarke has pointed out, inasmuch as man gained and holds power on earth by ingenuity in the creation of weapons he is living on borrowed time.[14] Any weapon is a stick sharpened at both ends.

The association of the new people with the destruction of the forest suggests another way in which the new people might serve as a warning to us of the dangers which, largely as a result of our successes, beset us. It is only in the decades since the publication of *The Inheritors* that awareness has become widespread of the threat that man poses to himself and to other forms of earthly life by his increasing ability to alter the nature of the environment in the peaceful pursuit of gain. Golding the prophet shows admirable foresight here. Today man is highly destructive of the world's tropical and equatorial forests, home to an immense variety of flora and fauna and also a source of much of the world's oxygen. Here again progress means destruction of others and may well be progress towards self-destruction. Today man can build a great highway through the fastnesses of the Selvas, the great Amazonian forest. This is a great tribute to his determination to gain control of all the earth but also a spectacular instance of his tendency to treat trees merely as green things that stand in the way. The new people's progress already shows this tendency to change and mar the face of nature, to crush without thinking the life that gets in the way:

> The trail had changed like everything else that the people had touched. The earth was gouged and scattered, the rollers had depressed and smoothed a way broad enough for Lok and Fa to walk abreast ... Fa looked mournfully at his face. She pointed to a smear on the smoothed earth that had been a slug. (p. 198)

The shrinking of the great forests of the tropics threatens the existence of higher creatures than slugs, endangers the existence of the great apes, whom we now know to be no fierce forest devils but affectionate, intelligent and gentle giants somewhat reminiscent of Lok, and threatens also the existence of primitive human cultures. The behaviour of the new people seems sadly prophetic of our indifference to the fate of or positive hostility towards those identified as outsiders, aliens or primitives. A catalogue of human crimes resulting from such hostility would be well nigh infinitely long. The new people have what has been described above as a laager or bunker mentality: they feel that whatever is outside of them poses a threat to them. They are in the grip of paranoia. Such paranoia, such readiness to defend the tribal laager by attacking those supposed to be a threat, may yet be the end of all of us. Even within the scope of *The Inheritors* this self-protective and self-advancing aggressiveness towards outsiders leads the new people to commit genocide. They wipe Lok's race from the face of the earth. In this context we should remember how in our own century an attempt was made to exterminate the Jewish race, a race identified by Hitler, as so often before, as a threat to the progress of civilisation and the all-round bogey men of history, the sort of role Wells gives to the Neanderthal men in the epigraph to the novel. The people are, indeed, at certain moments reminiscent of the Jews, as when Mal gives an account of their genealogy right back to a sort of Garden of Eden and, most poignantly, when Lok and Fa give expression to their feelings about the disastrous encounter with the new people in words which in their stark simplicity and power recall the most plangent verses of the Psalms or

the Lamentations of Jeremiah: '"They have gone over us
like a hollow log. They are like a winter"' says Fa, pointing
to the crushed slug (p. 198). With regard to primitive
peoples even our best intentions seem to have disastrous
consequences. Expeditions leave gifts in jungle clearings to
establish contact with primitive tribes, but once contact with
civilisation is established the influence upon the tribe is
generally baleful, leading quickly to the collapse of the
tribe's whole culture and way of life. The new people too
leave gifts for the forest devils, including the 'rotten honey'
(p. 200) that is their alcohol. Irresistable as honey, it is also
rotten, a poison that burns the mouth and transforms Lok
and Fa into imitators of the givers, so that the drunken Lok
can proudly make the horrible admission: '"I am one of the
new people."'(p. 204).

That we are, each of us, one of the new people is an
unpleasant truth which we cannot evade. As was the case in
Lord of the Flies we are confronted with a view of human
nature that is, on the face of it, profoundly pessimistic. Once
again we are shown the Yahoo in us. If, however, we
compare the methods used by Golding in his first two novels
to confront us with the reality of our own condition, we find
a resemblance not so much to Book Four as to the first two
books of *Gulliver's Travels*. In 'A Voyage to Lilliput' and
Lord of the Flies we are taken to a remote island peopled by
little men, whose behaviour represents in miniature our own
foibles and failings, our folly and outright viciousness. The
voyage to distant parts delivers some home truths. In 'A
Voyage to Brobdingnag' and *The Inheritors* we are made to
see ourselves through the eyes of an outsider (the King of
Brobdingnag or Lok), an 'innocent' who is exposed to
human nature for the first time. Seeing ourselves suddenly
from the outside, as it were, we are astonished at our own
wickedness. The King of Brobdingnag, who has greater
percipience and articulacy than Lok, sums up his reaction to
Gulliver's self-satisfied description of the life of civilised man
in a sentence of devastating frankness:

> By what I have gathered from your own relation, and the
> answers I have with much pains wringed and extorted from

you, I cannot but conclude the bulk of your natives to be the most pernicious race of little odious vermin that nature ever suffered to crawl upon the surface of the earth.[15]

We habitually think of ourselves as the pinnacle and triumph of nature, 'life's pride and cared-for crown', but to the eyes of the disinterested outsider we appear to be an affront to nature, our nature verminous and parasitic, our success that of a particularly virulent disease. Nature would be ashamed at us, would disown us: Fa speaks for Oa, we may be sure, when she remarks of the new people: 'Oa did not bring them out of her belly' (p. 173). Seeing ourselves through the eyes of innocence has the effect of making us ashamed of our humanity.

Such shame is perhaps the most abiding impression we take from *The Inheritors* and its outline of the *angst*-ridden psychology necessary in the struggle for survival makes it a deeply pessimistic work. However, as Kinkead-Weekes and Gregor have very clearly shown, the thrust of the novel is not simply to lament the disappearance of all things good and admirable in the shape of Lok's people and deplore the unqualified catastrophe of our own arrival and rise to power. It seems to Lok that the new people are like fire, but they also seem to him like honey. Their triumph involves much destruction and is qualified by the fear and grief which grip them mercilessly, but out of it may come a sweetness. One certain good which will arise from their costly advance is the creation of great art, a human contribution to the world which Oa's teeming belly could never produce.

The consciousness of the people may seem to us eminently poetic, but they themselves are no poets and the poetry in which Golding clothes them is limited to marvellous descriptions of nature and gains much of its power by contrast with our own fallen vision. Similarly, Blake's 'Songs of Innocence' derive much of their value from the strangeness we feel in a world of innocence; we are surprised by their joy. There can be no doubt, however, that when we enter the broken world of the 'Songs of

Experience' we move also into a world of deeper artistic vision and higher artistic achievement. Our fallen nature leads to many misfortunes and enormities but it also makes possible the creation of art which has the depth and emotional power of tragedy. Swift's Gulliver vaunts the poetic powers of the unfallen Houyhnhnms:

> In poetry they must be allowed to excel all other mortals; wherein the justness of their similes and the minuteness as well as exactness of their descriptions are indeed inimitable. Their verses abound very much in both of these and usually contain either some exalted notions of friendship and benevolence, or the praises of those who were victors in races and other bodily exercises.[16]

What chiefly impresses us, however, is the limitation, the shallowness, of their artistic vision: it is impossible to believe that a poem in praise of friendship or olympic achievement, however finely executed, could bear comparison with *King Lear* or *Paradise Lost* or even *Gulliver's Travels*. The fall was certainly fortunate for art.

Lok is left to die with only the little Oa for company. This is an image of the nature-mother and is itself a natural object. It is not an artifact, not a work of art: Lok merely found it lying around; he did not shape it or change it. For change, for creativity, for art we must look to the new people. Tuami is their artist and at the close he is meditating on the shape he will create on the haft of an ivory knife. His art cuts into the marble, is creative, exploratory as great art must be. It also grows out of the violent, quarrelsome, fallen nature of the new people. It is their nature to explore and we may see in their painful explorations the seeds of artistic achievements infinitely greater than Tuami's efforts with the knife-haft. The novel's twelve-chapter structure (though it is found in other Golding novels) might suggest the twelve-book epic achievements of Milton, whose *Paradise Lost* is similarly concerned with the cause and consequences of the fall, and of Vergil, whose *Aeneid* is built around a myth of the heroic migration of the founders of world-conquering Rome and is concerned not merely to trumpet the onward march of Rome but to show the bitter and tragic price of such success in terms of the sacrifice of love, in the rejection of Dido, and the unfortunate necessity of war and an 'us-and-them' mentality, in the killing of Turnus. The questing new people are enacting and creating the raw material of these epic achievements of the human spirit.

The potential in the new people for the creation of great and tragic art is perhaps one chink of light in the general gloom of *The Inheritors*. Another cause for cautious optimism is the adoption into the new people of 'the new one', the infant survivor of Lok's people. The baby can be suckled by a human, perhaps one day there will be interbreeding between the new people and this last Neanderthaler. Perhaps something of the goodness and gentleness will thus be introduced into human kind and thus we would be the inheritors of that race too. After all, the experience of reading the novel shows that we *can* feel sympathy for the alien Neanderthals and that we are also capable of shame at the excesses of our own kind. Our meeting with the new people is a little like the myth of Pandora's box: we uncover all the troubles and miseries in the world, but at the last there is still a token of hope.

·3·

THE DARK CENTRE
·PINCHER MARTIN (1956)·

"Justice". There's a large and schoolbook word to run directly
on like a rock in mid-ocean!

Rites of Passage

Who then devised the torment? Love.
Love is the unfamiliar Name
Behind the hands that wove
The intolerable shirt of flame
Which human power cannot remove.

T.S. Eliot, *Four Quartets*

Pincher Martin tells an enthralling and unlikely sailor's yarn
of a poor soul shipwrecked on the ocean, of his landing
on the lonely sea-stack of Rockall and his desperate and
ingenious struggle to combat madness and the elements in
that dreadful solitude of the sea. We sympathise with the
sailor's heroic efforts and are horrified as madness and
death seem to overwhelm him after a week of agony. In the
final chapter, however, Golding employs the shift of perspective that characterises his first three novels. A naval
officer arrives on a Hebridean island to identify the corpse
of Christopher Martin, the castaway, and reveals that he
could not have lived or suffered more than seconds in the
water. The whole story of courage and endurance on the
comfortless rock cannot be true or, at least, cannot be an
account of real events on the real Rockall in the real
Atlantic Ocean. On the rock itself Chris fails to remember
its name but recalls a humourous remark his captain had

made about it: '"I call that name a near miss"' (p. 31). A near miss for F— all, nothing at all.

Christopher Martin's adventures take place in some kind of nowhere or 'uncountry' (to borrow a word from *The Spire*) between life and death. It becomes clear that underneath the sailor's yarn there is a theologian's parable, a moral tale, it turns out, of unholy living and unholy dying. This parable is a puzzle, a dark conceit. What on earth, or anywhere else, are we to make of Chris's experiences on the rock? Careful reading reveals that the rock is Chris's own imaginative creation, his magnificent effort to avoid death at all costs. But there is an inimical presence on the rock that undermines and finally defeats his best efforts at remaining un-dead. This all-powerful enemy wins the day, but was Chris in the end accorded the sternest of divine justice or was he tormented and beaten by divine love and mercy? 'Pincher' Martin was a thief, but to which of the thieves of Golgotha was his fate similar? Was he saved or was he damned?

Once again an island looms large in the scheme of Golding's fable. *Pincher Martin* reaches an extreme of novelistic ascesis. The modern, urban, social world appears for the first time in Golding's fiction but only fitfully, as reels of film from Chris's bank of memories. The novel's focus is mainly on a single man on a rock in the lonesome ocean, a dot on the map at the extreme edge of things: the rock *is* virtually the novel's all. For much of the novel lack of human interaction makes scenery seem the real subject-matter. Much of the novelist's imaginative energy is used in creating in every detail the austere and awe-inspiring setting, which is, however, unreal, a creation of the energetic imagination of Chris in an attempt to avoid facing absolute privation and nothingness. Chris's triumph in creating and maintaining his world, while it lasts, is a novelistic one. As Gabriel Josipovici remarks: 'Pincher Martin's situation is in many ways similar to that of the novelist. The novelist also creates a world out of his own head and tries to believe in its reality in order to complete his story.'[1] But, once again, the novel's island setting focuses attention not on the complex world of

society and surfaces of men and manners, but on human
nature seen in its stark essentials. Kinkead-Weekes and
Gregor suggest that Chris must remind us of 'unaccommo-
dated man' in the harsh reality of the storm in *King Lear*, of
human nature stripped to the bone:

> Man is seen unromantically, clinically, for what he is in himself:
> Pharaoh without the ant-hordes who built the pyramids, the
> officer without the great machinery of his century. Yet for all
> this, man is not simply diminished: his qualities of endurance,
> courage, resourcefulness are also thrown into sharp relief.[2]

Here is a novel about man outcast from civilisation, left
alone with nature and his own nature, but the very fact of
its being a novel about a lonely castaway gives *Pincher
Martin* a literary background. Inevitably we are reminded of
other castaways and an examination of this literary background assists and enriches an understanding of Chris's
trials and tribulations.

Golding is rather fond of the significant name, the name
that tells us something of the nature of its bearer, a favourite
Dickensian device. Chris is particularly interested in his own
name as it seems to be something he can hang on to, a mark
of identity that reassures him in the midst of nothingness
that he exists. His problem and his name are reminiscent of
a character in a novel by the greatest of all tellers of sailors'
yarns, of Don Martin Decoud in Conrad's *Nostromo*. Don
Martin is a dandy, a popinjay, a man of dress and pose,
whose misfortune it is to be abandoned in the absolute
silence and solitude of the island of the Great Isabel. In little
more than a week he is driven to despair and suicide, his
sense of his own individual existence eaten away to nothing:
'After three days of waiting for the sight of some human
face, Decoud caught himself entertaining a doubt of his own
individuality. It had merged into the world of cloud and
water, of natural forces and forms of nature.'[3] Don Martin
has no identity unless he can dress a part; an amateur actor
in life, he soon dies where he is denied an audience.

Chris too was an actor in the social world. Like a good
pro, he is determined to put on a show to the grim death,

even realising the role of Poor Tom in *King Lear* as madness and the storm begin to crack his defences. Chris's agony on the rock is, however, intensified by his actor's need of others, of an audience. His sense of identity also begins to seep away, his powerful actor's voice dies into the cloud and water of the infinite and empty amphitheatre in which he finds himself: 'He stood up, facing a whole amphitheatre of water and sang a scale ... The sound ended at his mouth.' The air sucks up his voice 'like blotting paper' (pp. 79–80). It seems Chris is being punished in a pointed and appropriate way. For Chris the actor needed people in a sinister sense, needed to possess them, to feed off them: on the rock he is left entirely to himself and, since there is no-one to dominate or devour, that self is unable to confirm its own existence. It can no longer leave a mark on others, it is being blotted out, eaten away.

Chris's need for others, his fierce desire to be restored to the world and the flesh, is in marked contrast to the attitudes of another Conradian character, the island recluse Axel Heyst in *Victory*. Their likeness would be merely that of opposites were it not for the arrival of the naval officer to claim Chris's body at the close of *Pincher Martin*. The officer's name is Davidson, the same name as that of the naval officer who finds Heyst's body, or rather his ashes, in the final pages of *Victory*. This coincidence of names invites us to compare the two dissimilar castaways. Heyst's exile on his island is voluntary: there he escapes the world, the flesh and the devil, there his gentle and innocent nature can avoid the entanglements of life that he fears. Though accused of being a thief (and his name, perhaps accidentally, suggests theft), he is a man of utopian generosity and kindness; though a castaway, he is a rescuer of lost souls, saving Morrison from financial embarrassment and the girl Alma from sexual subjugation and exploitation. Heyst is less a thief than a Christ-figure. The name of Golding's castaway—Christopher—declares that he bears Christ within him, but this assertion is far from true.[4] Chris *is* a thief, stealing money, other men's wives, brutally attempting to force Mary into sexual intercourse. Chris entirely rejects the Christ within him in favour of the world, flesh and devil. In

Victory an evil triumvirate comes to the island to do battle with Heyst; their leader, Mr Jones, tells Heyst that he is ' "the world itself, come to pay you a visit" '.[5] His assistant, Martin Ricardo, who is troubled by lusts of the flesh, attempts to rape Alma. Mr Jones has an explanation for their voracious thievery: ' "It's the way of the world—gorge and disgorge!" '[6] This is certainly the way of Chris's world, a place where the god to be served is one's own appetite, where Chris is determined to outdo everyone else in engorging:

> The whole business of eating was peculiarly significant ... And of course eating with the mouth was only the gross expression of what was a universal process. You could eat with your cock or with your fists, or with your voice (p. 88).

It is for the sake of this sickening, cannibalistic world that Chris has suffered the loss of his own soul. In his obsession with food and with dominating and exploiting others he resembles that other wicked island-king, Jack in *Lord of the Flies*, the surname of whose original in Ballantyne's *The Coral Island* was also Martin.

On the rock the only food is utterly revolting and inadequate and there is no one over whom to exercise power. Chris's few possessions include a sliver of chocolate, which allows him an agonising memory of sweetness, and a few coins, the portable form of power over others: 'He took up the coins, chinked them in his hand for a moment and made as if to toss them in the sea. He paused. "That would be too cracker-motto. Too ham." ' (p. 77) Chris the actor does not want to play the castaway in a ham or cliché-ridden fashion. The idea of throwing the useless coinage into the sea recalls a moment when the most famous castaway of all, Robinson Crusoe, makes a very stagey speech to some coins he has discovered on the foundered ship:

> I smiled to my self at the sight of this money. 'O drug!' said I aloud, 'what art thou good for? Thou art not worth to me, no, not the taking off of the ground ... I have no manner of use for thee, e'en remain where thou art, and go to the bottom as a creature whose life is not worth saving.'[7]

However, after that ham apostrophe Crusoe's financial
prudence gets the better of him: 'upon second thoughts, I
took it away'. Like the still more worldly Chris after him, he
keeps his money by him. At this point in *Pincher Martin* we
are clearly reminded of the adventures of his famous fore-
runner but his experiences on the rock in general may
fruitfully be compared and contrasted with those of Crusoe
on his island.

The two resemble one another in their sheer determination
to survive, the force of will that impels them to go on, to
keep up the struggle, and the ingenuity which they bring to
that struggle. The inventiveness and dogged persistence of
Crusoe bring him in the end virtually all the comforts of
home, a desert island with all mod. cons. Chris's efforts at
construction, the dwarf, the seaweed-signal, the 'Claudian'
aqueduct, are much less successful, but his island is a great
deal poorer in resources than Crusoe's. Nonetheless, Chris
attempts to emulate what Angus Ross in his introduction to
Robinson Crusoe describes as Crusoe's 'success in building
up, step by step, out of whatever materials came to hand, a
physical and moral replica of the world he had left behind
him'.[8] The best Chris can do in this regard is to give to
features of the rock names which suggest home or, at least,
a world of social life, of food and drink: 'the Red Lion', 'the
High Street': '"I name you three rocks—Oxford Circus,
Piccadilly and Leicester Square"' (pp. 84–6). However, his
very presence on the rock outdoes all of Crusoe's inventiveness since Chris has invented the island upon which he is
stranded. It is impossible for us not to sympathise and
identify with both characters in their efforts to survive.[9]
This is partly through lack of competition, since neither is a
very endearing character. Chris is able to endure so long
because his nature is fierce, snarling ('"Help, curse you, sod
you, bugger you—Help!"'), predatory ('"All I have to do is
to endure. I breathe this air into my own furnace. I kill and
eat."') and dedicated to getting to the top (pp. 18, 115). He
can drive himself time and again up the mountain of his
island: he has the same frenzy for survival as the new
people, but as in *The Inheritors* such will to survive is by no
means an unmixed good. He wishes to cling to a world

where he can go on killing and eating, go on expressing his
need to dominate in violent sexuality, go on feeding the inferno within him. The desire to survive and be rescued, with
which we sympathise, is a desire to return to the world and
the flesh, the province of the devil, is a desire to reject God.

Such moral or theological interpretation of Chris's physical
plight is by no means alien to the spirit of Defoe's tale. For,
as Angus Ross remarks in his introduction to *Robinson
Crusoe*, the work is more than a mere sailor's yarn:

> The story is at once realistic (as far as Defoe went, or could go,
> at this time) and allegorical. The 'significance' is, however, put
> forward through a powerful imagination and the story consists
> of more than the dry bones of a parable: it has flesh and
> spirit.[10]

The allegory is in part theological. It was a special provi-
dence that saved Crusoe, alone of all the ship's complement,
and washed him up on the shores of the island, a particular
mercy, a token of salvation. Yet the sojourn on the island is
also a punishment for Crusoe's sins, a working out of divine
justice. The allegory in *Pincher Martin* is more difficult to
interpret, especially when it becomes clear that Chris has
created his own island, but here too we are dealing with a
story of retributive punishment for sin and expiation of sin,
of justice and mercy, of damnation and salvation.

'"Where the hell am I?"' asks Chris pointedly as he finds
himself miraculously at the base of a rock in mid-ocean (p.
30). This rock of salvation turns out to be a veritable hell
and Chris's sufferings are a miniature version of traditional
underworld horrors. Chris's attempts to build a cairn of
stones at the peak of the rock require dreadful physical
exertion:

> He scrambled back to the too heavy stone and fought with it.
> He moved it, end over end. He built steps to the top of a wall
> and worked the great stone up. He drew from his body more
> strength than he had got. He bled. (p. 80)

Struggling thus with a great stone up a mountain, he enacts
the punishment of Sisyphus, especially as he has just

accidently knocked the head stone of the cairn back down the cliff. Like Prometheus, another thief, he is pinned to a cliff in an abomination of desolation: '"I am Prometheus"' he declares, attempting to keep up the role of heroic God-defier (p. 164). Chris's supply of fresh water is preserved by a mere film of deposit, every sip he takes disturbs this vital dam the more: it is a tantalising situation. The exhausted man desperately needs sound, healthy sleep: 'He lay still and considered sleep. But it was a tantalisingly evasive subject' (p. 90). Like Tantalus he is punished for his greed by deprivation and disappointment. The water does not quench thirst and every drink is risky, the seafood is sickmaking, fitful sleep brings only guilty dreams. On the world of the rock these earthly goods and comforts are profoundly unsatisfying.

We learn from various flashbacks that there has been no shortage of sin in Chris's life. His last act on the ship is the attempted (and probably successful) murder of his friend Nat, a very damnable last act indeed. The predominant sin, however, is greed, the role Chris the mummer is assigned among the Deadly Sins in a Morality Play, though greed must be taken to include lust and envy, very prominent faults with Chris. The punishments meted out to him are, like Crusoe's 'particularly painful' and 'particularly apposite'.[11] Thus the 'personal and vicious' seas buffeting him at the foot of the rock attack the parts most deserving of chastising or punishment: they 'beat him in the crutch' and 'hit him in the guts' (p. 37). Eating, as we have seen, was Chris's sinful obsession; eating on the rock is a night-mare, an agony. He can pretend that his handful of red sea-anemones is a 'pile of sweets', but knowledge of the sickening truth provokes a cry of '"Bloody hell!"' (p. 66). The one sweet he has retained from the outside world, the grain of chocolate, proves to be a tantalising torture: 'The chocolate stung with a piercing sweetness, momentary and agonising, and was gone' (p. 83). Back on land, Chris was warned in the story of the Chinese box and the maggots that his voraciousness would turn him into a maggot, a filthy squirming knot of corruption and putrescence. The story becomes horribly, literally true on the rock, with Chris eventually hearing the spade crashing on the roof of his maggot-box. The food of the rock creates corruption and poison in Chris's bowels. 'All the terrors of hell' (p. 163) are unleashed inside Chris by that poison. To relieve the agony he is forced to administer an enema to himself, forced, in effect, to sodomise himself, a rather appropriate punishment for the sexual violence he used against the 'isled virtue' (p. 163) of Mary, indeed for his many sins of lust. The captain's implied near-miss name for Rockall might well have been the motto of Chris the sexual gormandiser.

Chris was not a great lover but 'a good hater' (p. 103), his relationships with others were devoid of love and coldly exploitative, a matter of 'grabbing a stuffed doll, plundering a doll' (p. 152). As he attempts to extort sex from Mary she exclaims: '"You filthy, beastly—"' (p. 152). Certainly the beast is rampant in him. On the rock the beast literally takes over his body as his hands become transformed to lobster's claws, the lobster being an object of particular distaste to Chris, a '"Beast. Filthy sea-beast"' (p. 112) which makes his skin crawl with worms of loathing. This is a hell to equal the most extreme medieval imaginings of infernal torture: as the gulls of the rock become flying lizards of nightmare, Chris is transformed to a vile thing of cold, hard exoskeleton and greedy, vicious claws, a thing he himself regards with particular and extreme horror and repugnance. It is an appropriate punishment of course, but it is more than that. It is a revelation of what sin had made Chris, even back in the social world. It is the true Chris, stripped down to ugly essentials. The hell that is the rock shows that it is the nature of sin to be self-punishing.

The rock is, after all, Chris's own creation, a little world he has cunningly made out of the memory of a carious tooth, another image of the rottenness that comes from bad eating. The rock is, indeed, Chris's all, an emblem of himself and his world. His world is one of Sisyphus-like struggle to be top of the pile. His behaviour as ravisher and glutton is reminiscent of Don Giovanni, who is dragged down to hell by a man of stone, of marble, an image of the cold, hard, loveless thing he has become. Chris *is* the hell in which he finds himself, an ossified phallus alone in an ocean of

emptiness: '"I'm so alone! Christ! I'm so alone!"' (p. 181).
But Chris has rejected Christ and now seems, like the
Ancient Mariner, to be alone on a wide, wide sea from
which the merciful aspect of God has disappeared. Chris is
fully responsible for that loneliness too: he betrayed and
murdered the holy fool Nat who was his one true friend. By
determined selfishness, by severing the ties of human love
and friendship, Chris has become what no man should be,
an island and the loneliest of islands at that. The rock is the
world Chris created or chose, or willed, his own will being
'like a monolith' (p. 163), a world where there is only the
self and the desires which torture that self, a world devoid
of satisfaction, fulfilment, peace, or love, a world where
God is rejected and crucified for sin; that world is Chris's
life in microcosm and it is hell.

Crusoe was punished for his sin, but he was also saved
alone of all his shipmates and took this to be a sign of
his eternal salvation through God's mercy and love. Chris
manages to save himself on an island of his own invention
but appears to have brought about his own damnation to
hell. The traditional view of hell has it that its torments are
eternal, of infinite temporal duration, but that is not so of
Chris's sojourn on the rock. The rock and the ocean are
torn to pieces on the seventh day to reveal a nothingness
that is 'three times real' (p. 200), real with the intensity,
the absoluteness of spiritual things. The hellish agony and
misery of the rock are temporary and that might suggest
that Chris is experiencing not hell but the tribulations
of purgatory, that he has been allowed by a power that
watches over and cares for him to create a place of trial
where his sins will be punished but also purged from him.
Chris himself is convinced that much of his suffering is
caused by a blockage in his bowels, by something he ate, by
a build-up of filth within him, and attempts to cure this by
administering to himself the enema, which has spectacularly
purgative results. The enema, however, shows Chris to be
still too much concerned with the physical rather than the
spiritual, more concerned with body than soul. The true
cause of his appalling condition is the spiritual filth of sin,
the moral corruption, within Chris. Sleep might offer some

respite from physical agony for the castaway, but for the guilty Chris sleep offers no comfort: 'Sleep is where we touch what is better left unexamined. There, the whole of life is bundled up'. Chris has great difficulty in achieving sleep, asks himself why, and answers his own question: '"I am afraid to"' (pp. 91–2). In sleep he is confronted with the spiritual filth of his own sin, the spiritual agony of his own guilt. That is a greater torment than the physical tortures of the rock. In sleep or delirium he must confront the whole of life, his all, and find that it is a series of films in which he is the villain, demonstrations that his life and precious self are rotten to the core. The torment forces from Chris an acknowledgement of the truth and an admission of guilt: 'Because of what I did I am an outsider and alone' (p. 181).

Such an admission of guilt and, in effect, of the justice of punishment is perhaps a step upwards on the mountain of purgatory, a first step towards salvation and freedom from torment. It is, however, the only step which of his own volition Chris makes. For him to be redeemed or saved he must lose his life, but he foolishly and misguidedly clings to it, vile though it is. The inimical presence which Chris feels to be stalking him on the rock attempts to force him to let go of the life to which he hangs with the tenacity of a lobster's claws. The presence, which finally destroys the rock and its painted ocean in a storm of black lightning and seeks to penetrate Chris's ugly crustacean exoskeleton, is identified at last as 'a compassion that was timeless and without mercy' (p. 201). That timeless compassion, merciless only in its determination to release Chris once for all from bondage to sin, is simply the love of God. God's love is seen in a negative way, as terror and black lightning, because it is opposed to Chris's will. Chris is entirely attached to, given over to the world, the flesh and the devil, so it is natural that the force that would take these from him and him from them appears as an enemy, an overwhelming threat. Golding has himself said that 'God is the thing we turn away from into life, and therefore we hate and fear him and make a darkness there'.[12] Thus, in a world of inverted values, God is the hated darkness, the feared nothingness. Chris to the very last refuses to let go, to die into life, and rejects and outrageously vilifies the compassion that batters at his dark heart: "'I spit on your compassion!'"; "'I shit on your heaven!'" (pp. 199–200).

The God who is lightning and love is not, however, to be rebuffed or denied. Despite his defiant blasphemies Chris is separated from the hell he would choose. His ultimate entry into nothingness might be taken to be the casting out into exterior darkness and nothingness of a soul so mercilessly self-assertive. It seems perhaps more reasonable to believe, however, that this very nothingness is Chris's salvation. It is forced upon him by 'a compassion' and an end to vicious and desperate struggle, a wiping clean of the slate of the guilty past, a complete cessation of the agony of existing, constitute the salvation that Chris requires, his heaven. Nat his true friend had warned him that heaven must seem to his perverse self a nothingness: "'Take us as we are now and heaven would be sheer negation. Without form and void. You see? A sort of black lightning destroying everything that we call life'" (p. 70). Chris is dragged kicking and screaming, unjustified and undeserving, into such a heaven. As such, he is the first in a line of characters in Golding's novels who live very reprehensible lives and yet, the novels suggest, may ultimately be saved or redeemed. There is Jocelin in *The Spire*, whose follies and sins are mercilessly exposed yet who nonetheless seems at the end to have some claim to salvation; there is Wilf Barclay in *The Paper Men*, who recalls Christopher Martin, as Don Crompton has pointed out, in possessing crustacean armour-plating and rottenness within but who is allowed at least a glimpse of heaven; and there is Sebastian Pedigree in *Darkness Visible*, who like Chris clings determinedly to his dreadful sin but whose grip on an evil life is broken by an inexorable and salvific love. In the extreme cases of Chris and Pedigree it is as if Golding would challenge us to set a limit to the mercy of an infinitely compassionate God. For all its bleakness and its almost unrelieved concentration on human wickedness, *Pincher Martin* is on this reading a more optimistic book than *Lord of the Flies*. Both novels involve characters who are saved from the sea yet remain in need of rescue. In the first novel the boys are saved or, at least, are found again by a very questionable *deus ex machina*. Chris, by contrast, is rescued from the world not back into it by a God who at first sight seems cruel and tormenting but whose mercy can extend even to so undeserving a case as Christopher Martin. Perhaps in the end all may be well.

The wise advice about learning to die, to give up the world, as well as a true prophecy that he has not long to live, Chris receives from his friend Nathaniel or Nat, the irritating gnat that Chris swats. Nat is not merely a prophet and purveyor of wisdom but a fool. His extraordinary height and slenderness make him ridiculous and awkward; on board ship he is an outsider, a laughing-stock, an unworldly innocent who is manifestly not cut out for survival on the rough seas of the world. Nat himself is not, however, very concerned with survival or getting on in this world. His foolish wisdom is that we must learn to renounce this world, that to philosophise is to learn how to die, the sort of insane philosophy discovered by Folly in Christianity, and indeed Platonism, in Erasmus' *Praise of Folly*:

> The happiness which Christians seek with so many labours is nothing other than a certain kind of madness and folly. Don't be put off by the words, but consider the reality. In the first place, Christians come very near to agreeing with the Platonists that the soul is stifled and bound down by the fetters of the body which by its gross matter prevents the soul from being able to contemplate and enjoy things as they truly are. Next, Plato defines philosophy as a preparation for death because it leads the mind from visible and bodily things, just as death does.

Thus 'the biggest fools of all' are those who are truly and entirely Christians, those who, like Nat, 'scorn life and desire only death'.[14] Such is the folly of Nathaniel, to whom Chris screams for help as he sinks beneath the watery floor: ' "Nat! Nathaniel! For Christ's sake! Nathaniel! Help!" ' (p. 13). The holy fool Nat is indeed to be associated with Christ, who by insanely generous example taught us how to renounce the world and accept death.

This sort of unworldly wisdom is seen as utter folly by

Chris, who is wholly given over to pursuit of the things of this world, though these things, as Nat perceives, fail to give him happiness. Devoted to this world, Chris is terrified by the thought or mention of death: when Nat reminds him of the plain fact that in only a few years he must die, Chris's reaction is incredulous outrage: '"You bloody fool, Nat! You awful bloody fool!"' (p. 72). But the fool has merely spoken the awful truth, as fools will. Nat forces upon Chris the unpleasant truth that death is a certainty and that he must change his attitude to life, but Chris does not like being irritated in this way: he kills the holy fool. For Chris is worldly-wise, determined to look after number one, to live it up, to make an impression and a killing. St Paul, in recommending holy folly, has a stern warning for such as Chris:

> Let no man deceive himself. If any man among you seemeth to be wise in this world, let him become a fool, that he may be wise. For the wisdom of this world is foolishness with God. For it is written, He taketh the wise in their own craftiness.[15]

But Chris cannot accept the truth Nat has to offer: at the very moment of his crafty attempt to rid himself of his friend he is himself taken by the death he so fears.

Chris himself is amazed at his capacity to hate, reject and kill Nathaniel in return 'for love given without thought' (p. 103). But Nathaniel wins the girl Mary, thus thwarting one of Chris's many desires, succeeding where he had failed. It is noteworthy in this context that Chris's violent desire to possess Mary seems to be fuelled by some kind of class bitterness. Chris is resentful of and yet attracted by 'the aspirations, prudish and social' (p. 148) of Mary's voice; he feels he has fallen in love with 'a front parlour on two feet' (p. 104). The origin of these feelings in Chris is obscure but once again in Golding class is at least partly to blame for some evil deeds. The involvement of feelings about class in erotic or romantic yearning will be seen again and much developed in the relationship of Sammy and Beatrice in *Free Fall* and the longed-for (on one side) relationship of Oliver and Imogen in *The Pyramid*. The mixture of erotic desire and class bitterness is a nasty one. Chris seems to associate Mary's refusal of his advances with some sort of class barrier: 'And here it comes quickly, with an accent immediately elevated to the top drawer. "No." There are at least three vowels in the one syllable.' (p. 149). Chris's true feeling, as he himself knows, is hate, his desire is to violate, to do violence to Mary, to drag her down into an imagined gutter where there is no love or decency but only beastliness and hate. He finds her out: 'Nothing out of the top drawer now. Vowels with the burr of the country on them' (p. 152). With this humiliating proof of her social pretensions Chris seems mildly satisfied. It is a conquest of a kind, a victory in hate if not in love.

The relationship of the attractive Chris and the awkward, unworldly, religious Nat is faintly reminiscent of the tragic friendship of Anthony Beavis and Brian Foxe in Huxley's *Eyeless in Gaza*.[16] In both cases rivalry over a girl leads to trouble in the friendship and ultimately to the deaths of Nat and Brian, characters who rival one another in benevolence and awkwardness. Chris's envy of Nat's success in becoming engaged to Mary goads him on to Nat's murder; Anthony's callous seduction of Brian's fiancée Joan leads directly to his friend's suicide. It is with this memory that Anthony has to live: like Chris his mind is haunted by pictures, snapshots, reels of film from his past that tell a sorry and guilty tale:

> A chalk pit, a picture gallery, a brown figure in the sun, a skin, here, redolent of salt and smoke, and here (like Mary's, he remembered) savagely musky. Somewhere in the mind a lunatic shuffled a pack of snapshots and dealt them out at random, shuffled once more and dealt them out in different order, again and again, indefinitely. There was no chronology. The idiot remembered no distinction between before and after,[17]

These pictures form much of the substance of the novel, they are the truth about himself he must confront, the rotten, sinful, ordinary self he wishes to transcend. Quoting Hopkins, Anthony suggests that that worldly self *is* hell:

> I see
> The lost are like this, and their scourge to be,
> As I am mine, their sweating selves; but worse.

Hell is the incapacity to be other than the creature one finds oneself ordinarily behaving as.[18]

Chris too is '"chasing after—a kind of peace"' (p. 105) but on the hell of the rock he misguidedly and determinedly hangs on to his ordinary self. He cannot accept, even when the actor's dress of everyday life is stripped away to reveal inner blackness and agony, that that sinful self must die if he is to achieve the kind of peace he needs.

For Anthony Beavis there is a way forward: the acceptance of his own responsibility and guilt and a determination to cultivate 'the difficult art of loving people'.[19] For Chris the only way out of his personal hell is death. This highlights the vast difference between the novelistic worlds they inhabit. In *Eyeless in Gaza* Anthony's wrongdoing is explained in terms of a highly complicated net of social and amatory entanglements: the novel's analysis of how he came to do what he did, some of which is done by Anthony himself, is of extraordinary intelligence and lucidity.[20] Where there is explanation and understanding there is hope. But in the savagely simple world of *Pincher Martin* there is virtually no explanation of Chris's wickedness. Chris is confronted with the darkness within him in all its terror and horror; the darkness that was in his cellarage even in childhood, but it remains essentially a darkness. There is really no light shed on the origin of Chris's evil: it simply *is*. Thus there seems some justification in Chris's outburst against his creator, which might almost be taken as blasphemously echoing George Herbert's 'Love III':

Yet suppose I climbed away from the cellar over the bodies of used and defeated people, broke them to make steps on the road away from you, why should you torture me? If I ate them, who gave me a mouth? (p. 197)

Chris is in fact a self-torturer, he flees from the goodness that seems to him darkness, but that, the novel insists, is his nature. God looks a little dark indeed. But the creator can also be the destroyer, can force upon Chris the peace he needs but cannot find in himself or his world. God's mercy, as Hopkins wrote in a poem on another shipwreck, can manifest itself with the violence and terror of storm and lightning:

> Thou art lightning and love, I found it, a winter and warm;
>   Father and fondler of heart thou hast wrung:
> Hast thy dark descending and most art merciful then.[21]

· 4 ·

RESPONSIBILITIES
·FREE·FALL (1959)·

Already of those hours a third was over
Wherein all stars display their radiance,
When lo! Love stood before me in my trance:
Recalling what he was fills me with horror.
                                    La Vita Nuova

I would wish my days to be separated each from each by
unnatural impiety.
                                    Eyeless in Gaza

The days of Sammy Mountjoy have indeed been separated
each from each by unnatural impieties, whether spitting on
the altar as a child or physically and psychologically abusing
a simple and loving girl in early manhood. Anthony Beavis'
line in *Eyeless in Gaza* wittily perverts healthy Wordsworthian
sentiment: the artist-hero of *Free Fall* is haunted by the
memory of a time when he was innocent and free, a childhood that, for all its squalor, was Wordsworthian. He is
separated from those days by his unnatural impieties. He is,
like Beavis and Christopher Martin, one of the 'guilty' (p.
232), haunted by the memory of his sins.

Free Fall, as critics have recognised, seems to grow out of
Pincher Martin. Its guilt-ridden hero-narrator seeks the ex-
planations for his behaviour that were lacking in the case of
Christopher Martin in the preceding novel. Where *Pincher
Martin* was eschatological, concerned in its unorthodox way
with the last things of death, judgement, heaven and hell,
Sammy Mountjoy is concerned to examine first things, the
fall from innocence to experience, the beginning of serious,

of perhaps irremediable sin and the responsibility for it.
Chris Martin put the blame squarely on God for his wickedness and we see little or nothing in the sketches of moments
from his life that would allow us to explain it in a more
human way, in terms of upbringing, circumstances, and
their influence upon personality. *Free Fall* with its detailed
account of Sammy's childhood and adolescence makes such
explanation possible: the responsibility for the fall and its
consequences may be sought and found within the human
world of the novel. Sammy's great sins resemble Chris's in
that they have sex at the root of them, the relationship of
Beatrice and Sammy seems to grow out of and develop the
sketchily drawn obsession of Chris with Mary, but sex for
Chris seems to be merely an appetite as uncomplicated and
frequent as hunger. In the case of Sammy we are given a
study of sexual desire as part of the complex nexus of
emotions and drives which we call love. The novel offers an
essay on the nature of love, but the subject is examined with
an absolute lack of sentimentality, with an honesty that
is frightening: Sammy's recollections of love fill us with
horror.

For the first time in Golding's work the setting is not
remote or exotic. The novel is set in England towards the
middle of the present century. This modern, civilised world
is a very unlovely place, a 'deep and muddy pool where
others lived' (p. 112), a rather shoddy and dirty place of
rural slums and urban grime the very skies of which seem
contaminated by man's business of living: 'the smokes and
glows and the spilt suds of autumn in the sky' (p. 79). The
overall unhappy feel of the modern world in *Free Fall* (and,
indeed, where it appears elsewhere in Golding) might be
aptly expressed in some lines of Hopkins:

> Generations have trod, have trod, have trod;
> And all is seared with trade; bleared, smeared with toil;
> And wears man's smudge and shares man's smell: the soil
> Is bare now, nor can foot feel, being shod.[1]

Against this ugly and inauspicious background the sordid
love-tragedy of Sammy and Beatrice is enacted. It is a

tragedy of such bitterness and cruelty that it may seem extreme or egregious, yet it is in keeping with a world where nations torture each other in a world war, where the Gestapo interrogator Dr Halde can boast that he and his kind 'have hung in a row the violated bodies' (p. 176) of Poland, Czechoslovakia, France and other subjugated countries. Sammy brutally violated the body of Beatrice but can ask in an attempt to put his own 'disease' in perspective: 'Why bother about one savaged girl when girls are blown to pieces by the thousand?' (p. 132). It is a world in which, on the grand scale, the love between human beings has failed.

It has been noted that characters' names in Golding often carry a literary resonance and this story of the love of a young artist for a girl called Beatrice who is associated with purity and religion cannot fail to suggest the love of Dante for Beatrice as recorded in *La Vita Nuova*. The comparison points up the sorry nature of modern love. *La Vita Nuova* is a work of extraordinary beauty telling a story and describing a world in which human love seems conducive to nobility, dignity and even holiness. Thus Dante can confidently write: 'Love and the noble heart are but one thing'.[2] This is in extreme contrast to Sammy's bitter experience of modern 'love in the mud' (p. 13), of the ignoble thoughts and deeds that spring from love.

On the opening page of *La Vita Nuova* Dante describes the effect upon him of his first sight of Beatrice:

> The moment I saw her I say in all truth that the vital spirit, which dwells in the inmost depths of the heart, began to tremble so violently that I felt the vibration alarmingly in all my pulses, even the weakest of them.[3]

Similarly, at the first meeting we witness between Sammy and Beatrice, Sammy suffers from 'wobble wobble heart' as Beatrice emerges from a girl's training college in the company of two 'blessed damozels' (pp. 82–3). The lovelorn Sammy has difficulty in timing his arrival because of the crowd of other students; this produces some less than noble feelings in his heart: 'I was in the gutter, sitting my bike, willing them to die, be raped, bombed or otherwise obliterated because this demanded split-second timing' (p. 82). His amatory obsession involves these war-like emotions. There are times when Sammy sounds quite the medieval love poet himself, as when he wishes to tell Beatrice how he burns, how there are flames shooting out of his head and heart. There are even moments when he achieves a *dolce stil nuovo* of his own, a dignity and lyrical beauty of language in describing love: 'She was so sweet, so unique, so beautiful—or did I invent her beauty? Had all young men been as I, the ways where she went would have been crowded' (pp. 93–4). For the most part, however, love in *Free Fall* partakes of the qualities of the modern world: it is dirty, cruel and violent. Even Sammy's unknown father in the act of begetting is imagined to be 'as specialized and soulless as a guided missile' (p. 14).

So different is the love of Dante for Beatrice in *La Vita Nuova*, so free of impurity or aggression, that one is tempted to say that he seems to inhabit a different universe from that of Sammy. And so, indeed, he does. For love is the motive force of the Dantean universe: the wheeling spheres of the heavens are driven by God's love. The whole universe is an expression, a manifestation of love, a love made flesh. Dante's indubitably idealised human love partakes of this divine love and raises the lover heavenward: the ultimate aim and meaning of love are given by religion. This is a very different universe from the modern one Sammy lives and suffers in. At school Sammy is torn between the world-views touted by two teachers, Nick Shales the science master and Rowena Pringle who teaches religion. For Miss Pringle, a most unpleasant character, God is still an active presence in the universe, God can take a hand in his world by working miracles. For Nick Shales ('Old Nick' (p. 210) but a good man), God has disappeared from his scientific world-view. The universe, marvellous though it is, is not driven by divine love but by physical laws. Sammy is attracted to Nick's kindly nature and chooses his world-view for the sake of the man. Clearly it is no longer possible to see love as Dante did. Indeed, the amatory world of *La Vita Nuova* does seem rather too good to be true, rather naive or innocent. Dante's attitude seems to proclaim no devil, seems so devoid of baseness as to be untrue to human experience of love. Dantean love and its circumambient universe are extraordinarily beautiful but beauty is not necessarily truth. Even Nick Shales, whose earthy name hints that he has no time for spiritual reality or beings, sees the sexual aspect of human love as a supreme piece of devilry:

> "I don't believe in anything but what I can touch and see and weigh and measure. But if the Devil had invented man he couldn't have played him a dirtier, wickeder, a more shameful trick than when he gave him sex!" (p. 231)

The innocence of the Dantean view is given the lie by experience. The adolescent Sammy, who can remember a time in childhood when the eye of innocence transformed a squalid slum childhood into a world of wonder and beauty recalling the childhood paradise evoked in Traherne's *Centuries of Meditations*, thirsts after the experience of sex but has thus far failed to realise the tragic cost of relinquishing innocence and its world. Sammy's world is secularised: his love for Beatrice, or for anyone else, is not ennobled or given meaning by the love of God but has become a poor replacement for the religious sense he has lost and yet needs: 'Therefore the tickling pleasure, the little death shared or self-inflicted was neither irrelevant nor sinful but the altar of whatever shoddy temple was left to us' (p. 108). Sammy is inclined to make a religion of love, he seems to worship Beatrice, yet the true object of his worship is pleasure or self-gratification. Sammy's love fails to raise him to the heavens. In fact its progress is a descending path, a route down into the sewers. As Virginia Tiger comments: 'whereas to Dante Beatrice becomes an instrument of contemplation, exaltation, and finally salvation ... to Sammy she is merely an instrument of lust'.[4] Beatrice is a coy and religious girl who does not respond to Sammy's sexual frenzies: she fails to give him the satisfaction or fulfilment he craves and this leads him to ever more desperate and extreme sexual abuse of her. He desecrates the object of his supposed worship, but it is still more a self-desecration. He remembers how after one particularly degrading exploitation he lay in self-contempt while the invulnerable Beatrice 'lay, looking out of the window as though she had been blessed' (p. 124).

Sammy's love, despite certain religious trappings, is thoroughly earthbound. He does wish (by the act of love) to break through the wall that divides people but seems to think that such a mystical union is merely a matter of physical movement and response, just 'salt sex' (p. 108). He fails to respect or appreciate Beatrice as a person. In *La Vita Nuova* Dante drenches 'the earth with bitter tears'[5] when Beatrice fails to give him a sign of greeting. In Sammy's world, where courtesy is of very much less moment, his extravagant tears and tantrums are provoked by the fact that Beatrice is reluctant to allow him to have sexual possession of her. For Sammy that tickling bodily need is all-important, driving him to violence and near madness. Thus his proposal of marriage (simply a means to the end of sex) contains the threat that if Beatrice does not agree he will kill her. He is under a compulsion, a dark and powerful god has come to rule over him, he is forced to use psychological torture upon the human being he supposedly loves:

> Once a human being has lost freedom there is no end to the coils of cruelty. I must I must I must. They said the damned in hell were forced to torture the innocent live people with disease. But I know now that life is perhaps more terrible than that innocent medieval misconception. We are forced here and now to torture each other. (p. 115)

The medieval vision, terrible though it is, seems innocent when compared with modern experience. Our hell, as in *Pincher Martin*, is the here and now in which God has been rejected and we are left with the dissatisfactions of human life, the positive agony of our capacity to inflict torture, our sense of helplessness in the face of our own evil. Human love, far from giving value to an otherwise sordid life, far from providing a satisfactory replacement for religion, is simply a particularly dirty and devilish aspect of the here and now, the torture-chamber.

Sammy is obsessed with the loss of his freedom. *La Vita*

Nuova also concerns itself with the loss of freedom that is a part of love. In a dream Love appears to Dante and, weeping, says: "'I am like the centre of a circle, to which the parts of the circumference are related in a similar manner; you, however, are not.'"[6] Dante himself feels that this utterance is very obscure: Barbara Reynolds, editor of the Penguin edition of *La Vita Nuova*, provides an explanatory footnote:

> Love seems here to be distinguishing between the general and the particular. Love in general is related to the whole of life and equally to all mankind ... In realistic terms, Dante feels a pang of regret on realizing that, though love is universal, he, an individual, cannot love diffusedly, but must love one and one only. He has reached the moment of choice, which for finite minds involves exclusion.[7]

For Dante the nature of love is determined from above. It is the nature of true human love that it is given to one and one only. Dante's choice in love has been made and he must stick by it. Dante's faithfulness to Beatrice, with whom he has achieved no greater intimacy than distant courtesies, remains steadfast even after the calamitous moment 'when the Lord of justice called this most gracious lady to partake of glory under the banner of the blessed Queen, the Virgin Mary, whose name was always uttered in prayers of the utmost reverence by this blessed Beatrice'.[8] Such are the words with which Dante calmly accepts her death, which he sees as a just promotion, earned by her innocence and virtue, to a higher, spiritual realm. Dante's love and fidelity are not defeated by death and in heaven he will again meet and be led upwards toward God by the lady Beatrice in *The Divine Comedy*.

Sammy's love for his Beatrice is, by contrast, strictly sublunary. It partakes of the changefulness of the world of the senses whence it springs, even as Dante's love has the unchanging quality of the heavenly or divine. The adolescent Sammy makes his choice: he wants something physical, something to satisfy a sensual longing, namely 'the white unseen body of Beatrice Ifor'. Even in this moment of dedication in love his desires include a most disturbing and violent element: 'for the pain she had caused me, her utter abjection this side death' (pp. 235–6). It is evident that this love does not include respect or care for Beatrice as a person. Sammy, however, is prepared to sacrifice 'everything', his own soul included presumably, to get the thing he wants. He is committed, he would agree with Dante that after his choice he has 'set foot in that part of life beyond which one cannot go with any hope of returning'.[9] Though he is embarked, however, on a course the consequences of which will indeed be irremediable, his love is not of the unswerving kind described by Dante. Sammy's choice is a decision to pursue the sexual possession of Beatrice at all costs, a decision which gives him into the power of his own sex-drive, allows his love to be shaped and controlled from below, as it were. Sammy the artist gives shape or form to his own nature by this choice, as the Florentine humanist Pico della Mirandola declared it is man's privilege to do in his *Oration on the Dignity of Man*: in this passage God is addressing man:

> Confined within no bounds, you shall fix the limits of your own nature according to the free choice in whose power I have placed you. We have made you neither mortal nor immortal, so that with freedom and honour you should be your own sculptor and maker, to fashion your form as you choose. You can fall away into the lower natures which are the animals. You can be reborn by the decision of your soul into the higher natures which are divine.[10]

Sammy chooses to fall and his behaviour towards Beatrice becomes ever more depraved, conducting him down into a guilty hell of his own making.

The choice made, Sammy is no longer able to behave with decency, even though he is aware of the wickedness of his own actions. His is the typical state of fallen man as described by Anthony Beavis, a man equally obsessed with freedom and the responsibility for evil: 'Five words sum up every biography. *Video meliora proboque; deteriora sequor.* Like all other human beings, I know what I ought to do, but continue to do what I know I oughtn't to do.'[11] The 'unruly member' (SP p. 77) has control of Sammy and when he tires

of seeking satisfaction with Beatrice he callously abandons
her for Taffy, an entirely secular creature, her first words
full of violence and swearing, who makes love with him
virtually on sight. Sammy has found a very suitable mate
but he has also given up Beatrice for toffee, for the merely
physical. The suggestion in her name is underlined by her
association with the Communist Party, where Sammy had
already found sex, 'a little furtive pleasure like handing
round a bag of toffees' (p. 91). His fall away from the
spiritual or divine could scarcely be more crassly emphasised.

Sammy sinks towards the animals but is also responsible
for dragging Beatrice down, for breaking her spirit.
Sammy's final reunion with Beatrice is in the house the
grounds of which he had experienced as the earthly paradise
when still an innocent child. 'Paradise' (p. 246), he ruefully
remembers as he stands in what is now a lunatic asylum, the
human zoo where what remains of Beatrice is kept. Their
reunion is in horrible contrast to that of Dante and Beatrice:
Sammy's Beatrice is not a soul in bliss but one who experiences a state '"rather like ... continual and exaggerated
worry"' (p. 247), a hell on earth. Sammy too is given a taste
of the deepest hell, as pictured by Dante, where Satan
himself is tortured in a glacier: he is 'up to the neck in the
ice on paradise hill' (p. 241).

Sammy chose a secular world, a world where the only
certainties were what could be weighed and measured,
where the only certain good was musk or salt sex, but finds
himself at last in a world where he is certain that there are
moral certainties, that there is sin and that one must face its
terrible consequences. One consequence of his sin is the
reduction of Beatrice to animal level. Sammy remembers
how at school a retarded child called Minnie had wet herself
in front of a school-inspector, revealing herself to the other
children as 'an animal down there' (p. 35) below them.
Beatrice, confronted suddenly by Sammy in the asylum,
repeats the act of Minnie, proving herself to be now only
minimally human and splashing Sammy with the fetor of
guilt for what he has done. His own punishment is momentarily reminiscent of Satan's because, for all Dr Enticott's
fence-sitting about the cause of Beatrice's wretched condition,

it is clear to us and to Sammy that he is responsible for the devilish wickedness of dragging her down into this hell. He treated her as something less than human and that is what she has become. At the first sight of more pleasurable and *simpatico* company Sammy abandoned Beatrice, removing in the most cruel way the prop that the fragile Beatrice needed to support her in life, but even in the time of their intimacy Sammy showed a crass insensitivity towards his supposed beloved. There is not merely the physical abuse and degradation, but his bullying interrogation of Beatrice, his attempt to force some intellectual response out of the taciturn and simple girl: 'Impatient and angry. Continue the catechism. "Aren't you human, then? Aren't you a person at all?" And with shudders of her wrists and shaking of the long fair hair she would whisper against me: "Maybe."' (p. 121). Beatrice's grip on her humanity is uncertain: Sammy breaks it once and for all.

It is painful to see the innocent tortured, especially as Beatrice seems sincere and devoted in her rather a-sexual love. Golding does not spare Sammy: after he has rejected her he receives a pathetic letter from Beatrice asking *his* forgiveness and bearing a desperately touching mark of her concern for him: 'In the top left-hand corner she had drawn a little cross. We were out of danger' (p. 130). This is their coded sign that she is not pregnant, but it might also be taken as a symbol of what Sammy has done to her: he has crucified her. Beatrice the rather dim, religious girl is this novel's holy fool, the innocent who is crucified for Sammy's sins. She is not the most interesting of Golding's exemplars of holy folly but she does nonetheless have one tiny piece of fool's wisdom to offer, her key word 'maybe'. Even Sammy recognises the importance of this little nugget of wisdom: 'For maybe was sign of all our times. We were certain of nothing' (p. 108). But Sammy fails, at that point at least, to take full cognisance of that grand Perhaps.

Sammy, as has been noted above, is torn in adolescence between the opposing world-views represented by his teachers Nick Shales and Rowena Pringle. This is the most explicit treatment of a debate, which runs through virtually all of Golding's novels, between a rational or scientific view of the world and a more intuitive and generally religious attitude, an opposition which has been treated of in many great works of English literature since the days of Blake, Wordsworth and Coleridge. The debate or tension between the two is often embodied in two characters: among these pairs might be numbered Piggy and Simon, Roger Mason and Jocelin in *The Spire*, Edwin Bell and Sim Goodchild in *Darkness Visible* and Edmund Talbot and Robert James Colley in *Rites of Passage*. The opposition in *Free Fall* seems to grow out of the contrast drawn in the final pages of *Pincher Martin* between the attitudes of the naval officer Davidson and the Hebridean Mr Campbell to the death of Chris Martin. Campbell wonders about the possibility of survival beyond death but Davidson, misunderstanding his drift, assures him that the drowned sailor could not have suffered much as he had no time even to kick off his seaboots. Ironically it is this earth-bound answer which opens the door to supernatural interpretations of the novel. But the two attitudes offer two ways of considering Pincher's death, two ways of reading the novel: as a disappearance into the great purple dark of nonentity or as an entry into a spiritual realm that is three times real. The novel may show a bias towards one of these readings but both seem possible and defensible. Any case one would wish to make had better be prefaced with a large 'maybe'.

The same is true of *Free Fall*. Sammy's feeling that the two world views are mutually exclusive is replaced at last by a conviction that miraculously both are true. Of each individually the best that can be said is 'maybe': a thorough conviction of the truth of one to the exclusion of the other yields a distorted and narrow view of the world. At the close of the novel, however, Sammy does not seem fully to have learned the lesson of 'maybe'. Overwhelmed by the consequences of his actions towards Beatrice, he biases the novel towards a reading which sees him as freely consenting to his own damnation, a reading which sees him as Samuel, the child called by God, as Moses was summoned by the burning bush in Miss Pringle's story, who rejects God for the world and is condemned for so doing. There is much to be said for this reading and this essay has so far been inclined to read the novel in this sort of way. But we must remember the fool's wise maybe. To read the novel exclusively in this religious sense is to impose an absolute pattern on the essential mystery of things, of Sammy's life. A reading is possible, of which, we may be sure, the kindly Nick Shales would approve, which sees Sammy's sin not as a damning mortal sin freely entered into but regards Sammy's whole involvement with Beatrice as an understandable mistake made by an immature young man which can be understood and forgiven as a result of the circumstances of his upbringing and his education. Was Sammy given free will by God to stand or fall? Did merely earthly factors of circumstance, chance, and genetic factors determine his actions? Were his actions predestined from all eternity by God? In a Godless world of atoms and forces which we can never fully understand was his choice free inasmuch that he seemed free at the time to himself? Maybe, maybe, maybe, maybe. Sammy's guardian, Father Watts-Watt, is writing a book on Pelagianism which would surely offer some views on free-will and determinism, but we are not told his attitude to Pelagianism so his view of what's what remains a mystery. But we must flesh out an *explanation* in terms of this world and his life for Sammy's sin or misbehaviour.

Just as the irreligious Nick Shales seems to be much to blame if we view the novel from a Miss Pringle point-of-view, so when we attempt to see Sammy's life as Nick might have seen it we find that Rowena Pringle has a great deal to answer for. Beatrice may represent purity, respectability and religion defiled, despised and rejected by Sammy, but the influence of Miss Pringle's uncharitable religious teaching did much to incline Sammy towards such desecration. A feature of Miss Pringle's religious lessons is that she likes to 'crucify' the boy Sammy (p. 210). She humiliates him, roasts him alive in front of the class. She instils guilt in Sammy about two things, two areas about which she seems herself deeply disturbed and unhappy: sex and class. Sammy is a growing boy; Miss Pringle knows he has a dirty mind. But then mere human flesh is dirty in the eyes of Miss Pringle: 'for Miss Pringle to touch human flesh would be a defilement'

(p. 195). Sammy is made to feel wicked for his mere humanity. But he gives particular offence to Miss Pringle because of his lowly origins, that taint seems the deeper and more vile: '"Do you suppose that I really don't know what you're like? We all know where you come from, Mountjoy, and we were willing to regard it as your misfortune"' (p. 203). But instead of simply making you feel ashamed of your birth and apology for a family (now mercifully deceased) by the charitable act of regarding it as a misfortune, we shall make you feel guilty as well by regarding your filthy nature as confirming our worst fears about life in the gutter whence you were uplifted. This is the treatment meted out to Sammy by Miss Pringle with her 'exquisite niminy-piminy lady-like air' (p. 194), whose sense of religion is so horribly entangled with her sense of class. But then that unseemly and unholy entanglement is a very prominent feature of Golding's English landscape: religion very often seems to be the handmaid not of the Lord but of the class system: 'Church of England was top and bottom; chapel was middle, was the class grimly keeping its feet out of the mud' (p. 101). Beatrice belongs to that middle class with its 'respectable devotion' (p. 80). Sammy makes sure that in the end her feet get dirty. But much responsibility for her crucifixion rests with Miss Pringle, whose lessons made Sammy's feelings about sex, religion and class such a deadly mixture of attraction and repulsion, love and hate. The guilt that was her gift to him prompted his guilty actions toward Beatrice: 'Guilty am I; therefore wicked will I be ... Guilt comes before the crime and can cause it' (p. 232).

Miss Pringle does not herself feel guilty about her treatment of Sammy, nor does she seem to suffer any punishment for her behaviour. She retires to a pretty little village and even congratulates herself, Sammy finds to his amazement and horror, that her 'care' of him may have been 'a teeny-weeny bit responsible for the things of beauty' (p. 252) that Sammy the artist has given the world. Perhaps she is more than a teeny-weeny bit right, for guilt, sin, a plunging into inner darkness do seem to contribute to the artist's creativity, as we shall see, in Golding's world. Sammy, however, does feel guilty about his treatment of Beatrice and does receive punishment both in the devastating confrontation with his victim in the asylum and in his interrogation by Dr Halde, the Nazi psychologist, in the P.O.W. camp. As was the case in *Pincher Martin* the punishment is appropriate to the sin. Sammy himself realises that his position as helpless victim of a cruel and intelligent interrogator is, as Kinkead-Weekes and Gregor point out, a reversal of his role with Beatrice:

> Sammy can say nothing; he is indeed, as a tiny but significant moment makes clear ('Do you feel nothing?' 'Maybe.') in the position of Beatrice responding to the catechisms he put her through, before he too is given over to torture.[12]

The boy who was tortured by Miss Pringle and learned to loathe himself, who tortured and threatened to kill Beatrice whom he admired, is now tortured by Halde, who tells him: '"I loathe myself, Sammy, and I admire you. If necessary I will kill you"' (p. 152). It is a grim vision of a world which is a vicious circle of self-loathing, torture and guilt, a pit full of scorpions or vipers.

Dr Halde continues his psychological torment of Sammy by locking him in an utterly dark room, (to Sammy) a pit of imaginary scorpions and vipers. Sammy feels he has been shut in with some invisible and unspeakable horror, and so he has: he has been shut in with himself. Sammy's mind creates terrors in the dark: he realises that it is a step by step process by which he must discover the dreadful truth or secret of the torture chamber, again a fit punishment for the steps of degradation down which he dragged Beatrice. The guilty Sammy is made to torture himself in the cell. It is rather like Orwell's Room 101 in *1984* in that Sammy inevitably conjures up out of the dark whatever is to him the greatest horror imaginable. Sammy is forced to explore the dark centre, the 'unfathomable and invisible darkness that sits at the centre of him' (p. 8). The darkness is made visible and fathomed in that Sammy dredges up as his greatest torture the image (indeed, he even imagines he detects the smell) of a severed penis. This grisly and gristly imagining reveals Sammy's priorities, shows that the god he serves is his own sexual appetite, and is also a comment upon them. The sexual organ is cut off, isolated from the rest of the living creature, it is no longer part of a whole human being. Being cut off, isolated, is another aspect of this 'thick, impenetrable cosmos', this world of walls, 'this wall and that wall and that wall' (p. 170). This abyss of deprivation and darkness is Sammy's world in its stark truth: Sammy creates the horrors of his own hell.

Dr Halde may be something of a devil, but devils may reluctanctly or inadvertently be instruments of good. He is also, in name, a doctor: he does seem to effect a partial cure of Sammy, who emerges from the cell into the open air of the prison camp to find a world transformed from sordidness and ugliness to the most radiant beauty. Sammy sees into the life of things, sees the world and describes it in terms recalling Traherne or the mescalin-induced ecstasies of Aldous Huxley: 'the mountains were not only clear through like purple glass, but living. They sang and were conjubilant.' It is the earthly paradise regained. The universe becomes positively Dantean: 'The power of gravity, dimension and space, the movement of the earth and sun and unseen stars, these made what might be called music and I heard it' (pp. 186–7). Sammy's experience of Halde's torture would seem to be a form of purgatory, that state which Dante imagines as a great mountain up which souls toil and strive towards bliss and beatitude, a mountain of pain and misery which is also a mount of joy. Sammy's most terrible war experience produces a vision that is in pointed contrast to that post-war pessimism Golding has described himself as experiencing: 'I returned to my fourth dimension and found that love flows along it until the heart, the physical heart, this pump or alleged pump makes love as easy as a bee makes honey' (pp. 187–8). This 'pentecostal' visitation of heavenly fire allows Sammy to create his finest works of art, the sketches of his fellow prisoners that look through the dirty surface of things to an inner realm of beauty and mystery, that sees grizzled P.O.W.s as Kings of Egypt.

But, though Sammy has escaped the nightmare cell into the realm of glad day, he is still a prisoner. He looks outward to a world of dazzling beauty but when he looks within himself he is appalled: the dark centre remains and its utter darkness is revealed by contrast with the diamond light in which the external world is bathed. Now he is aware of the nature of love, that sympathy for and enjoyment of the livingness and selfhood of the world and its creatures, he can see clearly the viciousness of his supposed love for Beatrice and appreciate, albeit too late, 'the beauty of her simplicity' (p. 191). The purgatorial process is not completed but merely begun. Sammy must face up to his guilty past, must examine with painful honesty his own behaviour as we see him doing in this novel. The result is partly an admission of guilt and partly an outline of extenuating circumstances, which may perhaps incline us to think that Sammy is worthy of the scalding mercies and diligent pains of purgatory. The irremediable consequences of his sin on earth remain in the form of Beatrice but at least Sammy is willing to face them and her in a final ordeal.

In the ordeal of the cell Sammy seems to go through a form of death and emerge a 'resurrected' man (p. 186). This pattern of symbolic death and rebirth, this descent into and emergence from darkness, is found elsewhere in Golding's fiction: Simon's confrontation with the embodiment of evil, the Lord of the Flies, culminates in his falling into the blackness of the hideous idol's mouth, descending through the jaws of hell in his prophetic fit; Matty, the holy fool of *Darkness Visible*, organises for himself in the Australian outback an extraordinary trial in the desert in which he submerges himself in the primeval slime and *ur*-darkness of a nocturnal billabong to emerge with renewed strength for his prophetic mission and ultimate self-immolation. These rehearsals of death, these plunges into darkness, seem to enhance the insight, the vision, the prophetic powers of those who undergo their agonies. Even Sammy, who seems in other ways no prophet, emerges with an intense religious apprehension of the world, a prophetic vision of his own filthiness and grievous sin, and wholly new artistic powers.

Free Fall, like *La Vita Nuova*, is something of a portrait of the artist as a young man. Sammy may bear little apparent resemblance to his creator but he does resemble

Golding in one important respect: his art grows out of and is galvanised by a fearless contemplation of the darkness of the human heart, an heroic delving into the muddy pool of human sin and depravity. As Jocelin discovers in *The Spire*, to build a work of art that towers into the heavens involves digging deep into the stinking pit of the self. The pattern of falling to rise again in art is found in perhaps the most famous *kunstlersroman* of all, Joyce's *A Portrait of the Artist as a Young Man*. Stephen Dedalus prefigures Sammy in his attraction to the pure religious girl, both the Blessed Virgin Mary herself and the earthly 'E—C—', and to the simple beauties of holiness. Stephen's human nature creates difficulties with the female who is like a *'Tower of Ivory'* and he is a rebel against the Church. Stephen defiles the image of the virgin by his determined devotions to prostitutes: he has his eyes on the stars but his feet in the gutter. However, Joyce makes it clear that this self-defilement, this plunge in 'the wild heart of life', is the key to Stephen's artistic development, his self-resurrection: it is Stephen's duty 'to live, to err, to fall, to triumph, to recreate life out of life'.[13] Dante looms large in the catholic and Catholic sensibility of Joyce and his name is mentioned on the first page of Joyce's 'Vita Nuova', but Joyce's young artist is a great deal earthier than Dante: where Dante pretended to be attracted to another woman to conceal his feelings for Beatrice lest Beatrice be affronted by his presumption, Stephen finds himself whores with whom to enact the fantasies that would shock his admired virgin. Cold, virginal women are a trouble to other Joycean characters who strongly resemble their creator: Gabriel Conroy in 'The Dead' is lectured to by the moralistic Miss Ivors and Richard Rowan in *Exiles* has for years been conducting an affair in fantasy with the Dantean Beatrice Justice.

The innocent Beatrice Ifor seems to owe a little to the Joycean background. But the corruption or destruction of feminine innocence is a feature of those artist heroes whom Stephen Dedalus admires and would like to think he resembles. Sammy's amatory career is also attuned to such conventions of the artist's life. There is the ambitious, God-defying Faust who seduces the simple and religious

Margaret. There is Stephen's favourite poet, Lord Byron. Sammy, once the young romantic whose obsession with the lovely Beatrice drove him 'forth on dark nights forsooth striding round the downs' (p. 115), can recall with bitter hindsight that his 'claims to evil were Byronic' (p. 232). Byron certainly set a standard of debauchery which has been difficult for young artists to emulate, but Sammy could without doubt say of his Beatrice what Byron has his self-recreation Manfred say of his beloved Astarte: 'I loved her and destroyed her.'[14] The role which fictional artists seem most inclined to play is, however, the plum role of them all, Hamlet. Joyce's *A Portrait of the Artist as a Young Man* and *Ulysses* are littered with references to and echoes of Shakespeare's masterpiece. The ambitious, proud, gloomy and sullen Stephen identifies with the philosophical and melancholy prince, the true prince and all-round renaissance man, the usurped heir to the throne and crown. Sammy too is likened to Hamlet, but the likeness is in terms of gloomy introspection and the wickedness or irresponsibility that drives a devoted girl mad. With reference to his strange guardian Father Watts-Watt Sammy asks the question, 'is a man who pretends to be mad completely sane?' (p. 160), a question which might well be levelled at Hamlet or at Sammy himself, who blackmailed Beatrice with his threat of madness. Locked up in the darkness of Halde's torture-chamber, Sammy's first words are '"Who's there?"' (p. 167), the nervy opening words of *Hamlet*. Another hint is found in the chapter describing the ordeal in the cell, which reminds us of the ill-usage of a girl for which this nightmare seems a punishment: 'Nothing communicated with nothing' (p. 172). The phrase echoes the mad, abused Ophelia.

Golding's artist, like Joyce's, is under an obligation to explore the dark underside of his (and everyone else's) humanity, to explore unflinchingly, in Auden's phrase, 'the bottom of the night'.[15] It is, unsurprisingly, a common determination among artistic explorers in this century of Freud, who pointed the way towards vast stretches of un-discovered, or at any rate poorly mapped, country in the psyche. Auden in his magnificent elegy for Freud praised him as an artistic hero who, like Dante, had dared to

descend into 'the stinking fosse'[16] of the Inferno, the underworld of the human mind. Joyce followed suit by sending
Stephen and Bloom down into the shifting phantasmagory
of depravity and beastliness that is the 'Circe' episode of
Ulysses. The artistic duty is to explore what man is, however horrible or painful the experience. This Golding has
himself set down as his artistic credo in terms which stress
the agony of the process: 'What man *is* ... that I burn to
know ...', like the 'burning amateur' (p. 5) Sammy, and
that he 'would endure knowing' (MT p. 199). The painful
duty of the writer, as of the psychiatrist, is to enable people
to understand and acknowledge their own humanity: 'The
greatest pleasure is not—say—sex or geometry. It is just
understanding. And if you can get people to understand
their own humanity—well, that's the job of the writer.'[17]
But the knowledge that the exploratory artist gains is a
source of guilt and shame: to acknowledge that one is a
human being, one would think from reading the first four
novels of Golding, is a dreadful admission to make in
public. The artist's knowledge makes him, in Dr Halde's
words, '"set apart from [his] fellows"' (p. 143). Yet the
artist is also like Halde himself, a ruthless pursuer of the
truth. Halde explains his role to Sammy:

> I shall explain you to yourself. No one, not a lover, a father, a
> schoolmaster, could do that for you. They are all inhibited by
> conventions and human kindness. It is only in such conditions
> as these, electric furnace conditions, in which the molten,
> blinding truth may be uttered from one human face to another.
> (p. 144)

Golding himself has admitted that his art tests people to
destruction to get at the truth; Sammy has thrown Beatrice
into the furnace with the carelessness Halde's colleagues
displayed in such immolations; Sammy the artist gains by
his debasement of and with Beatrice and in the clutches of
Halde. The artist for art's sake must be both torturer and
victim, but is artistic triumph worth 'everything', worth
even one's own soul?

The question troubles Golding, but he remains committed
to the exploration of the darkness at the centre of us 'that

hopes hopelessly to understand and to be understood' (p. 8). Hoping hopelessly is not a rational state but the dark is not rational, nor is it wholly explicable by rationality, by the clear light of reason. The darkness remains part of the mystery of man, that dark continent that defeats would-be cartographers, a mystery as insoluble as free-will or determinism. For Sammy and for Golding the systems man creates to describe himself and his life—narrative structures or even Freudian theory—falsify because they are selective. They are useful nets for trawling in the dark waters, but they do not catch the ocean upon which they are cast: 'Living is like nothing because it is everything' (p. 7).

·5·

DIVINE TRAGI-COMEDY
·THE SPIRE (1964)·

If the fool would persist in his folly he would become wise.
William Blake, *The Marriage of Heaven and Hell*

Because the foolishness of God is wiser than men; and the
weakness of God is stronger than men.
I Corinthians 1.25

'Only an aching heart', wrote Yeats, 'conceives a changeless
work of art'.[1] A church-spire rising above an English landscape is likely to inspire feelings of calm, peacefulness,
a gentle nostalgia: it is a changeless focus and symbol
of Christian community. Pre-eminent among the spires of
England is that of Salisbury Cathedral, a changeless work of
art that soars four hundred feet above the cathedral close.
Anyone with half an ounce of imagination who sees that
extraordinary structure must surely ask the question: how
on earth did they manage to build it? One might answer
oneself with the pious platitude that in those days they built
in faith, that the men of those times were spiritual giants
who simply piled stone on stone in the confident hope that
God would hold the structure up. Certainly it must have
taken a steely faith to dare so high above ground, but a
moment's reflection shows the explanation to be inadequate
and sentimental. Spires, towers and whole churches sometimes fell down: God did not always provide. What fear the
news or rumour of such calamities must have sown in the
minds of the masons! For these works were not, of course,
erected simply by prayer and faith but by the skill and
calculation of master-masons, by the muscle and sweat of

small armies of craftsmen and labourers. These men must have had great skill and courage, perhaps great faith, but they must also have known dreadful fear and awful aching of heart and limb in working ever upwards into unknown heights of air. They must have been mad! They must have been driven half-mad certainly. What storms there must have been in the creation of this calm! What tension there must have been between faith and reason, between the desire to trust in and glorify God to the utmost and the wordly but understandable wish not to be killed, between the spiritual aspiration that seeks to go as high as the very heavens and the common sense or calculation that says such ambition will bring the whole structure tumbling down in ruin.

The Spire recreates with a great deal more than half an ounce of imagination the stormy time that saw the spire of Salisbury rise above Golding's home county of Wiltshire. The tension between faith and reason is embodied in the fraught relationship of the novel's two central protagonists, Jocelin, Dean of the Cathedral Church of Our Lady, and Roger Mason, the skilful but sceptical architect who must struggle to make real and safe Jocelin's vision of skyward-thrusting stone. The tension in the work is not, however, simply between them but upon them. Locked in combat, they must bear upon the arch of their shoulders the appalling weight of the great spire, the colossal stone hammer that threatens to batter them into the ground. Both are physically and mentally broken by the pressure, driven into madness, Jocelin's back and Roger's neck giving way under the weight they have foolishly tried to carry.

The novel makes us intensely aware of the awful forces and pressures that must oppose each other and come to balance or cancel each other out so that the spire, that apotheosis of the pyramid, can reach into the heavens, can hang from the sky. And hang there, almost miraculously, it still does: we can go and see it, a vision made flesh in stone, an almost-miracle in the county of Wiltshire, a bridge between earth and heaven. That bridge is built by the combined forces of Jocelin, the fanatically faithful Dean who believes that the cathedral even before the addition of his spire is already a miraculous creation of giants of old, and Roger the worldly-wise and frightened expert in stones and stresses who knows that the Dean, by forcing them so high, may be heading for a great fall, but who contributes nonetheless to the scheme all that human ingenuity can. Neither man, neither world-view, alone could build so high. The world-view of each is too limited to achieve art of miraculous standing. Roger needs Jocelin's faith and will to thrust him ever upwards, to force him to set new limits to the possible: Jocelin requires Roger's expertise to make his dream a reality, but more generally he needs to have a little more reality, a little more of the earthly world, brought into the dream-world of his cathedral. For Jocelin's faith and the cheery optimism with which he sets out on the project are naive or childish. Jocelin has indeed been treated like a pampered child and knows very little of the muddy grown-up world outside the sacred battlements of the great church. The first stage of Roger's programme is to breach the cathedral walls, letting in both dirt and light. As the spire grows up, so too does Jocelin. The process of enlightenment involves becoming aware of the dirt and beauty of the human world his cloistered existence had kept at a distance.

That human world includes Jocelin and he comes to see how mixed were his own motives in wishing to build the spire. The spire is not merely a diagram of prayer or signpost to heaven, but a phallic image of his own desire for Goody Pangall, the lust that he had almost succeeded in concealing from himself. It is sexual energy as well as faith that creates the work, as is underlined by Roger's intercourse with Goody in the scaffolding of the spire, and by the fact that the financial support of the project is being provided by Jocelin's aunt Lady Alison, a king's mistress, a fallen woman. Nor is this the only admixture Jocelin discovers to the purity of the faith upon which the spire is built. The band of workmen that Roger precariously commands are not merely '"Murderers, cutthroats, rowdies, brawlers, rapers, notorious fornicators, sodomites, atheists"' (p. 167), but, '"worse"', are devotees of a pagan religion older than Christianity, worshippers, as Jocelin sees it, of Satan himself. To Jocelin it seems as though the spire built to the glory of God is threatened by Satan, who would like to bring it crashing to the ground, yet Satan and his minions do seem to contribute a very great deal to the spire's construction.

The Spire is a comedy in that it describes the ultimate triumph of the central characters: for all its imperfections the spire stands. Yet it is also tragic in that it describes the fall into disgrace and destruction of Jocelin and Roger, a true medieval tragedy in being *de casibus virorum illustribus*, a chronicle of the downfall of great men, the notable architect and the Dean of the Cathedral Church of Our Lady. The story of the building of the spire is tragi-comic, like the central events of the divine comedy of man's fall and redemption.'*It's like the appletree!*' (p. 223) is Jocelin's dying attempt to characterise the spire and the terrible experience of building it. It is, indeed, like the Tree of Knowledge of Good and Evil, whose mortal taste brought death into the world and all our woe, but which increased man's glory in that it led to the incarnation of Christ and his redemption of man. Jocelin tastes the bitterness of knowledge of evil in himself and all around him but succeeds in making incarnate his glorious vision of man's hopes. The spire also resembles the Tree of the Cross, typologically associated with the Tree of Knowledge, upon which mankind was redeemed through the tragedy of the sacrifice of an innocent and glorious victim. The glory of the spire redeems all but requires the sacrifice of the lives not merely of Jocelin and Roger but the ritual sacrifice of the scapegoat Pangall. Like the Christian account of history it is the tragi-comic story of a *felix culpa*.

The story of the *felix culpa* of Adam and Eve, the story of Original Sin, is one of a fall from innocence into experience. So too is that of Dean Jocelin. *The Spire* opens, like *The Inheritors,* in innocence, with joy and laughter, the ecstasy of innocent vision:

> He was laughing, chin up, and shaking his head. God the father was exploding in his face with a glory of sunlight through painted glass, a glory that moved with his movements to consume and exalt Abraham and Isaac and then God again. The tears of laughter in his eyes made additional spokes and wheels and rainbows. (p. 7)

Though already in this tragi-comedy there is a juxtaposition of tears and laughter, the overwhelming impression of the novel's first chapter is of sharing the beautiful and alien view of the world through Jocelin's innocent and medieval eyes. This effect is achieved, again as in *The Inheritors*, by a stylistic *tour de force*, by the creation of a prose style that expresses the world as seen by the medieval Jocelin. Golding avoids, however, the awful pitfall of writing a prose that is dressed-up in medievalisms: such an approach guarantees disaster, as in this extract from a 'translation' of the Middle English poem, Layamon's *Brut*:

> ... and so I will destroy the race that he of came. And if I evermore subsequently hear, that any of my folk, of high or of low, eft arear strife on account of this same slaughter, there shall ransom him neither gold nor any treasure, fine horse or war-garment, that he should not be dead, or with horses drawn in pieces—that is of each traitor the law![2]

One may say of this misguided translator, borrowing Jonson's words on Spenser, that 'affecting the ancients', he 'writ no language'.[3]

In general Golding sensibly avoids such period-costume treatment of language. 'If you go the the Hot Gates,' he wrote in a travel essay on Thermopylae 'take some historical knowledge and your imagination with you' (HG p. 16). In *The Spire* he follows this advice and imaginatively and convincingly creates a medieval world-view in a prose that is generally plain and unaffected. There *is* a certain formality about the prose: it is the product of a mind used to ceremony and decorum, to all things in their due place and order. The medievalism of the style is an expression of a way of thinking: 'Jocelin stood still and shot an arrow of love after him' (p. 8); 'As if the knowing was cue for entry in an interlude he heard a latch lift in the north-west corner and a door creak open. I shall see, as I see daily, my daughter in God' (p. 11). The metaphor of the arrow and the simile of the interlude are the products of some historical knowledge imaginatively employed. Once again Golding is displaying his ability to take us to a remote setting and convince us that we are thereby creating the atmosphere, the *feel* of the place and its people, in the novel's prose.

The world in which we find ourselves seems at first a Gothic Eden, a Ruskinian fantasy of a medieval world free from the religious doubts and self-questionings of the modern world, the kind of paradise of faith described by Carlyle in *Past and Present*, a work that has its source in the chronicle of another medieval Jocelin:

> Jocelin, Eadmer, and such religious men, have as yet nothing of 'Methodism'; no Doubt or even root of Doubt. Religion is not a diseased self-introspection, an agonizing inquiry: their duties are clear to them, the way of supreme good plain, indisputable, and they are travelling on it. Religion lies over them like an all-embracing heavenly canopy ...[4]

It may well seem to us, however, that religion really ought to involve some measure of introspection: the vision of the Pre-Reformation as prelapsarian paradise in *The Spire*'s opening pages is illusory, a product of the ludicrously naive and disgracefully complacent mind of Jocelin. The process of building the spire forces Jocelin into agonising inquiry about himself and his cloistered world. From the very outset, however, we can see, if we read with great care, not only through the eyes but, in Frank Kermode's apt phrase, 'over the shoulder of Jocelin'.[5] We see the fallen nature of his world and the flaws in him, though at first these are mere suspicions.

Jocelin enters the nave of his cathedral for the first time in the novel to find a blazingly beautiful world of 'solid sunlight', where the light pouring through the windows is made into seemingly tangible 'rods and trunks' (p. 10) by grains of fine dust kicked up by the masons. Jocelin sees motes and beams before him but is very disinclined to heed the warning about motes and beams in St Matthew:

> And why beholdest thou the mote that is in thy brother's eye, but considerest not the beam that is in thine own eye?
> Or how wilt thou say to thy brother, Let me pull out the mote out of thine eye; and, behold, a beam is in thine own eye?
> Thou hypocrite, first cast out the beam out of thine own eye;

and then thou shalt see clearly to cast out the mote out of thy brother's eye.[6]

Such Pharisaic behaviour is typical of Jocelin, who rebukes two gossiping deacons for accusing someone of pride and ignorance but who could not even begin to suspect in his ignorant self-complacency and pride that the subject of their backbiting is himself. For Jocelin, though he thinks himself a saint, one of God's chosen ones, is guilty of pride, that first and deadliest of sins. He is riding for a fall.

'All these years I have gone on, put the place on me like a coat' (p. 8) reflects Jocelin cosily and complacently, but there is sinful pride and vanity in his regarding the cathedral as an embellishment to himself. As he goes ostentatiously to prayer like the Pharisee in Scripture, he compares himself, addressing the dumb man who is carving his image for a gargoyle, to one of the four central piers, the pillars of the temple, that hold the whole cathedral up. Jocelin's enthusiasm for the heaven-reaching spire may therefore be attributable to a desire, of which he is himself perhaps scarcely aware, to glorify himself as well as God. The scheme is reminiscent of the Tower of Babel in Genesis, that monument to the folly of human pride: 'And they said, Go to, let us build a city and a tower, whose top may reach unto heaven: and let us make us a name.'[7] The association with Babel is reinforced by the varied languages of the masons, who have come from far and wide for the work. On his first visit to the vertiginous world of the spire's growing top Jocelin thinks how he 'would like the spire to be a thousand feet high' so that he might 'oversee the whole county' (p. 106). Even Jocelin is surprised by the self-aggrandising ambition in this. His ambition endangers many lives, but Jocelin is sure that God will provide and protect. This may be admirable faith, but Jocelin among the pinnacles of the tower also calls to mind the temptation of Christ by Satan at the pinnacle of the temple. Christ refuses to put his Father to the test by throwing himself down and rebukes Satan: 'Thou shall not tempt the Lord thy God.'[8] Jocelin's mad confidence in God puts God to the test: it is arguable that Jocelin's pride grows with the spire into the sin of presumption, the arrogant assumption or certainty of God's grace and favour.

Other deadly sins are also seen in Jocelin. There is anger in his argument with Anselm the Sacrist; there is envy of Roger's involvement with Goody Pangall; there is covetousness of Pangall's wife; there is lust for her. This last is at the bottom of much that is wrong with Jocelin. He fires an arrow of love, casting himself unknowingly in the role of Cupid or Eros, sexual desire personified. Desire for Goody, desire for self-glorification, these cupidities are at the root of much evil in Jocelin. He would do well to heed the stern warning of Chaucer's Pardoner: 'Radix malorum est Cupiditas.'[9] We learn of Jocelin's failings both through the direct evidence of his interaction with others and his thoughts and also by reading the book rather as a medieval might have read the symbolism of the form and images of a cathedral. Indeed, as Kinkead-Weekes and Gregor demonstrate, in the book's opening sentences we must interpret the significance of an image in the cathedral's glass: 'The meaning of the stained glass, that story of Abraham and Isaac and the cost of faith, passes [Jocelin] by'.[10] We must go back to the Bible to discover the image's relevance to Jocelin's story. Similarly, we ought to compare the spire-building to the Biblical incidents of Babel and the temptation of Christ and we must think allegorically to see the significance of Jocelin's arrow of love. We must see how the surface story of events is enriched and given meaning by relating it to the events of Holy Scripture and to a world of moral allegory.

Jocelin himself is not very skilled at reading or seeing the significance of his cathedral, or himself, or the world. He is not, as he later admits when beginning to learn humility, a learned man. He is both ignorant and obtuse. The significance of the image of Abraham and Isaac passes him by. The dumb stonecutter carves the gargoyle of Jocelin with 'wide, blind eyes' (p. 24), an image of innocent naivety and impercipience which Jocelin, as if to underline the point, misinterprets as representation of his spiritual vision. Jocelin's innocence is that of a wide-eyed child, of a big baby, who cannot see his own pride and who can lie

to himself about his motive in wishing to see daily his
'daughter in God', Goody Pangall. Jocelin sees his church as
an island of sanctity in a foul ocean of sin, a ship offering
rescue on the rough seas of the world: 'There is no good
thing in all this circle but the great house, the ark, the
refuge, a ship to contain all these people and now fitted with
a mast' (p. 107). Evil is a threat that comes from outside.
Satan is 'the beast' (p. 161) who batters at the walls of the
fortress-church in a storm. Jocelin, given to identifying
himself with his church, has a rather similar attitude to
himself: he is sanctified; sin and Satan are threats from
without. Thus a sexual dream is a visit from Satan not a
welling-up of something from within, some repressed part
of Jocelin's self. Even when he has gained much in self-
knowledge he falls back on blaming Goody Pangall's supposed witchcraft. Jocelin has been guilty, as were others
before him in Golding's novels, of externalising the devil.
This has allowed the devil a pretty free rein. As we have
seen, Jocelin is not so full of the beauties of holiness as he
would like to think. Nor, for that matter, is the ark of
salvation wholly perfect either: the Bishop, who ought to be
captain, has abandoned ship and is living it up in Rome,
while the Chancellor, one of those who must steer the ship
in his absence, has lost all sense of direction.

The building of the spire will educate Jocelin about himself and his house, will help the great child grow up. As he
himself comes to realise, there will be a lesson at every level
in the spire's growth. Jocelin's tears of joy at the outset
made him see rainbows, the rainbow being a sort of bridge
between earth and heaven but also a reminder of the catastrophe of the biblical Flood, brought about by human
wickedness. Jocelin's spire-building allows the filthy waters
of the world to invade the ark, the body of the cathedral. He
will learn that his own church and body partake of the sin
of the world which he observes from the tower. He will
learn the vital lesson that the beast is within him, but the
shock of this sudden end to innocence will break him.
His innocent faith and guilty ambitions and desires will
also leave the spire, magnificent though imperfect, as
their memorial.

Innocence and faith, however, are not in themselves enough to build the small mountain of the spire. Jocelin needs the experience of the master builder Roger Mason to achieve his ambition. Jocelin has his head in the clouds from the outset and finds himself at ease in the airy world of the ascending spire. Roger, by contrast, is in all ways a man of earth, practically-minded, physically powerful, but with a most unfortunate fear of heights. His name, as so often in Golding, declares his nature: Mason indicates simply his trade and skill as builder, Roger has the slang meaning 'to copulate with', indicating Roger's troublesome sexual energy, another aspect of his earthiness and creativity. For the spire is thrust upward by faith and craft, but also by sexual energy. The spire is a blatant image of Jocelin's desire for Goody Pangall, a substitute for consummation engineered by Roger, who with the connivance of Jocelin achieves that consummation with Goody within the spire, within the very house of God.

This is certainly a sacrilege, but Roger and Jocelin glorify as well as profane the sacred stones. Such ecclesiastic corruption and cupidity remind Don Crompton of Browning's poem 'The Bishop Orders his Tomb at St Praxed's Church'. Browning's poem exhibits the outrageous worldliness of a Renaissance clergyman, his lust for power, luxury, a woman and his desire for a glorious memorial in the form of a spectacular tomb with sumptuous embellishments:

> Some lump, ah God, of *lapis lazuli*,
> Big as a Jew's head cut off at the nape,
> Blue as a vein o'er the Madonna's breast.[11]

The casual cruelty is arresting, the sacrilegiously erotic reference to the Virgin Mary, surely indebted to a line of Shakespeare's Cleopatra, breathtaking in its blasphemy. Yet one is forced to think also of Renaissance paintings of the Madonna: the Renaissance church was corrupt and worldly and yet that very worldliness contributed to its stunning achievement in religious art. Golding's novel is similarly concerned to vindicate sexuality as contributing to great artistic achievement. Jocelin is in a hurry to build high but

Roger the man of earth insists that to do so they must dig deep. They must dig a pit at the centre of the body of the cathedral, dig down into the horrible and terrifying subterranean world:

> Some form of life, that which ought not to be seen or touched, the darkness under the earth, turning, seething, coming to the boil ... Doomsday coming up, or the roof of hell down there. Perhaps the damned stirring, or the noseless men turning over and thrusting up, or the living pagan earth, unbound at last and waking, Dia Mater. (pp. 79–80)

Jocelin is gazing down into a fecund and female world; to his way of thinking it is a realm of darkness and devils, an evil to be hidden away or walled out. But Roger's digging has broken open the earth, opened up the cathedral to the influences of this seething, boiling witches' cauldron, has tapped into the earth-magic of pagan religion. The old religion, the subterranean paganism of the masons and country people, will also play a role in the building of the spire. This is another way in which the spire is a rainbow-bridge between earth and heaven, a product of the combined if antipathetic forces of light and dark. The hull of the cathedral ark is holed to allow in foul stenches and the rising waters of a flood but also to admit more light; the great church is fallen into impious ways but the fall will further the flight in its stones.

Jocelin and Roger, though in many ways mighty opposites, are alike in that they are both engaged in colossal folly. The building of the spire, that giant 'dunce's cap' (p. 119), is 'Jocelin's Folly' (p. 35) and Roger merely tries to bring a modicum of sanity to the scheme. In terms of knowledge of the world Roger is no fool, but his experiences in Salisbury reduce him to a failed suicide, crippled, and helpless 'like a baby'. Roger is reluctant to be involved in the folly of building too high but he is dragged down, again with reluctance, into folly of another kind, folly in the archaic or occasional sense of sexual misbehaviour, the sense in which Jocelin employs the term when he thinks of the spire as 'a diagram of the folly they don't know about' (p. 128). The essentially decent and plain-dealing Roger is roped into, entangled in the folly of adultery with Goody Pangall. As Roger consents, defeated, to the murder of her husband, the two face each other across the mouth of the pit of hell. Jocelin too is involved with this unholy folly. Indeed, though their liaison is deeply painful to him, for he too is bewitched by Goody's beauty, he connives at it because he thinks it will keep Roger at Salisbury to complete his task. Jocelin must realise that Roger is imperilling his soul by his folly but Jocelin is determined he should be enmeshed for the spire's sake. One might almost say that Jocelin with his arrows of love plays Cupid to Roger and Goody. One might say that he allows the house of God to become an unruly house, that he himself becomes a pimp for the sake of the spire. Jocelin, who should look after Roger's soul with pastoral care, is prepared to use Roger as 'his tool' (p. 68) to get what he wants. Jocelin observes the folly of Roger and Goody not merely with the eye of the outraged keeper of God's house who connives at its desecration so that it may be glorified the more, but as a voyeur, an espy-er of pleasures or sins that he craves but dare only enjoy at one remove by watching them. He himself comes to understand the sordid role he has played:

> Once, standing lost in his private storm at the west end of the empty cathedral, he saw her cross the nave, heavily and clumsily with child; and he knew in himself a mixture of dear love and prurience, a wet-lipped fever to know how and where and when and what. (p. 127)

Jocelin feels that he may be able to hold up the spire by sheer force of will. But will is rather a Satanic quality: perhaps he half-consciously wills the entanglement of Roger and Goody too. He sees the shamed Goody after the disappearance of Pangall: 'But my will has other business than to help, he thought. I have so much will, it puts all other business by' (p. 97). This will pushes aside his pastoral care and duties. He boasts of having 'so much will', but there is an archaic sense of the word which signifies sexual desire:

Jocelin seems unknowingly to admit to a problem that plagues the Shakespeare of *The Sonnets*, 'Will in over-plus'.[12] Jocelin's will, the burgeoning sexual desire that may be attributable to the disease of the spine he mistakes for the ministrations of an angel, wills the supreme folly of Goody and Roger's intercourse at the crossways.

Jocelin's sight of this unholy sacrament of love is des-cribed in such a way as distantly to suggest the Crucifixion. Jocelin, who has played the pimp or pander to Roger and Goody, is associated (at the point of Goody's death in giving birth to the child of this union) with Judas, who sold Christ for blood-money. Jocelin brings money to Goody to ransom her from disgrace, but in the panic and horror of this dead birth 'there was blood over the money on the floor so that the world spun' (p. 136). The Easter carol that Jocelin recalls speaks of Christ as the 'true love' (p. 137). Jocelin has given his true love Goody in marriage to an impotent man, has connived at or even willed her adultery (while thinking it also a very grave sin): his will has been done. Roger too, put back firmly on the leash by his wife Rachel, seems to condemn himself as a betrayer or Judas by attempt-ing to hang himself. Jocelin hammers in the Holy Nail, an appropriate task since the sins of man are responsible for the crucifixion of Christ. But punishment for sin is heavy. Jocelin himself is nailed to the ground at the crossways by the giant stone hammer of the spire. Once again these punishments seem appropriate for the sin of desecrating God's house, for committing that dreadful folly.

God's house is also glorified by that folly, however: out of that moral compost-heap grows the spire. There is a holier kind of folly in Jocelin too, the kind indicated in the quotation from St Paul at the head of this chapter. Jocelin's foolishness in building so high is wiser than the wisdom of men, as exemplified by the cautious Roger. Jocelin 'built in faith' (p. 190) as well as folly, though for success there needed to be added to faith the good works devised by Roger. It is arguable that Jocelin emulates the faith and works of Abraham, illuminated in the novel's opening words, and suggested by St James as an example:

But wilt thou know, O vain man, that faith without works
is dead?
Was not Abraham our father justified by works, when he
had offered Isaac his son upon the altar?[13]

Jocelin's tendency to offer other people, to include them
in the cost of his self-aggrandising scheme, vitiates his
actions to a considerable extent, yet Jocelin above all· is
willing to offer himself: 'My will is in the pillars and the
high wall. I offered myself; and I am learning' (p. 97). He
imitates the sublime folly of Christ, 'God's Folly' (p. 121):
he is sacrificed, like Christ, of his own volition. Christianity,
in its lack of worldly wisdom and its spirit of self-sacrifice,
was folly to the Greeks, like Roger mathematicians and
builders of squat temples. But the fruit of self-sacrifice is the
glorious mystery of the spire: whatever the dubious origins
of the Holy Nail, the spire *is* nailed to the sky. Attempting
to nail something to the sky is an act of utter folly or
madness: a successful attempt is a miracle.

Jocelin's progress in the building of the spire is by no
means a simple matter of his sinking into a pit of sin. He
rises as he sinks. He learns humility; he can say to himself:
'I'm not very intelligent' (p. 140). He goes among the lowly
tradesmen, shares their work and their fears, becomes
a jack-of-all-trades, one of those trades being that of
carpenter. In so humbling himself he imitates Christ. '"I am
about my Father's business"' he twice remarks in the fourth
chapter (pp. 67, 69) where the self-association with Christ,
particularly as it is an excuse for neglect of priestly duty, is
prideful and sinful. It is as he learns to see the sin in his own
nature that he comes to seem more genuinely Christlike. An
unlikely Christ-figure he certainly is, but more unlikely yet
are to come in Golding's novels. He neglects his pastoral
duties, he neglects the sacraments altogether. To the other
clergymen of the cathedral he seems to have gone mad in
his obsession, to have reduced himself to a buffoon and
disgraced the dignity of his office by associating or mucking
in with the rag-bag of sinners and criminals who are the
workmen. But that reflects well on Jocelin and badly on
them. In his mad vision he towers above his fellow clerics

and Jocelin does seem like a giant of both faith and works when placed beside a 'minimal' (p. 202) priest like Anselm, a spiritual time-server and follower of the letter rather than the spirit.

Anselm does not wish to be humbled or to go among the humble: '"You must admit it capped everything, to try and make a man of my years and standing into a builder's mate"' (p. 203). Jocelin is, however, severely dealt with by more worthy men, the Visitor and Father Adam. Jocelin has misbehaved outrageously and so must forfeit his office, but in the interest of his soul he must be cared for and reformed. Jocelin proves to be a difficult object of reform. Having begun in pride and presumption he ends in the opposite, but subtly similar, sin of despair. The two sins are linked, as 'sins against the Holy Ghost', by another cathedral Dean, John Donne: 'The first couple is, *presumption* and *desperation*; for presumption takes away the feare of God, and desperation the love of God.'[14] Appalled by the vision of his own sinfulness, and the sinfulness of the world around him in its pride, he abandons hope in God. Father Adam encourages the dying man to re-affirm his belief that he might receive the sacrament and be saved, but Jocelin's reaction is ambiguous:

> Father Adam, leaning down, could hear nothing. But he saw a tremor of the lips that might be interpreted as a cry of: *God! God! God!* So of the charity to which he had access, he laid the host on the dead man's tongue. (p. 223)

But Father Adam seems absurdly like a spiritual banker or accountant and, even by his own system of accountancy, his withdrawal from the charity-bank comes too late to save the dead man.

Once again we are faced with the question: *was* he saved? Perhaps it is an improper question to ask of a character who has shuffled off the mortal coil and departed a *fictive* world, but it is one which Golding provokes time and again. He is in good company: Shakespeare in two of his greatest works, *Hamlet* and *Othello*, asks us at least to think about the post-mortal fate of his tragic heroes. In *The Spire* Golding seems to stress, as again he will later, the difficulty of such judgement: it is clear that the mechanical system of salvation credited by Father Adam is an absurd travesty of the mystery of a man's fate. At the close Jocelin may be in despair, but that despair is also a visionary scepticism: Jocelin can see deeper into the mystery, the tragi-comedy of the human condition than ever Father Adam, a man of genuine devotion, could. His vision of the awful unknowableness, the mystery of things, seems in a curious way closer to God than Father Adam's mechanical faith. His despair is, after all, the product of his profound sense of his own sin in all its seriousness and the physical devastation of his self-sacrifice. He may be in darkness, but perhaps that darkness is the Dark Night of the Soul described by St John of the Cross, that spiritual desert of uncertainty in God and self-condemnation so powerfully evoked in the 'Terrible Sonnets' of Hopkins, the darkness that is nearness to God.

This discussion has treated the fools and folly of the novel from a Christian perspective. The novel's religious vision is wider than that, however. When Christ the fool took the sins of the world upon himself and allowed himself to be killed to expiate them, to give new life to a sick world, he fulfilled a role that is found in pagan communities and beliefs. Jocelin thinks, even in the sunny early pages of the novel, that the changes wrought by the masons make the cathedral look like 'some sort of pagan temple' and that the builders themselves might be 'the priests of some outlandish rite' (p. 10). This idle imagining turns out to be near the truth, for Jocelin later discovers that the masons are practisers of pagan rituals. The first signs of their lingering paganism are seen in their superstitious mistreatment of the unfortunate and misshapen Pangall. Their galling of him for the sake of luck is an ancient superstitious use of the fool, as Enid Welsford describes in her social and literary history of folly, *The Fool*:

> ... misshapen, ugly, abnormal people are immune from the Evil Eye and ... images of them were ... employed as mascots in the Graeco-Roman world, apparently on the principle that

contact with the lucky brings good luck ... it is possible, therefore, that they and their masters were acting on the widespread belief that raillery is a protection against misfortune. But sometimes this idea might be developed in a way that tended to transform the fool from a mascot into a scapegoat, for it must be remembered that a scapegoat is not necessarily killed, he may be employed as a sort of spiritual whipping-boy.[15]

This role of mascot or lucky charm to the builders is later taken on by Jocelin, after he has begun to look like a mad buffoon and after the masons, feeling the need for more potent magic to keep their luck going on the insane project, have ritually slaughtered Pangall and thrown him as an offering into the pit at the crossways.

The spire is built not merely on Christian faith but on pagan human sacrifice. Jocelin offers himself, but Pangall is the first victim. His very name suggests the role, the bearer of all the cares and sorrows of the world: he is, after all, the church's caretaker. He is, as Don Crompton suggests, every inch the scapegoat: 'Scapegoat he certainly is, and even his deformity ... is one of the common characteristics of the tainted wether of the flock who must bear the sins of the many that all may live.'[16] Pangall is slaughtered because the workers are afraid that the whole kingdom of the cathedral will collapse around their ears: the threat to the kingdom is from its ruler Jocelin. Perhaps Pangall is a substitute for Jocelin, who is protected at the time of killing by the massive arms of the dumb man: such a substitution of fool for priest-king seems to be a convenience with a long anthropological history, as Enid Welsford describes:

There are traces in many parts of the world of periodically slaying the priest-king for the good of the whole community, which has been gradually modified by the substitution of a mock-king for the real ruler, and of a dramatic for an actual death. At certain seasons of the year people collect all their diseases and sins and misfortunes, and bind them upon some unfortunate animal or man whom they proceed to kill or drive off from the community. The killing of the king and the scapegoat ceremonial seem to have been originally distinct, but it seems probable ... that when the scapegoat was human he might prove an economical substitute for the king and so the two ceremonies would sometimes be confused with one another.[17]

So Jocelin and his spire rise at the expense of Pangall's death at pagan hands, the image of impotence is killed to bring new life in the sprouting wood of the timbers and the impregnation of Goody by Roger. Jocelin suspects that the sprouting wood is a sign of rottenness, the pagan doings of the masons brand them in his eyes as 'devilworshippers' and yet he persists in regarding them as 'good men' (p. 155). They remain good men to him because, despite or because of their paganism, they are able to complete the glorious work of the spire.

Jocelin identifies the pre-Christian earth-religion with devilry, with the forces of evil, to which infernal region he also consigns all stirrings of sexuality. He would exclude these from the body of the cathedral and the temple of the body. Yet these dark gods, this dark underside of things, seem to provide much of the energy, the will, that forces the spire upwards. The purity and light of Christianity seems to require foundations of earth-darkness to build the greater church. Indeed, it is arguable that the Christian story of the redemption from sin of the world by the crucifixion of Christ is itself built upon pagan myths of the sacrificial scapegoat, fool or priest-king.

Christianity itself has its roots in and derives strength from those pagan or pre-Christian religions which officially it would like to maintain it had driven out or slaughtered. In this context it is possible to see Pangall as symbolic representative of those pre-Christian faiths, destroyed by Christianity yet finding a place at its heart whence it derives much magical power. His name contains Pan, that goatish and archetypical (because all-embracing) deity of the pagan world who died, according to tradition, at Christ's birth.[18] He has his own little 'kingdom' (p. 17) of which he is fiercely defensive, and his ancient house, hard against the wall of the cathedral, grotesque and chaotic but built of older materials than the great fortress-like walls. His kingdom and house are taken over and wrecked by the masons:

Pangall's reactions sound like those of a Jewish prophet lamenting another take-over of the ancestral kingdom by blasphemous outsiders: '"It was our place. What will become of us?"' (p. 17). And that simplest cry of the afflicted and dispossessed '"How long?"' (p. 19). Pangall seems to represent also the Old Testament religion which Christianity replaced and whose recalcitrant adherents it has periodically persecuted or slaughtered. But Christianity built on the foundations of the Old Testament. The cathedral that seems to be a stronghold againt all outmoded faiths, beliefs and superstitions is rather more of an ark containing and preserving them all. It is rather similar to the shrine at Delphi as described by Golding:

> Yet, I thought to myself, Apollo was only a kind of front man at Delphi. Greek religion came in layers, each age super-imposed on an obscurer and more savage one. The layers existed together, since nothing is as conservative as religion. Dig down, and just below the surface you come on human sacrifice and, at the bottom, traces of cannibalism. (MT p. 37)

How typical of Golding to go digging for Dionysiac darkness even in the sacred precincts of bright Apollo!

In the cathedral world, too, religion is conservative and comes in layers. Pangall the fool is sacrificed to pagan gods, Jocelin the fool offers himself to the Christian God and is crucified by the stone hammer and nail, sacrificed on the great tree of the spire which grows out of these offerings. It is an eternal pattern of death and resurrection, dying to give new life, a pattern seen in the movement of the seasons, which the novel attentively observes. Jocelin also enacts the typical pattern of the Golding artist: to achieve the heavenly beauty of the spire he must encounter and explore his own darkness, he must suffer and die to rise again with new gifts of vision. It is out of the pain of his experiences that Jocelin gains insight: 'As far as some people were concerned, his eye had acquired a new facility. (Pain did it, pain did it, pain did it.)' (p. 139). In his final sickness, after his symbolic death, Jocelin can at last see clearly enough read the face of Father Adam:

Jocelin saw at once how mistaken they were who thought of him as faceless. It was just that what was written there, had been written small in a delicate calligraphy that might easily be overlooked unless one engaged oneself to it deliberately, or looked perforce, as a sick man must look from his bed. (p. 196)

'Until we are sick, we understand not' wrote Keats,[19] and it is a Romantic view of the artist that has it that he must suffer, must make the heart ache and break to achieve beauty, must fall and gall himself to gash gold vermillion. The reborn Jocelin is a visionary, experiencing a Blakean vision of an appletree as 'a cloud of angels flashing in the sunlight' though with 'a long, black springing thing' (p. 204) amongst its leaves. The joyous beauty contains also, and indeed grows out of, the darkness: the nature of beauty, like human nature, is terrible, mysterious and paradoxical. Golding himself has written of the novel's theme:

> If the reader, the critic does not understand that after all the theology, the ingenuities of craft, the failures and the sacrifices, a man is overthrown by the descent into his world of beauty's mystery and irradiation, flame, explosion, then the book has failed. The theme is not there. (MT p. 167)

Jocelin experiences explosive beauty but has a vision also of the ugliness and darkness of men, mad bones and vile bodies prancing absurdly in woven stuff and skins of dead animals. The achieved beauty of the spire which immortalises both Jocelin and Roger is flawed by the tilt it develops, is an image and product of human aspiration and imperfection. It is 'an upward waterfall' (p. 223) that impossible thing a fall upwards, a happy fall, a miracle in stone.

The miracle is achieved in stone and also timber; within the stone casing is a great timber framework, a huge tree growing from the fecund earth into the bright air. The whole is like the ash-boughs in May in Hopkins' fragment: 'it is old earth's groping towards the steep/Heaven whom she childs us by.'[20] The spire even sways, terrifyingly, in the breeze 'like a tall tree' (p. 133).The terror of the tree comes from the threat of a fall: the tree of the spire recalls the Tree of Knowledge of Good and Evil. Jocelin certainly comes to the knowledge of much evil and some good while climbing in its dangerous branches: 'He felt the same appalled delight as a small boy feels when he climbs too high in a forbidden tree' (p. 101). We are very pointedly reminded of another forbidden tree in the childhood of the human race and, more subtly, of the mixture of the delightful and the appalling that is knowledge of the truth of things and of our own nature. This tree brings about the tragic fall of both Jocelin and Roger. But the tree of the spire also recalls, as we have seen, the Tree of the Cross upon which the sacrificial victim Christ redeemed man from his fallen state. Christ likened the breaking of his body on the Cross and his resurrection to the destruction and rebuilding of the Temple in Jerusalem. Jocelin's body is torn 'from arse to the head' (p. 188) by the spire, rather as was the Veil of the Temple at the moment of Christ's expiring. The tragedy of the cross transforms history to a comedy by establishing again for man a bridgeway to heaven. The wood of the spire blossoms, suggesting rottenness and evil to Jocelin, but the final product is 'rosecoloured' (p. 223) suggesting the Rose on the Tree that is a symbol of Christ. The fruit of this tree is both mortal and salvific.

In bringing together the two trees, of fall and redemption, in the one tree of the spire, Golding is being true to the medieval setting of the novel, for it was agreeable to the iconographic mind of the Middle Ages to believe that the wood of the Tree of Knowledge was used to form the Cross. Christ was crucified at Golgotha, the place of the skull, a skull believed to be that of Adam. Thus the tree of sorrow becomes a tree of triumph and redemption through the sacrifice of the second Adam over the grave of the downfallen first. The triumphant tree of the spire soars out of a soil that contains the bones of Pangall, symbol of elder, pre-Christian things. The combination of these two trees would not have seemed in itself blasphemous or daring to a medieval. But in its all-encompassing nature, its being a many-branched image of our life, the spire also demands to be likened to a pagan tree, to the Life-Tree or World-Tree, Igdrasil. In *Past and Present* Carlyle suggests in a highly rhetorical peroration how by dealing with the Middle Ages he may illustrate the present, using this tree as an image:

> For the Present holds in it both the whole Past and the whole
> Future;— as the LIFE-TREE IGDRASIL, wide-waving, many-
> toned, has its roots down deep in the Death-kingdoms, among
> the oldest dead dust of men, and with its boughs reaches always
> beyond the stars; and in all times and places is one and the
> same Life-tree![21]

That sense of the eternal sameness of human experience is
also evoked in *The Spire*, that sense that despite spectacular
changes of costume, manners and even beliefs, we remain
the same tragi-comic creatures struggling between earth and
heaven.

The Spire dates from the era of the Second Vatican
Council, which went some way towards an *aggiornamento*
in the Roman Catholic Church, a bringing into line with the
modern world of somewhat ossified or petrified doctrine.
Jocelin too experiences a kind of *aggiornamento*. At the
outset he is an overgrown baby, childlike in the certainty of
his faith, childish in his innocence and ignorance of the
world and himself. His experiences in the course of building
the spire force him to grow up, though the shattering of his
initial certainties and delusions destroys him altogether. He
moves from childlike or childish certainty to a state where
he is certain of nothing and yet has gained a visionary
insight into the nature of things. The book requires of us
that our reading of its art should grow up in this way too,
that it should develop from the medieval to the modern. At
first the meanings are simple or, at least, clear: we can
read the meaning of the image of Abraham and Isaac; the
idea that the spire is a diagram of prayer is obvious and
commonplace; the body of the church (like our bodies or
minds) has a nasty underside, dig down a little and you
touch on hell itself.

Truth and goodness are contained within the fortress of
Holy Church and the holy church: the church and the world
are books to be read and the Church can provide the keys to
their clear interpretation and also a code of rules that, if
adhered to, will form a ladder to heaven. But, as we
progress, such certainties become untenable: the tree of the
spire which seemed a spear aimed straight at heaven turns

out to have many branches, truth and goodness seem highly complex and confusing. The truth cannot be simply a rigid stone book that is clear in its meaning to all or readily explicable by authority; goodness cannot be reduced to following a strict code of rules (look at the wretched Anselm and his Founder's Statutes!). Truth and goodness we might usefully combine in the word wisdom. Wisdom is glimpsed only out of the corner of the eye, it is elusive. It can be expressed only in daring and ambiguous metaphors and paradoxes: the spire itself is such a metaphor and paradox. Such daring threatens to bring the whole edifice tumbling down.

In his brilliant novel of the uncertainties of Roman Catholics in the era of the Second Vatican Council, *How Far Can You Go?*, David Lodge uses playful narratorial and personal interventions and comment to bring to our attention the fictive nature of the lives of his characters, the fact that they are not real. The effect on our willing suspension of disbelief is disconcerting in a way that resembles the jolts to the faith of the characters themselves engendered by radical new ideas in the Church. How far can you go before credence in the worth of the narrative or belief in the Church itself is irreparably shattered? Golding in *The Spire* is less radical, less playful and less funny, but we are presented with a narrative and religious vision the meaning of which is dark. Perhaps God has the key to meanings, the power to create light from darkness, perhaps he alone has clear and distinct ideas of truth and goodness, but '*God knows where God may be*' (p. 222). It is the paradox of Jocelin the visionary sceptic. Such scepticism alerts us to the dangers of certainty, warns us to beware of those twin sins of presumption and despair. The verses on motes and beams in St Matthew, quoted above, follow a direct warning of the danger of shutting up an open mind, a warning that is to echo through Golding's remaining novels and provide a secret motto to *Darkness Visible*: 'Judge not, that ye be not judged'.[22]

·6·

THE FLAT EARTH SOCIETY
·THE PYRAMID (1967)·

What life have you if you have not life together?
There is no life that is not in community,
And no community not lived in praise of GOD.

And the wind shall say: 'Here were decent godless people:
Their only monument the asphalt road
And a thousand lost golf balls.'

> T.S. Eliot, 'Choruses from *The Rock*'

Expect poison from the standing water.
The Marriage of Heaven and Hell

Stilbourne, the country town that is the setting of *The Pyramid*, is standing water. It is located in the heart of England, a heart that seems in the grip of sclerosis. *The Pyramid* stands at approximately the centre of Golding's *oeuvre* and it might aptly be described as the dead centre of his novels. It does seem to occupy a kind of no man's land between the first group of five novels and the late novels beginning with *Darkness Visible*: Gregor and Kinkead-Weekes regard it as the result of Golding's taking a step back so that he might again move forward. Don Crompton's essay on the novel does splendid work in showing hidden depths and revealing complex patterning, but it is not a work which readily elicits encomia. A pyramid might be a flattened spire and, though the settings of the two novels are similar in geographical terms, in moving from *The Spire* to *The Pyramid* we move forward some hundreds of years into a world that seems flattened out and deadly dull. In the former, for example, we watch as the fanatical Jocelin mercilessly drives the mechanic Roger into the vertiginous heights of the spire for the greater glory of God and to create a magnificent monument to them both; in the latter the mechanic Henry Williams is driven by a 'god without mercy' (p. 159), i.e. the desire to get on and up in the world, to build a business empire and ascend the social pyramid, but his success, measured also in stone, is more horizontal and less wonderful: 'There was a forecourt of concrete ... there was a garage and a pit for inspecting the entrails ... Behind the garage, in what had been long gardens running down to the river, the concrete spread' (p. 192). Henry's endeavours do not enhance the living landscape, they deaden it.

Henry is by no means the central character of *The Pyramid* but the comparison is illuminating and the contrast typical. Dealing with the dullness and lack of vitality, of life, in a backwater of the twentieth century, *The Pyramid* is itself rather unemotive: we miss the terrible harrowings of Golding's other fictions. The English have a reputation for emotional reticence and this is certainly reflected in the world of Stilbourne. The novel is emotionally rather flat: returning to his native town at the opening of the third section, Oliver, the rather unattractive hero and narrator, reflects: 'I examined my heart for emotion but found none. The determination never to return, lest I should find my heart wrung or broken by dead things, this I found replaced by a no more than mild curiosity' (p. 158). The emotional atmosphere, as Don Crompton indicates, is lukewarm. Even when there is violent emotion, it has difficulty in expressing itself, as when Oliver finds Bounce, his piano teacher, *in extremis*: 'She was down there in the dark ... trying to learn unsuccessfully without a teacher, how to sob her heart out' (p. 200). It is the same with Bounce's playing on the piano: expression is *not* her forte. Stilbourne is not an ideal spot for an *éducation sentimentale*.

This inability to express feelings is symptomatic of a general breakdown in communications and of community in Stilbourne. The inhabitants of Stilbourne live in isolation behind curtains and bolted doors, separated by absurd rules and prejudices of class, their attempt at social co-operation, the Stilbourne Operatic Society, leading only to disastrous clashes of temperament that make for even greater stand-offishness. Community is dead and Golding, like Eliot in the quotations above from *The Rock* and elsewhere in his morbid anatomy of the modern world, seems to attribute this deadness to the death of God. In Golding's own boy-hood in Wiltshire also God had been abandoned: 'we had thrown him out' (HG p. 173). Oliver is disconcerted when the Roman Catholic Evie makes the sign of the cross: 'She muttered, made some quick movements over her breasts with one hand. In our local complex of State Church, Nonconformity, and massive indifference, I had never seen anything like them' (p. 39). That massive indifference to God has much to do with the massive indifference and deadness of Stilbourne generally. God is love: love and indifference are antithetical feelings or states. In Stilbourne love seems to have died along with God. The first section of the novel shows us Oliver's first love, or rather his first sordid and loveless sexual adventure. The Godless, loveless modern world is treated by Golding with acute distaste.

For all that it is gloomy, *The Pyramid* is not tragic. Its emotions are far too muted and it tends, as with so much of Golding, towards the tragi-comic. The middle section in particular is clearly intended to be funny and the novel's humour in general is warmly appreciated by Don Crompton: '*The Pyramid* is undoubtedly one of Golding's funniest books, sometimes hilariously so, displaying not only a pointed verbal wit but a delight in the comic potential of awkward situations'.[1] But then Golding's books are not generally funny: the humour here might best be character-ised by quoting Hazlitt's remarks on the humorous aspects of Dr Johnson: '... his efforts at playfulness ... remind one of the lines in Milton: "—The elephant/ To make them sport wreath'd his proboscis lithe."'[2] The humour here is similarly elephantine, reaching a climax of clod-hopping predictability in the homosexual Mr De Tracy's spelling out of a *double entendre* on Oliver's attempts to force his halberd up 'the back passage' (p. 152). Crompton is right in suggesting that Golding's humour relies heavily on awkward situations: his is the rather heavy-handed humour of a practical joker. David Skilton, while describing the work as a 'comic masterpiece', admits that a number of its jokes are 'astonishingly heavy'.[3] At its worst this can be thuddingly inane and puerile; at its best, as in the stupendous embarrassments, the absolute tragi-comedy of Colley's misfortunes in *Rites of Passage*, it can be devastatingly funny, both funny and devastating. In *The Pyramid*, however, the humour is bitter and distasteful, like everything else.

The Pyramid is dedicated to Golding's son and growing pains might be said to be its subject matter. The very style of the prose suffers from adolescence. There is a callowness about it, particularly in the first section, which is distastefully true to the growing character of Oliver, but which might be used to justify Keats' strictures on the adolescent imagination.[4]

The book is much concerned with music, but music that is never quite right: there is an insistent out-of-tune, a 'vast disharmony' (p. 102) in the style as in the world. The opening sentences set the tone: 'It was really summer, but the rain had fallen all day and was still falling. The weather can best be described by saying it was the kind reserved for church fêtes' (p. 11). Wet summers are a disappointment, a let-down, the first of many in this novel, which will also concern itself with falling, with falls from innocence and grace. The novel is to be set in the sort of soggily boring England of the shires which Dickens tries to evoke in the Lincolnshire scenes in *Bleak House* by droning on about the fact that it is forever raining there (Lincolnshire is, in fact, quite a dry county). In the realms of cliché church fêtes invariably draw torrential downpours of rain, so Oliver, a sixth-form stylist, supplies us in the most fumblingly awkward way with that description of the weather in the second sentence, an infelicitous touch of acidulated adolescent wit. A little further on we are told: 'Eighteen is a good time for suffering. One has all the necessary strength and no defences' (p. 12). This seems fairly touching, but is also sympathy-seeking and self-pitying to suit Oliver's mood of frustrated infatuation: selfishness and self-regard are prominent features of Oliver's character and will help him to get on, to scramble up the social pyramid like Henry Williams, though they do not contribute much to the making of a novelist.

The olive is a symbol of martyrdom, but Oliver is a secular soul and certainly no martyr. He is not one for giving himself away: 'like Henry, I would never pay more than a reasonable price' (p. 217). This prudent instinct for self-preservation is seen in the sorry tale of Oliver's first love, or rather loves. Oliver at the outset would like to think himself a martyr to his love for the idealised, ethereal and engaged Imogen Grantley. He makes do for the time being, however, with the earthier and more available Evie Babbacombe. Though there is one sentence in the description of this affair that might remind us of *La Vita Nuova*, 'As if commanded by a master I stole out of the house' (p. 44), there is no *dolce stil nuovo* to evoke young love here. References to more spiritual or dignified treatments or visions of love in the past serve only to highlight the sordidness of the present love-story. In the third section Oliver finds the memorial to Bounce inscribed with her father's saying: 'Heaven is Music' (p. 213). This phrase might suggest the music of the spheres, but in Stilbourne ought to be interpreted as a substitution of a man-made art for the truly divine, the replacement of religious with secular values that typifies the Stilbourne world. Church fêtes are no longer religious feasts that inspire particular devotions but rather are dull and class-ridden social events frequently ruined by angry cloudbursts. More than a ton of monumental marble weighs the inscription down to earth and neither Bounce nor Oliver is a musician of such genius as to be able to suggest that sidereal music. The story of Oliver and Evie is one in which things constantly tend to get dragged down to earth. It is instructive to contrast Dante's reverential and beautiful compliments to Beatrice with Oliver's charming and courteous description of his down-to-earth girl as 'life's lavatory' (p. 91).

An English medieval backdrop to this sordid story is provided by the gold cross which Evie loses while cavorting with Oliver's rival Bobby Ewan. It is inscribed *Amor vincit*

omnia, the motto of Chaucer's ladylike Prioress. Evie, however, is no anchoress and her town crier father desecrates
the Latin in declaring the property lost: "'... Hay gold
cross hand chain. With the hinitials hee bee. Hand the
hinscription 'Hamor vinshit Homniar'. ...'" (p. 25). The
Prioress's noble, if mildly flirtatious motto, is dragged down
well and truly into the lavatory. A little later Oliver, who
is better educated than Sergeant Babbacombe, attempts a
translation of the motto: "'I think it means, 'Love beats
everything'"" (p. 37). Translation into the idiom of the
modern world reduces the phrase to utter banality. It also
gives it sinister overtones. There is a suggestion of violence
in the nature of *amor*, a hint reinforced by the fact that
one of those for whose benefit it is translated is Captain
Wilmot, who obtains sexual pleasure by beating poor Evie,
his pupil.[5] Love or desire can, indeed, beat everything,
can overcome and defeat all the claims of decency and
morality. This is illustrated not merely by Wilmot, the
'broken, heavily secreting gargoyle' (p. 90), but by Oliver's
shameful treatment of Evie and the sad misdemeanours of
Bounce and Mr De Tracy.

The world of Chaucer might suggest an imaginary Merry
England in the past, and it is not the only suggestion of
idyllic representations of England. *Merry England* is numbered
among the disastrous productions of the Stilbourne Operatic
Society. The nearby cathedral city is Barchester, a name
associated with Trollope; Stilbourne is a locale reminiscent
of *The Archers*; there is even a Mrs Miniver, the title-role of
a grotesquely sentimental war-time film about the whole-
someness of life in an English village. Jane Austen celebrates
the mild virtues of such an English rural world in *Emma*:
'English verdure, English culture, English comfort, seen
under a sun bright, without being oppressive.'[6] Golding
however, finds the comfortable life uncomfortable and the
atmosphere utterly oppressive, like that in a pyramid or
tomb. Don Crompton astutely quotes the Book of Revelation
on the lukewarm: 'So then because thou art lukewarm and
neither cold nor hot, I will spue thee out of my mouth.'[7]

The Pyramid is a spoiled idyll, a story of young love in a
rural setting that proves distasteful or even nauseating. Even

the landscape is verbally desecrated by the ludicrous *double entendres* in the place-names; Pillicock, Bumstead, Cockers. There are several references to idyllic or pastoral worlds in art: Oliver reads Edith Sitwell's *Bucolic Comedies*; the Operatic Society's dreadful and fractious production is set 'in Hungary or Ruritania or somewhere' (p. 118); Evie sings a snatch from a madrigal that casts her as a shepherdess. In this pastoral madrigal, however, the shepherdess declares that she daily weeps and Oliver thinks the song was written by Dowland, a musician whose motto was *Semper Dowland semper dolens*, a *mournful* lover and musician. The pastoral mode has been much used for elegies, but in *The Pyramid* allusions to idyllic art serve to point up the ugliness, vulgarity and tedium of Stilbourne and the mourning is for a world of the living dead, a ghastly realm of nightmare life-in-death. In this cold pastoral we discover that the truth about the respectable little town of Stilbourne is not beauty but filth.

This quintessentially English world of the country town that might be so idyllic, does not, in fact, bear much looking into. A close inspection reveals the sordid everywhere: Oliver's father voyeuristically trains his binoculars on Evie and his son exhibitionistically copulating on the downs above the town. The idyll is spoiled by the sorry paths into which its characters are led by victorious *amor*; incest, sadism, transvestism and, according to Evie, rape. It is middle England seen through the Sunday papers, a shocking revelation of reality which the people of Stilbourne privately and pruriently like to read about: 'We were our own tragedy and did not know we needed catharsis. We got our shocked purging from *The News of the World*' (p. 114). Mr De Tracy dresses as a ballerina; Bounce Dawlish walks down the street wearing a hat, gloves, flat shoes and 'nothing else whatsoever' (p. 207); Evie is sexually abused by her father and by the crippled Captain Wilmot. Wilmot has the surname of the Earl of Rochester, Restoration court buck and scurrilous poet, another Merry England figure. Rochester was a libertine, but Captain Wilmot is a sinister, cruel and disgusting figure in his sadistic games with Evie. Evie, after her first sexual liaison with Oliver, glumly taunts him

(' "That's all I s'pose" ' (p. 72)) in a way that momentarily
calls to mind Rochester's 'The Imperfect Enjoyment', a
marvellously funny poem which nonetheless conveys a sense
of disgust at sexuality which is quite ferocious. *The Pyramid*
does not have such ferocity, but it is pervaded by a similar
disgust at human sexuality: its pastoral idyll turns out to be
a nauseating tour of the human farmyard.

The forms of sexual misbehaviour listed above are not
equally heinous. Don Crompton suggests that the ex-
hibitionism of Evie and Bounce is a healthy antidote to
Stilbourne's attitude to sex as a dirty little secret:

> Discussing *The Scorpion God*, Golding has observed, 'Herodotus
> says that the Egyptians do everything in public that other
> people do in private.' Perhaps within the stifling Stilbourne
> pyramid, it is Evie and Bounce who prove themselves true
> Egyptians, rejecting the death of the heart and struggling
> towards another mode of being where love may some day
> conquer.[8]

Stilbourne could well do with having a few taboos broken.
None of the proclivities commonly regarded as perverse or
deviant which we see is as horrible as Oliver's 'normal'
treatment of Evie. This first love affair for Oliver is
thoroughly devoid of love. It is more a matter of antagonism
and hate, of struggle and violence: ' "Damn you, Evie!" ' (p.
79) and threatening to break her neck are samples of the
amatory language of Oliver. It is no wonder that the much
put-upon Evie is thoroughly sick of the business of love and
can say from the heart: ' "I hate men" ' (p. 80). Evie is
consistently presented, in contrast to the spiritual Imogen
Grantley, as being all body and no soul. When she appears
in the darkness and wet of the novel's opening she is
all scent, eyes like plums, and physicality: 'She convulsed
silently. Farted. "Pardon." The plums glanced up at me over
her hands'. (p. 14). Her physicality is not all attractive!
However, though Evie is not very refined, Oliver would like
to enjoy closer acquaintance with this luscious fruit. Her
appeal is utterly basic and atavistic: she seems to Oliver
to have the ability, seen in Lok and Fa, to control the
exhalation of her own scent; she inspires caveman thoughts

in Oliver: 'Evie was girl, much girl' (p. 51). But all these thoughts are Oliver's. He is the narrator and it is he who presents Evie as all body. That is how he chooses to see another human being. Evie, a Roman Catholic, is in fact aware of the existence of the soul and has some worries about its state:

> "You wouldn't care if I was dead. Nobody'd care. That's all you want, just my damned body, not me. Nobody wants me, just my damned body. And I'm damned and you're damned with your cock and your cleverness and your chemistry—just my damned body—" (p. 88)

Oliver is unabashed by such considerations and by such a justified onslaught. It is he whose thoughts are all of the body, at least where Evie is concerned. Oliver is afraid that he will be dragged down into embarrassing disaster by the cave-girl Evie, but it is he himself who does all the dragging down, both literally and in the slanders and condescension of the narrative. Oliver, her lover, fails to treat Evie as a human being:

> "You never loved me, nobody never loved me. I wanted to be loved, I wanted somebody to be kind to me—I wanted—"
> She wanted tenderness. So did I; but not from her. She was no part of high fantasy and worship and hopeless jealousy. She was the accessible thing. (pp. 88–9)

Oliver excludes her from the realm of tenderness because she uses double negatives in her speech. He is afraid that she will drag him down not into damnation but merely a step or two on the social ladder. At the root of the considerable evil of his treatment of her is class.

Oliver fails to treat Evie as a human being because she is socially beneath him. Tenderness, high fantasy and worship are reserved for the socially exalted Imogen. A sexual liaison with Evie is vitiated by fear, fear that Oliver will be forced into a marriage that is beneath him, below the middle station so tenaciously held by his respectable parents. He is terrified that he and his family will be dragged down into the lower-class gutter of Chandler's close:

> My father, so kind, slow and solid, my mother, tart, yet with such care of me, such pride in me—I would kill them. To be related even if only by marriage, to *Sergeant Babbacombe*! I saw their social world, so delicately poised and carefully maintained, so fiercely defended, crash into the gutter ...—Yes. I should kill them. (p. 82)

Class is taken seriously in these parts: a social fall is death. Oliver's father is, indeed, a kindly and rather admirable man, but he finds professional, pharmaceutical reasons to warn his son off Chandler's Close and Evie: '"... There's— disease, you see"' (p. 100). Once again Evie has been reduced to 'life's lavatory'. Oliver, who had used her as a public convenience because she 'was accessible', now avoids her 'as if she had been one of the diseases my father had talked about' (p. 101).

It is not, however, Evie that stinks and is diseased, it is the mentality of Stilbourne. The class-ridden attitude of Oliver reifies Evie, she is not a person but a member of the lower classes, a 'thing'. Oliver feels pride that he 'had *had*' Evie (p. 73), 'the ripest apple on the tree' (p. 39) who is also, in a moment of less rosy enthusiasm, 'life's necessary, unspeakable object' (p. 91). This may seem sexist rather than classist, but Oliver's attitude to Evie contrasts pointedly with his veneration of Imogen:

> Even the thought of Imogen, though she caused me my usual pang, brought no more than a covered one, a pang with the point blunted. I pinned the memory of a scented, white body over it. I found myself ... wishing that Imogen might know I had *had* Evie; that she might see ... this hot bit of stuff through which I had achieved my deep calm.(p. 75)

Evie is regarded simply as an object, to be used as a means to an end, the achievement of deep calm and the blotting out of the memory of the sacred Imogen. Evie is exploited, used 'to stick like a plaster' over the thought of Imogen's wedding (p. 96). These may be deeply sexist attitudes but they are born of class. The much abused Evie is, however, virtually the only person to emerge with much credit from the Stilbourne world. Evie, as we have seen, has desires and aspirations that are admirable; she is a rebel against the exploitation and hypocrisy of Stilbourne; she struggles to find or maintain some human dignity for herself amidst the abuse which her good looks and lowly social standing bring upon her. Stilbourne, with typical hypocrisy, ejects her, but the town is the poorer for her going: 'Evie went, and the coloured picture of Stilbourne was motionless and flat again' (p. 101). Evie escapes and manages in London to make some weary progress on the social ladder. It is by no means clear that her experiences in the great world have improved her, but she is able on her return to do battle with Oliver, to take revenge for his outrages, to outrage Stilbourne by forthrightness, by bringing out into the open air what Stilbourne thinks should be buried and secret. Evie at least wants to awaken the dead: she admires the Savoy Orpheans, though Oliver, who no doubt would have preferred a liking for Monteverdi's *Orfeo* or Gluck's *Orfeo ed Euridice*, sees in this only an opportunity for intellectual and social sneering: '"You're like—the Savoy Orpheans!"' (p. 62). Oliver and Stilbourne stink. Inside the pyramid it is very stuffy, the atmosphere is stifling and fetid, and the very air that one breathes is class.

Golding has spoken with some feeling of the class-ridden society of his own boyhood in Marlborough:

> It was about as stratified a society as you could well find anywhere in the country, and I think that the pyramidal structure of English society is present, and my awareness of it is indelibly imprinted in me, in my psyche, not merely in my intellect but very much in my emotional, almost my physical being. I am enraged by it and I am unable to escape it entirely ... it's fossilised in me.[9]

Rage as one will, the dead world of class is fossilised within one. There is no escape from the vast tomb. The evils of our class-system form the principal theme of *The Pyramid*. Stephen Medcalf doubts this and thinks the title a little inappropriate: 'after all the social structure has little to do even with the fate of Evie ... and nothing at all with those of Mr de Tracey or Miss Dawlish.'[10] But the social structure has *everything* to do with the fate of Evie, class bitterness and snobbery are very much in evidence in the story of Mr De Tracy's musical production, and Bounce is destroyed by the exploitations of Henry Williams, who manages to scramble quite a few notches up the social pyramid at Bounce's expense. Class is the very air the characters breathe: the narrative itself is extremely class-conscious and assumes that we are too. Oliver introduces us to Evie:

> I had seen Evie often enough, and for years; but I had never spoken to her ... I knew she worked next door, in Dr. Ewan's reception room ...—knew she was the Town Crier's daughter and came from the tumbledown cottages of Chandler's Close. But of course we had never spoken. Never met. Obviously. (p. 13)

It is only obvious how two such people could never have met or spoken if we are aware that social standing is everything in this society and that Evie is beneath Oliver. To be so prejudiced is for Oliver as natural as breathing. The system is bred into him: 'I understood that the son of Dr. Ewan couldn't take the daughter of Sergeant Babbacombe to a dance in his father's car. Didn't have to think. Understood as by nature' (p. 18). Class inhibits communications and prevents the treatment of whole classes of people as human beings. This is quite normal: Oliver *of course* has never spoken to Evie and any liaison between Bobby Ewan and Evie must, one knows as if by instinct, be a matter for secrecy and fear.

Islands are not a prominent feature of the Wiltshire landscape, but snobbery and class-consciousness create artificial islands for people in that landlocked county. Golding remembers the isolation caused by class-consciousness in his own boyhood:

> My father was a master at the local grammer school so that we were all the poorer for our respectability. In the dreadful English scheme of things at that time, a scheme which so

accepted social snobbery as to elevate it to an instinct, we had our subtle place ... In fact, like everybody except the very high and the very low in those days, we walked a social tightrope, could not mix with the riotous children who made such a noise and played such wonderful games on the Green. (HG p. 168)

Golding, like Oliver, knew by instinct his own place and the place of others in this scheme and felt it a constraint. The children on the echoing green seem to play in a Blakean innocence from which Golding has been expelled by the serpent of class. Stilbourne is full of invisible class barriers, barriers against the meeting of other human beings, lines on the street which Oliver must walk like a tightrope.

These lines extend into Stilbourne's involvement with art, as the unspoken rules of casting in the Operatic Society make clear:

Though Evie sang and was maddeningly attractive, she would never have been invited to appear, not even as a member of the chorus. Art is a meeting point; but you can go too far. So the whole thing had to rise from a handful of people round whom an invisible line was drawn. Nobody mentioned the line, but everyone knew it was there. (p. 114)

The role of art is perverted. Instead of bringing people together and thus enriching their lives, it merely emphasises the isolation of people from one another and creates new bitterness, poisons the atmosphere still more. The *King of Hearts* ought to be a harmless love story, but the title itself allies class with romance and Oliver is enraged to find himself as accompanist to a love-scene between Imogen and Mr Claymore, who seems to have won his place both in life and in the play more by birth than talent. The light romance is turned to class war by the antagonism between Oliver and Mr Claymore and, though Oliver wins the day by drowning out Mr Claymore's gnat-like voice, it is again a failure of Stilbourne people to make harmonious music together.

Though Oliver may enjoy a brief public triumph over Claymore and though he succeeds in getting on in the world, he is nonetheless very much a victim of the system, seeing the world and himself in classist terms. As an adolescent he is depressed by the fact that he has the looks of a milkman and fears that this will hinder him in his amatory rivalry with Bobby Ewan, who has an aristocratic profile. Though Oliver manages a win in this fight too, the process is self-defeating because he feels that his knee-jerk method of winning reveals him as an oaf. Don Crompton points out that this fight resembles that between Pip and Herbert Pocket in *Great Expectations*, a supreme study of the terrible disease of the spirit that is snobbery and revelation of the corruption that underlies so much respectability. One can win, one can get on, but one's origins are always going to show through. The system is the inevitable victor. Bobby and Oliver are scarcely out of their prams when Bobby lays down the law about the nature of their relationship: '"You're my slave." "No I'm not." "Yes you are. My father's a doctor and yours is only his dispenser."' (p. 23). So much for innocence. Oliver may knock Bobby over, but the system itself is not so easily beaten and Oliver's attitude to Evie, whom he calls 'my slave' at one point (p. 91), is rather similar to Bobby's attitude to him.

Oliver is a victim of the system in that he has learned to victimise. Everyone is affected by this pervasive poison which perverts or destroys human relationships and community. Oliver's mother's relations with the other inhabitants of Stilbourne are on a wartime footing. She senses the goings-on of other people by 'radar' and she has 'a secret weapon as well as radar' (p. 117), i.e. the young Oliver who is sent on errands to spy in the enemy territory of other people's houses. Evie's mother is a deviant from the system, since her indomitable friendliness leads her to greet quite openly persons whose social position compared to her own is stratospheric:

> Naturally these greetings were never acknowledged or even mentioned; since no one could tell whether Mrs Babbacombe was mad, and believed herself entitled to make them, or whether she came from some fabulous country where the Town Crier's wife and the wife of the Chief Constable might be on terms of intimacy. (p. 43)

'Naturally' again, but nature has little enough to do with the highly artificial barriers between people that exist in Stilbourne. Mrs Babbacombe is either mad or else she comes from some inconceivable never-never land where people treat one another as human beings: 'The first alternative seemed the more probable' (p. 43).

A certain forthrightness and lack of restraint seem to be characteristic of the Babbacombe family, but other Stilbourne-dwellers are very concerned not to go too far. Indeed, there is not much going at all. Oliver's mother, standing a yard behind her curtains, is one of many such watchers cut off from community and vitality. As Oliver makes an escape from his stuffy and stifling home, we see that this English-man's castle is elaborately defended: 'I was wrestling with the chains and locks and bolts of the front door' (p. 67). Restraints, constraints and chains, mind-forged manacles are everywhere in Stilbourne, the inhabitants of this Ruritania are all prisoners of Zenda, all are locked up in the suffocat-ing atmosphere of inside a pyramid. Stilbourne, like the London of the opening of *The Waste Land*, is inhabited by the undead, by those who have no living relation with others, whose life has dwindled to an absolute minimum.

Oliver describes the brief flurry of social activity aroused by the revival of the Stilbourne Operatic Society as 'always a time when my mother came to some quite extraordinary level of life' (p. 113), emerging temporarily from cryogenic subsistence. The Orphean Evie, returned from the big city, finds Stilbourne rather lacking in life: '"There must be someone!" "What d'you mean Evie?" "Someone alive!"' (p. 105). In this environment Evie's wearing of the 'celebrated, the notorious cross' (p. 69) about her neck seems almost a hint that she fears the vampiric attentions of these undead tomb-dwellers. Vampirism may just be hinted at, but cannibalism is strongly suggested in the ghoulish gossip that Oliver's mother is so fond of. She apprises him of the news that his rival, Bobby Ewan, has been injured while riding his motor bike: '"Badly?" "They don't know yet. Took him to the hospital." I helped myself to HP sauce.' (p. 58). Oliver receives the news with relish. A little later, Evie tells Oliver that Bobby may be crippled for life: 'Then we were silent, ... I digesting this news according to my nature. I felt properly shocked of course; on the other hand I felt a little of Stilbourne's excitement and appetite at the news of someone else's misfortune' (p. 63). He is a true son of Stilbourne: beneath the public front of propriety there is baseness, there is the pleasant process of digestion of another's injury and an increased appetite for such fare.

That such ghoulish and cannibalistic appetites are found in every Stilbourne in England is suggested by some embittered remarks of Sammy Mountjoy in *Free Fall* concerning his friend Philip Arnold:

> He liked to inflict pain and a catastrophe was his orgasm. There was a dangerous corner leading to the high street; and in a freeze-up, Philip would spend all his spare time on the pavement there, hoping to see a crash. When you see two or three young men on a street corner, or at a country cross-road, at least one of them is waiting for just this. We are a sporting nation. (FF p. 48)

The inhabitants of Stilbourne are trapped in their nightmarish little world. Their horizons are extraordinarily limited and they have difficulty in imagining a world beyond them. Bounce, who suffers much from the narrowness and constraints of Stilbourne, boasts to Oliver of her thrilling explorations in her new motor car: '"I've been right round the downs—oh almost as far as Devizes—by myself, Oliver! Think of that!"' (p. 180). That Bounce should be cock-a-hoop about the excitement of almost reaching Devizes says much about the limitations of her experience! Oliver's father later comments on the money Bounce must have made from Henry Williams' business: '"Why, with what she gets from the money she put into his business she could live like a— she could live in Bournemouth if she wanted to."' The highest and most extravagant felicity that Stilbourne can imagine is living in Bournemouth. Small wonder that Oliver's comment on this is 'I was getting bored' (p. 204).

The little world is shut in by those surrounding downs, almost as securely as is the bizarre pharaonic kingdom by the palisades in 'The Scorpion God' and, though the world of the ancient Egyptians seems very strange to us, it is also strangely similar to the world of Stilbourne, as Don Crompton points out: 'The microcosm of the upper kingdom, narrow both geographically and intellectually, with its rigid code of behaviour, is not ... so unrecognisably different from that of Stilbourne, though the relationship is largely one of reversal.'[11] The Egyptians believe that the roof of the sky is held up by their religious observances and rituals. They are intensely religious, believing this earthly life to be a state of death compared to the true life of the next world. The people of Stilbourne have no such vision, are highly irreligious or, rather, they have a religion which is entirely man-made and which fills the flattened heavens with disharmony: that religion is the worship of class. The difference between Imogen and Evie, a difference of class, is put succinctly by Oliver in religious terms: 'Evie had none of Imogen's sacred beauty. She was strictly secular' (p. 16). The religion of class, with all its rituals, observances and commandments, dominates life in Stilbourne almost to the extent that Egyptian life is dominated by religion in 'The Scorpion God'. The Liar, who has experience of a world beyond the upper Nile valley, thinks that the Egyptian religion has confused life and death, but in the religion of Stilbourne there seems to be nothing but deathliness. The Egyptian world is destined, we know, to produce those stupendous religious and funerary monuments, the Pyramids; the best Stilbourne can manage is Henry's horizontal tarmac spread and Oliver's contribution to creating the tools of germ warfare.

It is hard to find positive or hopeful elements in the dull and stuffy world of *The Pyramid*. There are, as usual, characters whom we may describe as fools but they are not particularly holy and do not have a great deal of wisdom to offer. Bounce's final flouting of Stilbourne taboo, her experiment in urban naturism, lands her in a lunatic asylum and our final view of her is of an old woman both mad and bad, though very much the victim of her environment. Mr De Tracy is another taboo-breaker, but his escape is into the realm of farce. It is hard to feel there is much wisdom in a man's dressing as a ballerina. Mr De Tracy's philosophy is negative indeed: life is 'an outrageous farce ... with an incompetent producer' (p. 148). Perhaps this is the truth which Oliver tells Mr De Tracy he wants desperately to find but it is the bitterest, the most deflating truth imaginable. Evie, who is made a fool of by men and made a scapegoat by Stilbourne as a whole, is effective in exposing many of the vices of the town's life. Evie wants to live: '"Oh I should like to fly more than anything! And I should like to dance— and sing, of course—and travel—I should like to do everything!"' (p. 55). The burgeoning vitality of Evie is attractive and positive but is thwarted or abused by Stilbourne. Evie has a good voice, but her class excludes her from the town's musical productions. She does succeed in travelling as far as London and returns briefly, having 'hitched herself up a couple of degrees on our dreadful ladder' (p. 103).

This physical escape has not, however, been spiritually beneficial to Evie. She has hitched herself up by exploiting her sexuality for gain. She has not escaped: Stilbourne, as Oliver discovers rather late in the day, is, alas, 'like anywhere else after all' (p. 157). Yet the returned Evie provokes Oliver into recognising the spoiled potential in her, the human potential that he ignored or abused:

> I stood, in shame and confusion, seeing for the first time despite my anger a different picture of Evie in her life-long struggle to be clean and sweet. It was as if this object of frustration and desire had suddenly acquired the attributes of a person rather than a thing; as if I might—as if *we* might—have made something, music, perhaps, to take the place of the necessary, the inevitable battle. (p. 111)

It is a moment of extraordinary vision and insight that allows Oliver to see his ex-lover as a human being rather than a thing. Such an attitude might have enabled them to make love rather than war, to make real human contact through all the lines, barriers, locks and bolts of Stilbourne. Oliver's language is cliché-ridden, but that love might, indeed, have been a sweet music amid the vast disharmony of their loveless environment. But the chance is lost, Oliver's momentary urge to be reconciled is stillborn. Evie walks away, no doubt to run that endless gauntlet of sexual abuse to which she is condemned by birth and looks, condemned to struggle on for survival or progress in this vile society with whatever weapons are given her, to crawl on, like everyone else, up the dreadful social pyramid that is a mountain of purgatory with no heaven at its summit.

·7·

CHIAROSCURO
·DARKNESS VISIBLE (1979)·

And when I looked, behold, an hand was sent unto me; and, lo,
a roll of a book was therein;
And he spread it before me; and it was written within
and without: and there was written therein lamentations and
mourning and woe.

> Ezekiel 2. 9–10

And then shall many be offended, and shall betray one another,
and shall hate one another.
And many false prophets shall rise, and shall deceive many.
And because iniquity shall abound, the love of many shall wax
cold.
But he that shall endure unto the end, the same shall be saved.

> St Matthew 24. 10–13

... no defences and no remedy but simply to endure.

> *Darkness Visible*

Darkness Visible is a book in which we find lamentations
and mourning and woe, the prophetic book of an author
who once described himself as 'a pint-size Jeremiah'.[1] The
opening chapter, describing a fire-storm in London during
the blitz, makes explicit reference to the Apocalypse and to
the destruction of Pompeii and implicitly recalls various
visitations of divine displeasure upon the sinful Jerusalem
called down or lamented by the prophets. The novel is a
fierce Jeremiad against the modern world, but is by no
means simply a reactionary grumble against the decline of
traditional values in the moral mayhem of recent decades.

This prophetic utterance, Sibylline in the scattered nature of its narratives, is itself dark at heart, not a simple parable of moral black and white, but an agonised exploration of the perils of judgement in moral matters, a work in many ways deeply mysterious and ambiguous.

The condemnation of the modern world is not in much doubt however. Golding is at pains to remind us that the interlocking stories of Matty and Sophy are set in a very specific time. There are exact dates in Matty's journal, 6/6/ 66 for example, at the dark heart of the sinful Sixties, and there are many references to recent events and developments in British life, all of them disheartening or appalling. Thus at Matty's school Mr Pedigree looks from the window to the horizon 'where the suburbs of London were now visible like some sort of growth' (p. 32). The growth is in one sense a burgeoning of life but the sentence asks us to think of it as a tumour, a great wen, expanding outwards to engulf the Greenfields of England. We are reminded of another disaster for England's green and pleasant land much later when Edwin Bell refers to 'the elms they haven't cut down yet' (p. 201). Even the narrative voice can swing with the times, infected by the all-pervasive canned music and trash-culture in this description of the twins, Sophy and Toni Stanhope: 'they were as different as day and night, night and day you are the one, night and day' (p. 105).

Christianity is on the decline, is pretty well moribund: Matty, a fanatical devotee of the Bible, is shocked to find that Christian England is being infiltrated by what he regards as heathen faiths. Christ issues very severe warnings in the Scriptures concerning those who harm or mislead children, but the modern world of *Darkness Visible* is particularly harmful to children. The child Matty appears in the book's opening pages, horribly burned and scarred by the fire of modern war. Robert Melion Stanhope disgrace-fully neglects his children, the twins, in pursuit of slightly older young ladies: when Sophy weeps at his announcement that he intends to marry one of these he roars out in anger '"Christ! Children!"' (p. 125). His casual blasphemy succinctly suggests his own lack of any sort of Christianity. The effect is repeated later when Stanhope's daughter Sophy begins to hatch her plot to kidnap and murder a child: '"Where do they send their children to school?" This time the pause was even longer. Gerry broke it at last. "Christ all bleeding mighty. As Bill would say. Christ!"' (p. 159).

The mismanagement, maltreatment and abuse of children is a major concern of the novel. Matty has no known parents and is brought up somewhat haphazardly by society; the son of Sim Goodchild, the goodhearted and philosophical bookseller, has somehow ended in an asylum. These are misfortunes and perhaps nobody's fault. But the book is set in the age of 'free love', of 'anything goes': the darkness is most intense in the realm of Eros. The schoolgirl Sophy gives herself to passing motorists in scenes of spectacular sordidness, but discovers that violence is what turns her on: her number one fantasy, which she tries very hard to realise, is to torture and mutilate with a knife a helpless child. Sebastian Pedigree's life is dominated and ruined by his passion for young boys, a passion which makes him a child-molester. Golding deliberately chooses to concentrate on aspects of human sexuality which it is difficult not to characterise as particularly vile and evil, presents the age of free-love and 'doing your own thing' as one of particular and extreme depravity, of terrible crimes against innocence.

Golding's presentation of modern Britain is thus savage, but we are frequently reminded, especially by the frequent Biblical references of that extraordinary Scriptural scholar Matty, that the prophets of the Old Testament were wont to condemn their own time for similar wickedness. Ezekiel addresses the city of Jerusalem as a beautiful woman fallen into sin, in terms which might suggest the lovely and gifted Sophy, symbol of the corrupt and whorish modern world:

And thy renown went forth among the heathen for thy beauty: for it was perfect through my comeliness, which I had put upon thee, saith the Lord God. But thou didst trust in thine own beauty, and playedst the harlot because of thy renown, and pouredst out thy fornications on every one that passed by; his it was.[2]

This rather aptly describes Sophy's sexually voracious hitch-hiking habits. Perhaps more frighteningly, Ezekiel also condemns the killing of God's children:

Moreover thou hast taken thy sons and thy daughters, whom thou hast borne unto me, and these hast thou sacrificed unto them to be devoured. Is this of thy whoredoms a small matter: That thou has slain my children, and delivered them to cause them to pass through the fire for them?[3]

Ezekiel (or God's voice through the prophet) condemns crimes which are comparable to those meditated or executed by Sophy and Sebastian and reminiscent of the violence visited upon the child Matty.

The Scriptural or typological background to the novel has been well documented by Crompton: this Biblical background serves to remind us that man's wickedness and depravity is no modern development but is an eternally present threat. Golding is still weeping over the darkness of man's heart. The captain of the wartime firemen who in the book's opening chapter is granted a momentary insight into 'the workings of things' amidst the ruins of a blazing city experiences extraordinary 'grief' (p. 16), the theme and emotional keynote of Lord of the Flies. That grief might recall that of Jeremiah's lamentations over the desolate Jerusalem: 'For these things I weep; mine eye, mine eye runneth down with water, because the comforter that should relieve my soul is far from me: my children are desolate, because the enemy prevailed.'[4]

This sense of the eternal nature of man's wickedness notwithstanding, Darkness Visible does convey a sense of prophetic urgency, a sense that evil in our time is burgeoning, is spiralling towards some awful end, that the foul brew of the cup of abominations is brim full and about to bubble over. Such, at any rate, is Matty's view in his journal of May 1966: 'I tell myself the cup is full but not yet pressed down and overflowing' (p. 88). For what such evidence is worth, the messages supposedly vouchsafed by the Virgin Mary to various visionaries in the twentieth century (at Fatima and Garabandal, for example) convey a similar sense of the extravagant growth of evil and impending doom. Such doom-laden prognostications have at least the comfort (if comfort it be) that they derive from a specific view of history and a fairly clearly defined set of moral values. Thus, the course of history is foretold in the Bible: all history is moving towards a great Apocalyptic conclusion in which God will enact a final judgement upon mankind and the evils and darkness of the modern world ('free love', 'the permissive society', 'anything goes') are symptomatic of the fact that the end is nigh.

Some remarks made by Golding with regard to future possible themes in his work suggest that he is aware, like Matty, of the darkness of evil but that for him there is also the darkness of uncertainty and bafflement about the course of history: he is describing the Singing Stones of Memnon in Egypt:

> These huge stones that once sang are seated kings. Ruins as they are they may yet convey by a meta-language what we have left for a future and what we may build on. I say their faces have been struck away as if blasted by some fierce heat and explosion. All that is visible there is shadow. Their heads preserve nothing but a sense of gaze, their bodies nothing but the rubble of posture on a royal throne. Here might be an image of a humanity indomitable but contrite because history has broken its heart. It may be that in a reading of these broken stones lies an image of a creature maimed yet engaged to time and our world and enduring it with a purpose no man knows and an effect no man can guess. (MT p. 168)

The passage is clearly related to *Darkness Visible*, where the captain of firemen feels grief for the 'maimed creature' that is himself as well as the 'maimed child' (p. 16) Matty who has been blasted by fierce heat and explosions, and suggests an absence of any sense of a divinely ordered course of history, of any confidence in the light of revelation, the appropriate symbol for the condition of modern man being no more than a heap of broken images.

In the pictorial technique called *chiaroscuro* darkness is used to enhance our sense of light. It is arguable that the surrounding darkness in this novel is used to emphasise the light that is in Matty. One of the finest exponents of *chiaroscuro* is Caravaggio and one of the most famous examples in his *The Calling of St Matthew*, where the light of Christ falls on the future apostle who is doggedly engaged in his tax-collector's task of counting money. The dogged Matty, like the saint after whom he is named, is also an evangelist of a kind, the author of a spiritual journal or testament, and a study of the Gospel according to St Matthew contributes a good deal to an understanding of the novel. St Matthew's traditional symbol is the face of a man and, though it is debatable perhaps whether Matty's damaged features quite constitute a man's face, it is undoubtedly the case that Matty's face draws more attention than anything else about him. Matty may well be the light shining amidst darkness, but though he emerges from the darkness of war in a blaze of light, that light is nonetheless 'shameful' and 'inhuman' (p. 11): as we shall see, Matty is himself unreasonably full of shame and somewhat inhuman or inhumane in certain of his attitudes. Though he comes forth, like the voice of God, from a 'burning bush' (p.9) and walks, like one elected and protected by God, through a fiery furnace, there are certain aspects of the presentation of Matty which provoke scepticism about his prophetic mission. Matty may be a prophet and evangelist, but he is also a grotesque and a fool, a saint perhaps, but perhaps a religious maniac. Passing judgement on Matty and his career is no easy matter.

In a book entitled *Darkness Visible* we may well expect to find mysteries. The life of Matty presents some of the most obviously mysterious elements in the book. That he is the novel's holy fool is abundantly clear, but it is a more difficult act of interpretation to establish what wisdom this fool has to offer us, to what extent we should regard his life as an example to us. We may well feel that certain aspects of his life and attitudes are not fool's wisdom at all but simply the sheerest folly, the most benighted religious atavism. This man in black is a presence of silence and darkness, a walking mystery: one might well apply to him certain properties described by Golding as constituting the heart of his Egypt: 'to be at once alive and dead; to suggest mysteries with no solution, to mix the strange, the gruesome and the beautiful' (HG p. 80). The first mystery about Matty is his 'birth', his apparently miraculous emergence from the white-hot flames of the blitzed dockland streets. His parentage is wholly unknown and there is no explanation of how he could have come to be there in the first place, still less how he could survive such a trial in the furnace. It is a birth and baptism by fire. We should perhaps recall the words of John the Baptist in St Matthew's gospel: 'I indeed baptize you with water unto repentance: but he that cometh after me is mightier than I, whose shoes I am not worthy to bear: he shall baptize you with the Holy Ghost, and with fire'.[5]

Matty's baptism of fire does seem to be a baptism in the spirit, since throughout his life he is possessed of spiritual gifts. Matty's actual christening, his being given a name, is also a teasing mystery, since Golding is very reluctant to give away exactly what his surname is, though evidently it has something to do with wind. This is again suggestive of his spirituality and his prophetic role: the visions of Ezekiel in which the word of the Lord comes to him are introduced thus by the prophet:

> And I looked, and, behold, a whirlwind came out of the north, a great cloud, and a fire infolding itself, and a brightness was about it, and out of the midst thereof as the colour of amber, out of the midst of the fire.[6]

It is from such a firecloud that Matty Windrove (this is the final and perhaps definitive form of his name) comes walking 'with a kind of ritual gait' (p. 14), miraculously protected, we may well imagine, to fulfil some prophetic mission, entrusted, it may well appear, with the word of the Lord. His name is itself prophetic of his end in a whirlwind of flames, as a pillar of fire.

This baptism into the spirit is bought at a dreadful price, however. Matty's face is terribly scarred on one side, making him a loner, a figure of fun or horror, an outcast among men. He is, as Kinkead-Weekes and Gregor point out, 'burnt all down the imaginative side of the brain ... so literal-minded as to be almost a "natural"'[7] and this folly of literal-mindedness is further to isolate him, as when it leads him to tell tales on his fellows at the Foundlings School. His foolishly literal reading of the Bible leads to much more serious trouble at school when Matty is involved in the tragic death of the beautiful boy Henderson of whom the paedophile schoolmaster Mr Pedigree is much enamoured. Golding shrouds the incident in mystery, but it seems that Matty's throwing of a gymshoe, an enactment of a phrase from the Psalms, contributes by physical or magical force to Henderson's fatal fall. Matty, with good reason perhaps, feels that he was putting a stop to 'Evil' (p. 36), but there is nonetheless in this action a strong element of jealousy and rivalry for the love of Mr Pedigree, for Matty is in need of love and has mistaken some sarcastic remarks of Pedigree's for affection. Mr Pedigree, certainly the main villain of the piece, ignobly puts all the blame on poor Matty: '"You horrible, horrible boy! It's all your fault!"' (p. 37). Matty is psychologically scarred for life by the incident, for he still loves and trusts Mr Pedigree as his only friend and so takes him at his word. Pedigree is thus doubly guilty, but it is Matty who feels an overwhelming sense of guilt and sin. As Don Crompton has suggested, his role in the death of his rival and his marked face associate him with the biblical Cain. The spiritual beings who communicate with him later in his life tell him that his 'spiritual face' is so badly scarred by a sin that they can scarcely bear to look at him and they confirm that this sin is 'the terrible wrong I did my dear friend' (p. 93).

From a common-sense point of view, we may feel that Matty's view of himself has been warped by the incident, that his guilt-feelings are psychological scar-tissue and that the wicked Pedigree is much to blame. But we should also be aware that there *is* a guilty aspect to Matty's role in the death of Henderson and that Matty, in stark contrast to Sophy or Pedigree or even Sim Goodchild, openly acknowledges his own guilt and its attendant grief, humbles himself, dresses in mourning, makes his darkness visible. There is no smug self-righteousness or hypocrisy about him. Indeed, he takes the guilt of Pedigree upon himself, he continues to love and care for the enemy who has so severely damaged him and loathes him, ultimately he triumphs over death and sin by returning to heal Pedigree's sickness, to tear out the devil from his heart: he establishes thereby his likeness to the supreme holy fool as characterised by St Matthew:

...they brought unto him many that were possessed with devils: and he cast out the spirits with his word, and healed all that were sick: That it might be fulfilled which was spoken by Esaias the prophet, saying, Himself took our infirmities, and bare our sicknesses.[8]

Matty is also ultimately willing to give himself as 'a burnt offering' (p. 238) that the innocent may be protected and saved from evil, atoning for the disastrous effects of his youthful attempt to stave off evil. He is unhesitatingly willing to take up the cross in imitation of Christ.

Darkness Visible cannot be read without a highly positive view of Matty, without the feeling that he is intended to be a Christ-like example to us all. Don Crompton has demonstrated that his life and career seem to re-enact the progress of biblical history from its beginnings to the Apocalypse and Matty's own religious views and sense of his own role develop so that he comes to think of himself as a prophet of Armageddon and perhaps the guardian of the youthful King of the Last Days who will defeat the beast and bring about the Kingdom of God. But if we take Matty at his word, if we accept his warnings as the literal truth, which would be in keeping with his own general attitude to the Bible, we create a novel of similar moral thrust and value to the pamphlets proving that the end is nigh forced upon unwilling passers-by by those whose religious enthusiasm has wholly outstripped their reason. Perhaps Matty is a false prophet, a religious simpleton or even maniac. At any rate, St Matthew's gospel warns us to beware of false prophets, as in the passage quoted at the head of this chapter which prophesies the Last Days when the love of many shall wax cold: 'And many false prophets shall rise, and shall deceive many.'

Matty's naive manner of reading scripture was a contributary factor in the death of Henderson, which left Matty so badly scarred within. Matty associates that incident with his adolescent hankering after the attractive girl in Frankley's shop: both involve sexual desire and for Matty such desire is a thing of darkness, a defilement. The guilt he feels with regard to this aspect of his human nature is grotesquely exaggerated, as is the portion of blame he takes upon himself for his role in Henderson's fate. He is far too severe upon himself. In Australia he is made impotent by the vicious attack of an Aborigine known as 'old Harry' (p. 65), seemingly a sally against one of God's prophets in the wilderness by a representative of Satan. As he attacks, the Aborigine shouts: '"Fucking big sky-fella him b'long Jesus Christ!"' (p. 64). But it would be possible to interpret this 'crucifarce' (p. 68) as symbolic of Matty's gelding by his own religious attitude. His disowning of his own sexuality, though sadly understandable given his own ruined looks, establishes a curious likeness among Matty and those other extremists, Sophy and Sebastian Pedigree. It is, indeed, on 'the seamy side' (p. 48) that the connections are. Matty avoids what he regards as sinful, dangerous and vile; Sophy cultivates the dangerous, violent and sordid in her sexuality; Pedigree, though in theory an enthusiast for pure youthful beauty, comes to get his kicks out of the sheer filth and degradation of his public lavatory world. All three are haters of the body, who despise and dishonour their own capacity for sexual love. This benighted attitude is a source of much darkness.

Matty's religious life becomes even odder and more disconcerting upon his return from Australia. He begins to receive nocturnal visits from spirits and divines that they have come to warn him of the fatal day '6/6/66' (p. 89), the sort of crackpot pseudo-religious goings-on wryly dismissed by T.S. Eliot in *Four Quartets*:

> To communicate with Mars, converse with spirits,
> To report the behaviour of the sea monster,
> Describe the horoscope, haruspicate or scry ...
> ... all these are usual
> Pastimes and drugs and features of the press ...[9]

Matty's simple-minded numerological divination proves incorrect (as have all such to date, needless to say), a fact which causes him to feel 'a great emptiness': 'What am I for, I ask myself. If to give signs why does no judgement follow'

(p. 90). He is not alone in this embarrassment: the prophet Jeremiah himself experienced just such a setback to his career: 'O Lord, thou hast deceived me, and I was deceived ... I am in derision daily, every one mocketh me.'[10] But the affair inspires no confidence in Matty's adequacy as an interpreter of Scripture.

The tutelary spirits, perhaps sharing such a view, order Matty to throw away his Bible. This command, which strikes at the very mainspring of his faith, causes Matty great perturbation, for he knows that 'Satan may appear as an angel of light so much more easily as a red or blue spirit with hats' (p. 92). The dreadful step does seem to be a necessary one: Matty must get beyond his obsession with the letter of the Bible. The spirits thus seem to contribute positively to Matty's spiritual development. He bears at this stage a certain resemblance to George Fox, the founder of the Quakers, who advocated the discarding of the Bible in favour of direct communication with God through the 'inner light' of Christ in each individual's heart. Matty's communion with the spirits may be a self-communion; perhaps their advice to throw away the Bible reflects some subconscious disgruntlement at the failure of the 666 theory. The spirits certainly seem to reinforce some of Matty's own obsessions. They confirm and perhaps worsen Matty's guilt in the matter of 'the terrible wrong' done to Mr Pedigree and this does appear a very odd position for the agents of supreme justice to adopt. Their answer to Matty's worried questions about the nature of his purpose and whether it is to do with children is strange indeed:

> It is a child. And when you bore the awful number through the streets a spirit that is black with a touch of purple like the pansies Mr Pierce planted under the rowan was cast down and defeated and the child was born sound in wind and limb and with an I.Q. of a hundred and twenty. (p. 101)

The spiritual realm seems to be coloured by Matty's peculiar and peculiarly circumscribed knowledge and interests; the fate of the world turns on one man's bizarre advertising campaign in Cornwall. Matty in his next journal entry supplies the amazing fact that '120 was the I.Q. of Jesus of Nazareth'. The authority for this statement is not clear, as the Scriptures are silent on the matter of Jesus's I.Q. It is, however, a statement of quasi-historical fact and describes Jesus from a twentieth-century standpoint. It may be argued that more respectable historical theories about the life of Jesus and the assessment of that life and mission from our modern standpoint are helpful in passing judgement on the curious career of Matty.

These statements about the Christ-like child keep Matty's mind running along Apocalyptic lines. Indeed, 'the red spirit with the expensive hat' is identified by Kinkead-Weekes and Gregor as 'John of Patmos utterly divested of poetic symbolism'.[11] St John the Divine is himself a rather atavistic figure in early Christianity. His Revelation or Apocalypse is somewhat lacking in the Christ-like spirit of forgiveness and rejoices in the thought of a forthcoming separation of sheep and goats, triumph of the justified and trampling down of sinners, persecutors and rivals. There is a good deal of such intolerance in Matty himself: returned to Greenfield on his bicycle in 1966, he is surprised to find that the community has become multi-racial and that various religions are represented:

> There are many more black and brown men and women ... There is a heathen temple built right next door to the Seventh Day Adventists!! When I saw this and also the mosque I was torn by the spirit. I had a great desire to prophesy Thou Jerusalem that slayest the prophets and sitting on the saddle with one foot on the pavement I had to clap both hands over my mouth to keep it in. (p. 96)

Matty re-entering Greenfield in the saddle might faintly recall Christ's Palm Sunday entry into Jerusalem, but in this case it is difficult not to feel that it is Matty who is the ass. The Adventists, who believe that 'signs' of the Second Coming of Christ are multiplying and that upon this coming believers alone will be saved, seem deliberately chosen to look shabby, parochial and small-minded beside the great faiths which Matty chooses to regard as mere heathenism. Without honour in his own country, Matty quotes Jesus on Jerusalem's persecution of the prophets and no doubt regards the arrival of these heathens, remembering Ezekiel, as a punishment for the nation's sinfulness and a sign of impending doom: 'Wherefore will I bring the worst of the heathen, and they shall possess their houses ... and their holy places shall be defiled. Destruction cometh; and they shall seek peace, and there shall be none'.[12]

The ecumenism of the sixties is lost on Matty. He would no doubt make nothing of the ideas of that apostle from the heathens, Vivekananda, whose view that 'all religions are one' is mentioned in *Darkness Visible* by that veteran but still hip pursuer of strange gods or spiritual enlightenment, Edwin Bell. Though Sim Goodchild's reply, '"Try telling them that in the mosque"' (p. 203) points to some major difficulties with the notion, Edwin's theology has at least a liberalism which makes Matty seem ridiculously narrow and bigoted. The study of comparative religion does indeed tend to show that there are common elements or a common essence to the great world-religions and helps in separating what is essential and vital in a religion from what is accidental, local, cultic, the product of superstition and bigotry. Matty's own religion is vitiated by its 'non-conformist' insularity, its literal-minded lack of sophistication and scepticism. Such a world-view, 'assured of certain certainties', may be a source of harm beyond anything contemplated by the wicked Sophy or Sebastian Pedigree. The final exchange between the friends Sim and Edwin hints at this: '"We think we *know*." "Know? That's worse than an atom bomb, and always was."' (p. 261). The last verse quoted from Ezekiel above sounds grimly like a warning of the nuclear holocaust. Matty's prophetic gesturings and posturings in Darwin are interpreted by the kindly government official as a warning of the dangers of the atom bomb and a nuclear disaster. But what is more dangerous and worse than the bomb itself is the certainty in the rectitude of one's nation, tribe or faith that would persuade one to use it. The point was movingly made by Jacob Bronowski with regard to a holocaust of those identified as children of darkness that has already been carried out:

This is the concentration camp and crematorium at Auschwitz. This is where people were turned into numbers. Into this pond were flushed the ashes of some four million people. And that was not done by gas. It was done by arrogance. It was done by dogma. It was done by ignorance. When people believe that they have absolute knowledge, with no test in reality, this is how they behave. This is what men do when they aspire to the knowledge of gods.[13]

Certain contemporary fundamentalists in America seem almost to relish the thought of a nuclear war as it may be the beginning of the 'blessed event' of the Apocalypse. Those who believe, in certain approved ways, will be spared the hell on earth of such a death and Hell in the hereafter: whoever is not of the elect will be reduced to ashes as a prelude to eternal torture. 'I feel bad that he is not a Godly man', Matty writes of one of his employers, 'What will become of him I ask myself' (p. 95). Matty is kindly as usual, but there are aspects of his religion that seem both mad and bad.

Golding has deliberately made his evangel ridiculous and Kinkead-Weekes and Gregor pose the inevitable question:

> ... can we accept his Revelation, his world of spirit ... that certainty of Apocalypse, that cranky fundamentalism, beyond even the Brethren in discarding Scripture and taking his mission only from direct messengers of God. Matty's language permits no figurative compromise. The world for him is literally governed by a spiritual force, a wind that roves through him, a spell that is God's ... the news is good. Or else it is idiotic, Matthew's gospel; not truth of nature but the foolishness of a 'natural'. Which? There can be no ducking the question.[14]

The question of judgement upon Matty is not, however, necessarily a simple one of all-or-nothing acceptance or dismissal. It is necessary to separate the elements of wisdom from the folly, the universal from the cranky, the sort of process that is vital to any reading or interpretation of the Bible that can have any claim to seriousness. Certain elements that seem worthy of condemnation or at least question have already been discussed, but before proceeding to more obviously positive aspects of Matty's prophetic mission, it is necessary to say a little more about his expectation of an Apocalypse and its relevance to his status as Christ-figure.

That Christ's self-sacrifice in the crucifixion may be regarded as an act of sublime folly is a notion touched on earlier. The historical researches of the young Albert Schweitzer led him to be more specific about the nature of that folly. For Schweitzer, Jesus believed that the coming of the Kingdom, the Apocalypse, was at hand, was indeed overdue. To hasten its coming and to take upon himself the woes and sufferings traditionally regarded as preceding this event, he offered himself as 'a ransom for many'[15] to be sacrificed. The implications of Schweitzer's theory are described thus by Don Cupitt:

> ... the heroic effort of German biblical criticism to define the essence of Christianity by recovering the original Jesus had failed in the moment of its success. It had found him—and he was a figure utterly alien to the modern world.

On this reading Jesus is just the sort of misfit, cranky millenarian that Matty is, Matty who ransomed a kidnapped child with his life:

> For Jesus had after all been mistaken. The kingdom he expected had never come. Schweitzer's Jesus was a tragic hero, a figure of extraordinary nobility and moral grandeur inspired by a sense of destiny, who had taught an ethic of brotherly love and had voluntarily taken it upon himself to endure the tribulations of mankind in the hope of seeing the coming of a new order.[16]

Jesus and Matty would seem to have been similarly mistaken but, grotesque though the suggestion may seem, of similar nobility and moral grandeur. If we take their careers and intentions literally, they may well seem insane, but (as Edwin Bell reminds us) 'the letter killeth' (p. 203), the spirit giveth life. Matty's life, like the life of Jesus, presents us with an example of selfless love which may not bring about an end of history, but may be regarded nonetheless as a personal Apocalypse, a realisation of the Kingdom in his own person which gives to Matty the last and greatest of his spiritual gifts, the triumph over sin and death.

Matty's triumphant example must be measured against the darkness of the age, a darkness embodied in Sebastian Pedigree and, still more, in the beautiful but vicious Sophy. If Matty is a lonely and unheard herald of holy folly, Sophy, as her name declares, is a symbol, for all her extremism, of the unholy wisdom of the world and the times. Dark though she is, she is possessed of much that the world admires and desires: she has beauty, intelligence and class. Sim Goodchild cannot help but love the 'Misses Stanhope' (p. 120), Sophy and Toni; the Pakistanis who chase a black from their shop fall over themselves to serve the lovely girls. In a world impressed by surface show and given to lust of the eye, Sophy is courted and Matty shunned: 'And this is the condemnation, that light is come into the world, and men loved darkness rather than light, because their deeds were evil.'[17] Sophy is out for what she can get, out to get what she wants, and does not care what she has to do to get it or for the fact that her needs and wants are profoundly evil.

Matty's religious morality may be ridiculously severe in certain respects, but Sophy presents us with the unsavoury spectacle of a human being who has rejected moral values altogether, whose life is entirely governed by appetite, a hunger and thirst for degeneracy and outrage. Sophy resembles Matty, however, in that there is a sort of metaphysical substructure to her moral attitude. Matty communicates with spirits, but Sophy, child of the Sixties as she is, likes to spend time with her ear pressed against the speaker of a transistor radio. It is thus, through the medium of a product of scientific ingenuity, that Sophy hears a message on the ether, a scientific theory of the end of the world which accords with her instinctive feelings: 'One was about the universe running down and she understood that she had always known that' (p. 131). Things are falling apart: the world's one great end is not to be the manifestation of God but a mere nothingness of entropy without even a whimper.

This view that everything is running down, that traditional values are being abandoned or are a spent force, is one that is frequently heard on radio and television. *Darkness Visible* provides a good deal of evidence that would seem to support the view. Thus Frankley's the ironmongers is in the grip 'of something uncontrollable, an inevitable decline' (p. 41); Sim Goodchild's old-world bookshop can scarcely manage to 'limp after inflation' (p. 193); Sophy's house, according to the tedious Roland, seems to have been degenerating for some time: '"It'll have been for the coachman and the grooms and ostlers. You see? They must have built it before the canal because now you couldn't get a coach out. That's why the house went downhill." "Downhill? Our house?"' (p. 143). Evidently this touches a chord with Sophy. Old-fashioned Matty if told to do a job on his own goes off promptly and does it rather than take the opportunity to loaf around, but Sophy is an enthusiast for decadence. 'One joins the movement in a valueless world'[18] wrote Thom Gunn and Sophy is keen to get in the swing and be outrageous.

Sophy's attitude to sex is modern in its lack of inhibition: 'she does not care if her jewel is lost or not' (p. 236) as Matty reflects. But this lack of inhibition reflects a lack of care for her own body, indeed a hatred of it. Her initial sexual adventures are an abuse of her body, an expression of that hatred and distaste. After her first intercourse she explores inside herself:

> ... she came on the other shape, lying opposite the womb but at the back, a shape lying behind the smooth wall but easily to be felt through it, the rounded shape of her own turd working down the coiled gut and she convulsed, feeling without saying but feeling every syllable—*I hate! I hate! I hate!* There was no direct object to the verb, as she said to herself when she was a little more normal. The feeling was pure. (p. 138)

It is not *odi et amo*, but simply *odi*. This capacity for pure feeling is one shared by Matty, but Sophy's feelings are at bottom negative and violently destructive. This Sixties determination to 'be yourself' is by no means a wholly unworthy ideal, but Sophy is a warning of the perils of this pursuit of freedom. Don Crompton writes:

> If freedom means anything to Sophy, it is something which involves putting aside all silly posturing and pretending and simply being, simply taking the brake off and allowing the spring to uncoil, because that, in her view, is to be in sympathy with the process of untangling and running down which is the universal law.[19]

Sophy's honesty allows her to discover that she hates 'the inside of her own body', that she doesn't care about 'being a whore' but does care about 'the roll of blue five-pound notes' (p. 139) it earns her. She will do anything for monetary gain because money means power: sex in itself has no attraction for her, but eventually she discovers that what turns her on is violence, is the most naked, honest and terrible expression of power over others. Anything goes in satisfying this lust for naked power, and that includes child-murder. Sophy's scheme of kidnapping and murdering the immensely wealthy child will kill two birds with one stone, so to speak. It will also be a triumph of self-expression and self-realisation.

Though Sophy is remarkably honest with herself, she is anything but honest towards other people, winning over people by duplicity and, even when caught in the execution of her evil plot, managing to display to effect the much-admired virtue of cooking excuses and getting away with it. She is bought by a newspaper, one of the newspapers she had earlier identified as the source of vicarious pleasure in outrage and evil for the general public:

> ... with *their* great newspaper stories of hideous happenings that kept the whole country entranced for weeks at a time ... all unable to stop reading, looking, going with the feel of the blade sliding in, the rope, the gun, the pain—unable to stop reading, listening, looking— (p. 147)

There is crystallised in Sophy the very worst of human nature and the very worst of the age. Matty thinks that she is literally 'the terrible woman ... in the Apocalypse', the great whore of Revelation with her cup 'full of abominations and filthiness of her fornication', the 'woman drunken with the blood of the saints',[20] his diabolic opponent in the struggles and tribulations of the Last Days. Taken as a metaphor, there is much in this: Sophy is the spirit of the age, symbol of the modern Babylon. The god she serves is her own appetite. Having overturned all moral values, she has come to worship the Beast. The age is obsessed with the pursuit of worldly gods, with the satisfaction and indulgence of appetites, and yet is wretched and empty. In the words of Revelation: '... thou sayest, I am rich; and increased with goods, and have need of nothing; and knowest not that thou art wretched, and miserable, and poor, and blind, and naked ...'[21] Sophy herself, despite having everything, is full of a sense of her own darkness and an intense self-loathing: it is as the word of the Lord prophesies in Ezekiel: '... I am broken with their whorish heart, which hath departed from me, and with their eyes, which go a whoring after their idols: and they shall lothe themselves for the evils which they have committed in all their abominations'.[22]

Matty succeeds by his fiery and terrible death in thwarting the designs of Sophy, but frustrating her ends is as far as he can get with her. Even his spiritual guides seem incapable of reaching her, as they confess. The spiritual powers of Matty make much greater headway with the novel's other main characters, Sim Goodchild and Edwin Bell, the 'decent', 'average' bystanders, and even with Sebastian Pedigree, the pederast whom the public at large regards as the wickedest of men, the very lowest of the low, the perpetrator of sins beyond forgiveness.

Sim Goodchild is the central figure in the third book of *Darkness Visible*: after two books dominated by the bizarre Matty and the 'weird' Sophy, Sim offers a more normal, everyday sort of viewpoint. Sim is, however, an educated and cultivated man. His world-view is that of a secular humanist, his nature for the most part kindly and benign. He believes in 'the life of Jesus' as he believes in 'the battle of Hastings', as a historical event and nothing more: 'It is a kind of belief which touches nothing in me' (p. 200). His friend Edwin Bell, however, is an enthusiast for religions, a devotee of '"Transcendentalism"', a man inclined to speak 'like a character in one of Huxley's less successful novels' (p. 200). It is yet another manifestation of the Piggy/Simon rivalry. To the rationalistic and sceptical Sim the enthusiast brings Matty as his latest guru or avatar, his latest solution to the problems of life.

The title of the third book, 'One is One', encapsulates what is for Sim probably the greatest problem and misery of the world, his sense of the isolation of people from each other, of the walls 'less penetrable than brick, than steel', the 'walls of adamant' that lie 'everywhere between everything and everything' (p. 83). Even he and his friend Edwin Bell live on different islands, see the world in very different ways and find communication problematic. This sense of alienation, of isolation within the crowd is an experience that recurs frequently in the art of the past two hundred years. Arnold's lines:

> Yes! in the sea of life enisled,
> With echoing straits between us thrown,
> Dotting the shoreless watery wild,
> We mortal millions live *alone*.[23]

encapsulate perfectly Sim's unhappy sense of lonely insulation. Though one of Greenfield's churches has been converted into a community centre (where they are rehearsing Sartre's *Huis Clos*, which contains the line 'Hell is just—other people'[24]) there is no sense of community, perhaps as a result of the ebbing of the sea of faith. It is a particular gift of Matty's that he has the ability to break through these interpersonal walls, to bridge the gap between islands. Even in his childhood his nurse feels the power of his 'wordless communication': 'Being, it seemed, touched being' (p. 18). Matty almost wholly abjures language, but thus avoids the meaningless gabble of so much of human speech; he favours places of silence where a true peace and true communion may be found. Speech may be used to avoid communication, as when Pedigree returns to Greenfield and buttonholes Edwin Bell: 'both of them talked at once as if silence would allow something else to be heard, something deadly' (p. 81). But Matty rejects such linguistic camouflage, communicates silently and with great intensity his *feeling*, his extraordinary grief at human wickedness and sin, and yet also the joy of his love for humanity.

Edwin persuades a reluctant Sim to participate in a kind of seance with Matty. Before they begin Matty silently reads Sim's palm: the whole affair seems a piece of spiritualist fakery. We learn later from Matty's journal that his own view of the occasion included 'green and purple and black' evil spirits (p. 235). Yet despite these embarrassing trappings, Sim is given through the medium of Matty a revelation. Matty's Apocalypse is here and now, his revelation is that the Kingdom is at hand in the beauty of what is immediate to us. The men join hands in a communion where being touches being, where their circle expands to embrace millions, a whole country, where Edwin's voice, or a voice that speaks through Edwin, intones an ecstatic word or note that seems to last an aeon:

> ... and the semi-vowel of the close was not an end since there was, there could be no end but only a re-adjustment so that the world of spirit could hide itself again, slowly, slowly fading from sight, reluctant as a lover to go and with the ineffable promise that it would love always and if asked would always come again. (p. 233)

Gazing into his own 'pale, crinkled' palm, not to the ordinary eye a thing of beauty or a joy forever, Sim sees 'a gigantic world' and knows that it is holy (p. 231). Crompton points out that Matty makes real for Sim and Edwin the Blakean ambition of seeing a world in a grain of sand and holding infinity in the palm of your hand. As Huxley argues in *The Doors of Perception* and *Heaven and Hell*, this seeing into the life of things, into the radiant beauty of the commonest objects, this transformation of the shoddy world of here and now into a heaven of eternity, is the common goal of many mystics. Thomas Traherne, for example, speaks of how in his visionary childhood, 'Eternity was manifest in the Light of the Day and something infinite behind everything appeared'.[25] Huxley quotes one authority who states that: 'The Dharma-body of the Buddha' *is* 'the hedge at the bottom of the garden.'[26] Matty is, indeed, the 'treasure' that Pedigree jokingly calls him, the treasure hid in a field that is the Kingdom of Heaven. The world of Greenfield is no longer for Sim a brazen prison, a torture-chamber or madhouse-cell of impenetrable walls, but a world transformed in a revelation to a beauty beyond words, a world where the lonely man feels suddenly loved, where the very fabric of the world seems suddenly to welcome him and make him at home with the warmth and sweetness of a lover.

Sophy's natural advantages and breathless pursuit of the objects of her appetites bring her no peace: plenty makes her poor. Matty's ascesis, his rejection of appetite, his abnegation of pleasures, bring him the supreme gift of a world transformed to beauty and an ability to show to others that beauty which words cannot express. Sim at the seance finds that his nose itches agonisingly and that this interferes with or gets in the way of his sense of communion, vision and ecstasy. Matty records how he saw evil spirits clawing at Sim and Edwin. Perhaps this 'itch' or 'tickle' is a troublesome lust that clouds Sim's vision: he finds that it helps 'to detach oneself from the desire to scratch' (p. 232), though it must be said that he does eventually get rid of the problem by scratching. Detachment from desire is also a traditional method of the mystical seeker: if we could achieve freedom from those obsessive desires that dominate our lives and leave us unsatisfied we might find with Matty and Shakespeare's Timon that nothing brings us all things, might rediscover those powers we had wasted in getting and spending.[27]

Matty breaks down some walls for Sim, cleanses the doors of perception for him, but Sim is very reluctant to agree to Matty's wish that Pedigree should be drawn into the magic circle. One has to draw the line somewhere. Matty is, however, determined to try to redeem or save the enemy whom he loves, to break through to Pedigree, that creature of walls, to break down his lavatory wall, to cleanse him of filth and give him freedom. Edwin and Sim especially are very unwilling to get involved with an infamous sinner and criminal like Pedigree, but Matty's determination to cure the beastly man follows the example and the advice of Jesus in St Matthew:

And when the Pharisees saw it, they said unto his disciples, Why eateth your Master with publicans and sinners? But when Jesus heard that, he said unto them, They that be whole need not a physician, but they that are sick.[28]

Sebastian Pedigree is a hard case for the spiritual physician. He persists in his folly, refuses whatever help medicine can offer him. He and his kind are the object of especial and extreme loathing on the part of the public at large. Even Sim, who is kindly and looks upon Pedigree as a 'sick' man (p. 121), can scarcely bring himself to name his condition. Even the narrator approaches 'old Pedders' (p. 24) in his days at Foundlings by means of schoolboy jokes: 'Mr Pedigree had no intention of interfering—none whatever' (p. 25). But interfering with little boys *is* Mr Pedigree's intention and obsession and because of this he is the object of much righteous anger. Ordinary, 'nice' English ladies with names like Mrs Allenby and Mrs Appleby attempt to 'maim' him on the streets of Greenfield. Their violent animus towards the 'ghastly old creature' reassures them that they are on the side of the forces of light against darkness and evil, but their vigilante enthusiasm for maiming and scratching eyes out seems fairly sinister in itself (pp. 84–5). They, and we, would do well to heed those words of Bishop Wilson which Matthew Arnold so admired:

"First, never go against the best light you have; secondly, take care that your light be not darkness." We show, as a nation, laudable energy and persistence in walking according to the best light we have, but are not quite careful enough, perhaps, to see that our light be not darkness.[29]

They show that English trait, upon which Golding has remarked, of believing that evil is elsewhere and in someone else. They know they are right ('"We think we *know*"') in judging and condemning Pedigree and that certainty of their own rectitude allows a devil of murderous violence to take them over without their even noticing it. It is the oldest Golding theme: the sins of the community are imposed upon a scapegoat who may then be destroyed by the mob. For Matty, Pedigree resembles the supreme scapegoat in that he is 'despised and rejected' (p. 96). Judgement, Golding reminds us once again, is not the easy matter we might think. Perhaps Pedigree differs from ordinary people not in being more wicked, but merely more unfortunate, an object worthy of pity rather than hate. However, 'It is not recorded anywhere if there was a single person living in Greenfield who pitied him' (p. 85). It is in *this* regard that Greenfield compares unfavourably with Sodom and Gomorrah.

The attitude of Sim towards Pedigree is somewhat Pharisaic. Sim Goodchild's very name seems to declare that he is a good knight and true, a very model of decency and respectability: *he* does not want to be seen in the company of a sinner like Pedigree. Sim's involvement with Matty, however, reveals that Sim is deserving of the denunciation handed out to the Pharisees by Jesus in St Matthew:

> Woe unto you, scribes and Pharisees, hypocrites! for ye are like unto whited sepulchres, which indeed appear beautiful outward, but are within full of dead men's bones and all uncleanness.
> Even so ye also outwardly appear righteous unto men, but within ye are full of hypocrisy and iniquity.[30]

Sim, shiny white on the outside, has within him his own well of darkness and shame. He has a particular reason to shun Pedigree: Pedigree reminds him of the truth about himself which he would rather not face in so naked a form. For Sim too has paedophile inclinations. Young girls are his thing and he particularly dotes upon the angelic, upper-class-ish Stanhope twins, though, as Crompton points out, 'his illicit feelings for the Stanhope girls are insulated by invoking Wordsworth'.[31] Pedigree, in his earlier days, employs a similar dressing-up of his desires as an enthusiasm for youth, beauty and purity. But Sim's enthusiasm for Sophy Stanhope is, from Matty's point of view, a thraldom to the Great Whore herself. The seemingly pure and angelic little girl is not what she seems and Sim's sentiments are by no means pure either. When Sim and Edwin stumble on evidence that the grown-up Sophy is *'into bondage'*, into '"Sexual games, private and, and shaming"', they are in fact revealing the truth about Sim's private and shaming sexual fantasies, for the scene before them is 'like something out of the furtive book in his desk', is a 'brothel image' (pp. 246–7). His involvement with Pedigree, which is forced upon him by Matty, and his entry into Sophy Stanhope's territory for the seance force out of Sim a confession to Edwin about the Stanhope girls: ' "I used to be in love with them" ' (p. 224). A 'part of the generation-long folly of Sim Goodchild' (p. 223) is revealed, a little of the darkness, the 'vast heap of rubbish, of ordure, of filthy rags' (p. 194) that is within him is made visible. Matty manages to 'pierce a partition' (p. 225), the lavatory wall between them is breached to show the shaming similarity of Sim and Pedigree.

Sim regards Pedigree as 'sick', but Golding seems to favour the Freudian view that we are all sick. Such was his belief at the time of *Lord of the Flies*: 'I believed then, that man was sick—not exceptional man, but average man' (HG p. 87). *Darkness Visible* provides little evidence of any change of heart or mind. The idea is not a new one: 'all have sinned, and come short of the glory of God' says St Paul.[32] Those who mob Pedigree would do well to recall Christ's words to those who intended to stone the woman taken in adultery: 'He that is without sin among you, let him first cast a stone at her.'[33] It may be argued that Pedigree is a much greater sinner than Sim, a much more wicked man, since he has been unable to restrain his illicit desires, has allowed those desires to be translated into actions, whereas Sim has merely indulged in fantasies about little girls. It is a serious argument, but the answer given to it by Christ in St Matthew is clear enough and terrible:

Ye have heard that it was said by them of old time, Thou shalt not commit adultery:
But I say unto you, That whosoever looketh on a woman to lust after her hath committed adultery with her already in his heart.[34]

Christ takes the thought for the deed. Viewed from such a standpoint judgement upon Sim and Pedigree is no longer the simple matter of black and white that at first it may appear.

Matty wears his darkness outwardly, like another man in black he insists on and grieves for the darkness of human nature: 'Use every man after his desert, and who shall scape whipping?'[35] Mr Pedigree, insisting that he himself is 'nowhere near the worst' when compared to Sophy, also quotes from *Hamlet* but the words are those of Ophelia, a 'favourite character' of his, presumably because her particular love was also despised and rejected: 'We know what we are but not what we may be' (p. 260). These words of a wise fool are analysed by Anthony Beavis, a character in one of Huxley's more successful novels:

> Mad, Ophelia lets the cat out of the bag ... Polonius knows very clearly what he and other people *are*, within the ruling conventions. Hamlet knows this, but also what they may be— outside the local system of masks and humours.[36]

The profoundly unsophisticated Matty forces Sim to remove the mask and see what he may be, find his Pedigree, find out what's what. As *Hamlet* illustrates, this can be a harrowing experience, a descent into primeval filth such as Matty forces upon himself in the wilderness of Australia, the abomination of desolation. After such a painful but salutary encounter with one's own darkness one may well find it more difficult to condemn the likes of Pedigree, less easy to cast the first stone. King Lear, after an experience of stripping down to basics in a howling wilderness, has similar warnings to offer on the hypocrisy of judgement:

> Thon rascal beadle, hold thy bloody hand!
> Why dost thou lash that whore? Strip thine own back;
> Thou hotly lusts to use her in that kind
> For which thou whipp'st her.[37]

Mrs Allenby, one of those who would cast stones at Pedigree, remarks to Mrs Appleby that 'it was lucky for Mr Pedigree this was England' (p. 84). This reflects a rather rueful chauvinistic pride that the English are more civilised than some races she might care to name, but her remark is incorrect in that the horror with which Mr Pedigree's sin is regarded is the product of the mores of particular times and places, of 'the ruling conventions' rather than any absolute law. At least, so the narrator would have us believe, for we are told of Mr Pedigree only a few pages before Mrs Allenby's remark that 'except for his compulsion—which in many countries would not have got him into trouble—he was without vice' (p. 79). Pedigree is extremely unlucky to be living now and in England. As Nietzsche points out in *Thus Spoke Zarathustra*, the historian or geographer of law and morality finds anything but consistency: 'Much that seemed good to one people seemed shame and disgrace to another: thus I found. I found much that was called evil in one place was in another decked with purple honours'.[38]

The particular loathing with which Pedigree's condition is regarded in his particular time and place contributes to his degeneration:

> He was developing. Over the years he had moved from a generous delight in the sexual aura of youth to an appreciation of all the excitement attendant on breaking taboos if the result was sufficiently squalid. There were public lavatories in the park of course ... oh there were public lavatories dotted round the place ... (pp. 79–80)

What is sexually delightful for Pedigree is regarded by all around as filthy and shameful and so what is filthy and shameful becomes for him sexually exciting. He becomes a prisoner of life's lavatories. He is driven on, despite himself, to ever new disgraces, knowing that one day his fears may make him a child-murderer as well as a child-molester. It is hard not to feel outraged by child-molesting, but if we condemn Pedigree and regard him as damned or unspeakable we run the risk of being dealt with equally severely ourselves, for Pedigree's sin may be no more dreadful, from a God's-eye point-of-view, than a number of others, some of which our society regards as mere peccadilloes or even approves of as worthy behaviour. As Don Crompton has pointed out, Matty's names, Matthew Septimus, point us to a clear and terrible warning regarding the passing of judgement upon others in the opening verse of the seventh chapter of St Matthew: 'Judge not, that ye be not judged.'

The second verse expands on this: 'For with what judgement ye judge, ye shall be judged: and with what measure ye mete, it shall be measured to you again.'

The novel's final pages present us with one last mystery, though a mystery not sorrowful but joyful. The last episode, in which Pedigree finds the park transformed to a sea of gold and sees the dead Matty come floating on that light sea to redeem and rescue him, is dark with excessive bright. In a scene that recalls the end of Christopher Martin's island life Matty comes as a 'loving and terrible' angel (p. 265) to bring freedom to Pedigree and drag him kicking and screaming into heaven or, at least, to cut him loose from his pitiful subservience to his passion. Pedigree scarcely seems deserving of this strange rescue: he still blames others and is reluctant to accept the wound of death that will cure him, though it must also be said that he does call out to Matty for help, for salvation. We see now most clearly the appalling struggle that goes on inside Pedigree, see that he is by no means simply a beast. He fights as best he can against the 'graph' (p. 262) that rises within him, the 'wave motion' (p. 260) of desire that he cannot hold back forever. These images suggest the world of human intellect: whatever saves Pedigree must transcend this. What saves him is the love of Matty, that love that has remained loyal to his enemy, that offers himself to be a burnt offering for the sake of others, a love beyond reason, a love that passeth all understanding.

Matty may be said to represent Christ's sacrifice which made possible the salvation of even the likes of Pedigree, which opened the gates of heaven to all of us, insofar as Pedigree represents the innate propensity to sin, the Original Sin, present in all humans. It may seem impossible, beyond the wit of man, to heal Pedigree, yet Christ's self-oblation made such a salving possible. The last devilish no-saying of the specific Mr Pedigree may seem a bar to salvation, but he does also call for help. He cannot win the struggle within himself alone and unaided, but perhaps the love that overwhelms him is prepared to give him credit for trying. Once again, it is not for us to judge. We have all sinned and come short of God's glory: if Pedigree may be forgiven it is good news for us all.

Such might be a fairly orthodox, conservative, Christian reading of the ending, a Rowena Pringle sort of interpretation. The sceptical, unreligious voice or view is also, as ever, present as the park keeper approaches Pedigree knowing 'the filthy old thing would never be cured' (p. 265). Perhaps the vision of salvation was simply an hallucination of the dying Pedigree, the resurrected Matty a mere fantasy. But perhaps a middle way of interpretation is possible. Perhaps we may say that salvation and redemption for Pedigree is the simple knowledge that he is loved and forgiven: this it is that provokes tears of joy, that turns a world of hellish filth and guilt to golden light and warmth. Matty hates sin but loves the sinner. In imitation of the example and teaching of Christ he forgives the man who has trespassed against him. This transforms the world, this breaks down the adamantine walls that keep us each in his cell. Only by forgiving others do we earn the right to be forgiven, to forgive ourselves, only thus can *we* be cured. To love and forgive the sinner transforms the world *and* us. In certain ways Matty resembles Blake and perhaps his epitaph might be the sublime words of that half-mad genius:

> Mutual Forgiveness of each Vice,
> Such are the Gates of Paradise.[39]

·8·

DARK TROPICS

·RITES OF PASSAGE (1980)·

'Tis a sad thing, I cannot choose but say,
    And all the fault of that indecent sun,
Who cannot leave alone our helpless clay,
    But will keep baking, broiling, burning on,
That howsoever people fast and pray,
    The flesh is frail, and so the soul undone:
What men call gallantry, and gods adultery,
Is much more common where the climate's sultry.

                                              Byron, *Don Juan*

The Prince of Darkness is a gentleman.

                                              King Lear

Rites of Passage purports to be the journal of Edmund
Talbot, a lordly young buck of Byron's time, as he sets out
confidently and optimistically on the great adventure of his
adult life. He hopes that the voyage to Australia upon which
he is embarked will provide material for some entertaining
entries and episodes to amuse the godfather and patron to
whom the journal is written. Talbot spots as one source of
humour and diversion the maladroit young parson, Robert
James Colley. Colley's comic misfortunes grow ever more
extreme, so that he becomes the central figure in Talbot's
story: as the ship sails through the waters of the torrid zone,
Colley is brutally humiliated and abused in the 'Crossing the
Line' ceremony and dies of embarrassment and shame after
he makes a drunken fool and exhibition of himself the next
day. The full extent of his folly, of the horror at the heart of
his farcical career, is discovered by Talbot as he reads

Colley's own journal of the voyage and as he assists the captain in his enquiry into the cause of his death. Colley's ultimate mistake is a sexual misdemeanour, a folly brought on in part no doubt by the baking, broiling, burning heat of the tropics and the fiery liquor he is given to drink. The voyage towards the underside of things and through the heart or centre of the map of man's world reveals the dark truth about Colley's nature. But not merely Colley's, for Talbot very gradually becomes aware of the darkness in himself, of the beam in his own eye, and we are made horribly aware of the darkness and filth below decks on the ship of state and of the soul. Though all at sea, we are very much in the Golding country.

'Long live illusion,' says Talbot. 'Let us export it to our colonies with all the other benefits of civilization!' (p. 123). He is thinking of Mr Brocklebank, who keeps two women but keeps up appearances by pretending that one is his wife and the other his daughter. Talbot's view may well be prudent: his exploration of the truth of the Colley affair, his vision of human nature under too searching a light, leaves him, like the Ancient Mariner's wedding-guest, a stunned and very much sadder, if wiser, man. To borrow a phrase from Thomas De Quincey, whom Talbot faintly recalls in that he tipples some laudanum on the voyage, he is forced to 'see the things that ought *not* to be seen',[1] sad and fearful truths about ourselves and our world the discovery of which may shake our very sanity.

The novel is set, however, in the age not only of Byron, Coleridge and De Quincey, all producers of sighs from the depths of human experience, but of Jane Austen, a novelist much concerned with manners and the class-system, with temperate zones of human experience but not with its dark tropics. Talbot is keen on preserving illusions, particularly the illusion that civilisation (i.e. things as they are in Britain) is a benefit to man, though it is pretty plain that most of its benefits are given only to people of his elevated station or class. Colley is undone in part by the illicit desires which are of his very nature but also by his being an upstart, a man who has risen from the lower orders to the gentlemanly station of a Church of England minister. Kinkead-Weekes

and Gregor detect a specific echo of Jane Austen: 'Colley ...
betrays the *parvenu* in every detail of appearance, manner
and speech and, like his counterpart in Jane Austen's Mr
Collins, is riding for a fall.'[2] Colley's fall is rather more
spectacular and tragic than that of the execrable toady of
Pride and Prejudice however. Golding's novel seems to
mock Austen's novelistic world by revealing those embarrassing areas of human life which Austen so signally ignores. It
is impossible to imagine any Jane Austen character using the
lavatory: in *Darkness Visible*, however, the personages of
Jane Austen's England are shown as their sweating selves
and, worse, their vomiting and defecating selves as well.

In *Persuasion*, a novel which reaches sublime heights of
formality and reticence when its naval-officer hero proposes
by letter to the heroine though they are both in the same
room at the time, Louisa Musgrove delivers a paean of
praise of the navy:

> Louisa ... burst forth into raptures of animation and delight on
> the character of the navy—their friendliness, their brotherliness,
> their openness, their uprightness; protesting that she was con-
> vinced of sailors having more worth and warmth than any
> other set of men in England; that they only knew how to live,
> and they only deserved to be respected and loved.[3]

In the classist world of Austen's novels it goes without
saying that Louisa has in mind naval officers and not
common sailors: the lower orders are kept hidden almost as
rigorously as visits to the lavatory. The sailors home from
the sea in *Persuasion* are, indeed, a well-mannered and
pleasant lot. Golding's officers are a good deal more rough-
and-ready: the nautical *argot* which Talbot delights in learning is called 'tar' and it is the habitual filthiness of their
language which drives the prim and perhaps Austen-like
governess Miss Granham from their table. No obscenities
are to be heard in Miss Austen's world.

Golding in *Rites of Passage* is characteristically unafraid
of crossing the bounds of decorum in pursuit of the truth,
however filthy. This is in stark contrast to Austen. The novel
resembles Austen, however, in that it is obsessively interested
in class. Austen habitually condemns open and blatant

snobbery while endorsing snob or classist values by mocking and humiliating the *parvenu*, and by quietly dismissing the greater part of mankind as beneath the regard or interest of well-bred readers. To Golding such classist values are an obscenity and one might argue that such values are the one obscenity that is glaringly visible in the pages of Austen. The ship with its rigid segregation of classes, its lines on the deck which are dangerous to cross, is manifestly Britain in miniature, and it stinks: 'the sand and gravel of Old England' (p. 9) that make up its ballast create a 'fetor', a 'stench' (p. 4) which is nauseating, though one soon gets used to it. Talbot is in many ways a decent, well-meaning and generous young man, but his automatic classist attitudes are hateful and harmful. To him the common sailors of the fo'c's'le are scarcely human creatures who are generally unworthy of his notice and he unthinkingly insults the excellent Lieutenant Summers who has achieved the astonishing feat of rising from the ranks. He finds the *parvenu* Colley contemptible and risible, regards his tragedy as one of simple class-regression: Colley was dragged 'back towards his own kind' (p. 277), back into the savagery of the fo'c's'le. Yet Talbot's instinctive sense of his own status contributed not a little to Colley's death, for his entry to the forbidden territory of the Captain's quarterdeck, protected by his own status and his godfather's name, enrages Captain Anderson and causes the explosion when Colley sub-sequently blunders in the same way. Class is a way of life, but also a killer.

This concentration on class suggests a contrast, quickly detected by the critics, between *Darkness Visible* and *Rites of Passage*: where the former is inward, mystical, distrustful of language and almost unrelievedly sombre, the latter has much lightness, is full of imagery from the theatre, is frequently comic (though it bears saying that the funniest moment is also the most appalling). *Rites of Passage* seems to have been dashed off, as Crompton suggests, with a certain *sprezzatura*: it is, one might say, an example of passage-work, is a spell of virtuosic showing-off on the part of its author. In reading the novel we partake of the highly civilised pleasure of watching a skilful artist creating the illusion that his work is a product of a past age in art. It is a splendid piece of forgery, a marvellous pastiche of early novelistic techniques and styles. Golding apes early devices aimed at creating verisimilitude: the book purports to be the 'true story' of the adventures of a young hero on a strange sea voyage, with some reflections on life, death, morality and the well-being of the body politic; it takes the form of a journal-epistle written by the hero and includes also the journal of Colley, which proves to be a book of confessions. Golding's skill helps to win our credence, but we do not believe the tale is literally true, we feel that it is true to its supposed time, that we have been placed if not in the world then at least in the world-view (or views) of the early nineteenth century.

Talbot makes great efforts in his journal to communicate the feel of the alien world of the ship to his godfather by his attention to its workings and the 'tarpaulin' language of its crew. Golding, standing behind his narrator as it were, is still more assiduous in his efforts to recreate the style of his classically-educated and classist young man of 1813–14. In this he is very successful, but the success is in the production of a biased account of the voyage. Certain aspects of the pastiche, the antiquated type-set and 'olde worlde' design of the title-page for example, serve oddly to draw attention to the fact that the novel is an elaborate fake, a stylistic forgery. Golding insists on the fact that his novel is not what it purports to be, is not a true history of a sea-voyage at all. The novel seems to mock the naive belief that a novel or a work of narrative historiography can be successful in telling the truth, the whole truth and nothing but the truth.

'"Tell all, my boy! Hold nothing back!"' (p. 11) were the bluff instructions given to Talbot by his unnamed godfather whose name is such a potent charm, but they prove quite impossible to carry out. It is scarcely a week into the voyage before Talbot has lost track of the date, for example. 'Circumstances', as he complains 'are all against careful composition' (p. 11). Though precise positioning in time and space is a tricky business in navigation, as the rite of 'shooting the sun' (p. 35) indicates, chronology is a minor problem when set beside the traditional narrative and historiographical habit of attributing agency and causation. Talbot is asked the innocent and natural question '"Who killed cock Colley?"' (p. 248), but the answer is elusive and anything but simple. Perhaps Colley was his own executioner, bringing about his own end by sheer force of will like a member of the 'savage peoples' (p. 153) Summers mentions. The captain's log records that he died of 'a *low fever*' (p. 263), but Captain Anderson has reason to falsify history for he is himself surely in part to blame for conniving at the abuse of Colley. Cumbershum and Deverel must bear some of the guilt for they select Colley as the victim in the equatorial tomfooleries and drag him off to the throne of judgement. Talbot himself sets off the captain's explosive temper which contributes not a little to the parson's demise and Golding has himself suggested that Colley is killed 'in a subtle way' by Talbot.[4] The common sailors assault him brutally in the 'Crossing the Line' ceremony and they are a party to the act which finally wrecks his sanity and will to live. It seems that the whole damned crew, the entire little world of the ship must partake of the guilt of Colley's death. The answer to Talbot's simple question would not be a statement of fact but an interpretation, an act of judgement, and judgement, once again, is no simple matter. The very act of telling or reading a story, it may be argued, is itself an act of interpretation and necessarily a biased one at that. The act of narrating, of shaping the facts into a story, is one which necessarily distorts the truth, as Talbot hints in reporting with disappointment that he has failed to spin out the story so that it neatly fits the journal his godfather has given him: 'All was of no avail. His was a real life and a real death and no more to be fitted into a given book than a misshapen foot into a given boot' (p. 264). Talbot's narration or any narrative is a framework or net by which we may make some sense of what went on but, once again, it does not catch the ocean upon which it is cast.

Don Crompton has suggested a resemblance between Talbot and Colley in this exploration of dark tropics and Marlow and Kurtz in Conrad's *Heart of Darkness*: in both cases the would-be missionary discovers the darkness within himself in the steamy world of the equatorial regions.

Talbot, like Marlow, finds that he cannot 'tell all' to the unfortunate's relative back home because the truth is 'too dark altogether'.[5] Conrad himself refuses to come clean about the precise nature of the abominations perpetrated by Kurtz in the darkness of Africa, though we may all perhaps be able to fill in the blank on the map on our own behalf. Golding is more forthcoming. Both these sailors' yarns, however, describe a voyage from innocence to experience and the shock of their narrator's discovery of the darkness of man's heart. *Rites of Passage* seems also to owe something to a lesser Conradian tale of the passage from youth to maturity undergone in a tropical inferno, *The Shadow Line*. That tale is set in 'that twilight region betwen youth and maturity'[6] and describes an ordeal of that critical and dangerous phase of life:

> Only the young have such moments ... one perceives ahead a shadow-line warning one that the region of early youth, too, must be left behind ... What moments? ... Rash moments. I mean moments when the young are inclined to commit rash actions, such as getting married suddenly or else throwing up a job for no reason.[7]

The young sailor hero of *The Shadow Line* successfully crosses the mysterious line in the thick murk of the Gulf of Siam which seems to stand as a barrier between him and further progress in life. Colley too comes to a line in the ocean but is judged to be unworthy; in the 'Crossing the Line' ceremonies he has rashly crossed the invisible lines of class which so interest Golding and still more rashly he crosses the visible demarcation lines on the ship's deck. Drunk and back with the lower orders in the fo'c's'le, he crosses with disastrous results further lines or bounds of decency and propriety, descending like Kurtz into abominable acts.

This tropical descent into primitive savagery has been seen before in Golding: the unclasping of the snake-belt of society's inhibitions releases the powers of darkness within the boys in *Lord of the Flies*. Yet the act which destroys Colley is a great deal less lethal than those perpetrated by

Jack and his cohorts or by Kurtz. The precise nature of that misdemeanour in the fo'c's'le we learn only in the novel's last pages when Mr Prettiman and Miss Granham reveal to all and sundry the 'fact' that Colley 'chewed tobacco', this being their ludicrous misinterpretation of a lavatorial conversation between two sailors:

> Billy Rogers was laughing like a bilge pump when he come away from the captain's cabin. He went into the heads and I sat by him. Billy said he'd knowed most things in his time but he never thought to get a chew off a parson! (pp. 272–3)

The drunken vicar disgraced himself with a sailor, that is the filthy truth which kills a sobered Colley and which Talbot understandably thinks unfit for communication to the unfortunate man's sister back in England.

Colley dies of shame at this, feeling no doubt that he has utterly betrayed and disgraced his cloth, even as the suicidal former captain had betrayed his uniform of office in *The Shadow Line*:

> Yet the end of his life was a complete act of treason, the betrayal of a tradition which seemed to me as imperative as any guide on earth could be. It appeared that even at sea a man could become the victim of evil spirits. I felt on my face the breath of unknown powers that shape our destinies.[8]

Colley is overwhelmed by an unknown power, a devil within him; he commits what Captain Anderson describes as 'beastliness' (p. 253) with Billy Rogers; as Talbot puts it, he makes 'a beast' (p. 150) of himself. It seems that, like Kurtz, he lets the devil, the Beast within him, loose. Yet Marlow, though aware of his degradation, continues to consider Kurtz 'a remarkable man',[9] to admire his terrible honesty in a world that easily matches him in viciousness but cloaks its wickedness in the most nauseating hypocrisy and self-satisfaction. Talbot is a rather more reactionary moralist than Marlow, but he too is aware that the rottenness in the ship is not confined to poor Colley.

Colley's reaction to his experience, while he is still under the influence of 'the devil's brew' (p. 237), as he calls it, is not shame but wild, ecstatic joy: '"Joy! Joy! Joy!"' he exclaims and flings out his arms 'as if to embrace us all' (p. 117). He would kiss the whole world and has a blessing for everyone and everything. Colley seems momentarily to have discovered an equatorial paradise of innocence, the 'earthly' or 'oceanic paradise' of which he had written in his letter (p. 187). He has realised his true self, brought into being what had been hidden away perhaps even from himself: small wonder that this self-realisation should be a source of joy. He has felt the power of a dark and unknown god whom his everyday, dishonest self would regard as the very devil. He is drunk out of his mind and the governing deity of such madness and ecstasy is Dionysus. Some remarks of E.R. Dodds in his classic study *The Greeks and the Irrational* provide a useful commentary on Colley's brush with that dangerous god:

> He was essentially a god of joy ... And his joys were accessible to all, including even slaves ... Apollo moved only in the best society, from the days when he was Hector's patron to the days when he canonised aristocratic athletes; but Dionysus was at all periods demotikos, a god of the people ... he is Lusios, "the Liberator" — the god who by very simple means ... enables you for a short time to *stop being yourself*, and thereby sets you free ...[10]

Among the common people and in the power of the demotic god, Colley finds the joy of liberation, is able to strip off the lies and self-denials that are the essence of his quotidian, social self and find the truth beneath: *in vino veritas*. The fleeting sense of paradisial love for all which he seems to discover is described by Nietzsche as one of the gifts of Dionysus: 'Under the charm of the Dionysian not only is the covenant between man and man again established, but also estranged, hostile or subjugated nature again celebrates her reconciliation with her lost son, man.'[11]

Colley's paradise is poisoned, however: its joys are taboo. Dionysus may deliver 'the fundamental knowledge of the oneness of all existing things', in Nietzsche's words,[12] but such knowledge may well be a dangerous thing, a threat to the very fabric of law and morality. Dodds' haughty Apollo would enjoy the company of Talbot and, for Nietzsche, though he is also a god of dreams, Apollo is a god of bounding, of lines and limitations: 'But also that delicate line, which the dream-picture must not overstep ... must not be wanting in the picture of Apollo: that measured limitation, that freedom from the wilder emotions, that philosophical calmness of the sculptor-god.'[13] Talbot conducts his own *amour* at sea with elaborate discretion and a certain rather distasteful coldness; it is in his interest, and is second nature to him, to observe and preserve the differences between people and casts of people rather than celebrate their oneness; he would have decencies and decorums honoured, would not be seen 'arm in arm with a common sailor' (p. 51), much less in attitudes of greater intimacy. Patrician that he is, he stands for the moral legislators of our society, those who draw lines or weave circles around those areas where a man may not stray, those who would presume to decide even which acts are natural and which (as the law would have us believe that Colley's is) unnatural. Kinkead-Weekes and Gregor have pointed out that the rivalry between Talbot and Colley may be seen as a clash between Augustan and Romantic world-views, the learned and urbane against the naive, the patrician against the demotic, the socially-oriented against the nature-worshipping, the decorous against the exploratory. Underlying this we may perhaps perceive the struggle between Dionysus and Apollo, the tension between instinctive drives and the forces of law and morality which repress them, forces which would see in the Dionysian only filth, darkness and devilry, forces which divide us from ourselves. Out of the agony of this repression is born tragedy.

Colley discovers what he truly is and that experience is joyous, a liberation; but his true nature is something which both his society and his sober self reject as vile. For, having broken the taboo, he passes judgement upon and punishes himself with death. He cannot be, cannot live with, what in reality he is and so must die. The shock of the sudden, overpowering manifestation of what was repressed in him is too great for recovery: Dionysus denied can become a destroyer. His fall is surely a tragedy, yet Talbot seems unsure whether his story is worthy of that noble title:

> It is a play. Is it a farce or a tragedy? Does not a tragedy depend on the dignity of the protagonist? Must he not be great to fall greatly? A farce, then, for the man appears now a sort of Punchinello. (p. 104)

Though this is written before Colley's death and before Talbot's discovery of his final impropriety, even at the very last Talbot still regards Colley as 'clownish' and the whole affair 'by turns farcical, gross and tragic' (p. 276). Moreover, his classical and classist demarcation line would still apply even after Colley's death. Such a snobbish ordering of the world of literature must seem absurd to an age that has learned, from Wordsworth among others, that men who do not wear fine clothes can feel deeply, that there may be tragedy in the death of a salesman. Yet it is undeniable that the manner in which we learn of Colley's catastrophic lapse is extremely funny, amusing in a gross and brutal, almost Python-esque way. The blackest moment in the novel is also the funniest.

The exaggeratedly tragi-comic nature of Colley's misfortune serves to vindicate Talbot's preference for Shakespeare over his godfather's favourite Racine. Racine rigidly excluded the comic from his tragedies, while Shakespeare took no heed of such neo-Classical strictness and freely mixed the tragic and the comic. Life does not come neatly divided up into tragedy and comedy: 'real life' and 'real death', those misshapen feet (to adapt Talbot's own metaphor), refuse to fit neatly into one style of boot or the other. Shakespeare at times, in the madness of King Lear and the filthy jokes by which Iago unleashes a killer in Othello, seems to hint that at bottom tragedy and comedy are inextricably linked. Even the noblest of tragic heroes may be seen as the victim of some divine practical joke, even the most heart-breakingly tragic lines may have a ghost of laughter, a spirit of black farce, about them:

EDGAR ... Look up a-height; the shrill-gorg'd lark so far
    Cannot be seen or heard: do but look up.
GLOUCESTER: Alack! I have no eyes.[14]

The unravelling of the story of Colley shows life to be the
sort of grotesque commingling of tragedy and comedy that
Jocelin feels is exposed by the 'gross impropriety' of the
gossip Rachel in *The Spire*: 'She stripped the business of
living down to where horror and farce took over; parti-
coloured Zany in red and yellow, striking out in the torture
chamber with his pig's bladder on a stick' (SP pp. 59–60).
Things, as Conrad's Winnie Verloc has it, do not stand
much looking into:[15] we are all in the grip of some mad
cosmic jester who tortures and kills us for sport.
    Laughter and tragedy do, however, make fairly strange
bedfellows. It is, to say the least, difficult to identify oneself
wholly with the sufferings of a person at whose misfortune
one is laughing. Laughter, as Bergson points out in his
classic essay on the subject, has the tendency to alienate its
object, to mark him out as deviant, to put a *cordon sanitaire*
round the odd-ball.[16] It confirms in those who share the
laughter the sense of their own normality. It consolidates the
sense of community by providing a common object of
derision, an enemy. Colley's class-move has made him a
natural butt or target, for no class has a particular feeling of
his belonging to it: he is, in the terms of his *sors Biblica*,
'"not of Israel"' (p. 223). In the ritual of the 'badger-bag'
Colley feels that he has become '*the foe*' (p. 237) and,
indeed, he is made to suffer as a scapegoat for the sins and
uncleanness of the whole sea-going community. This
creation of a scapegoat or enemy, as is usual in Golding,
makes the community more vulnerable to takeover by the
common Enemy of man. Colley the buffoon and butt provides everyone with a jolly good laugh and makes each feel
happy that he or she was not selected as the victim, but the
laughter is at a brutal humiliation and violation of the
dignity of a fellow human being (an aspect of Colley which
has been forgotten by the audience). Colley makes a 'beast'
of himself with Billy Rogers, but the Beast is rampant in
most of those who casually persecute or condemn him. 'The

devil is in it' (pp. 11,23) is Talbot's oath in the unpleasant early days of the voyage and his words have more truth than he knows with regard to the ancient ship with its 'damned Captain' (p. 91) and its air stinking, like Marlow's boat in *Heart of Darkness* with its rotting hippo-meat, with the odour of corruption from its ballast and the unavoidable flotsam and jetsam from the 'natural functions' (p. 5) of its crew and passengers. At the outset Talbot can complacently congratulate himself that he is 'a good enough fellow at bottom' (p. 4) while he sneers at the loathsome Colley, but the novel as a whole shows that there is at least as much of the beast in Colley's persecutors as in their victim and involves us in that guilt and darkness by the laughter which makes of us their accomplices in his persecution.

Colley dies of shame when he remembers the obscene nature of his actions while drunk. According to his own lights he has defiled himself and his cloth. After his victimisation in the 'badger-bag' he writes to re-assure himself: 'I can scarcely hold this pen. I must and will recover my composure. What a man does defiles him, not what is done by others — My shame, though it burn, has been inflicted on me' (p. 235). He falls foul of his own quite sensible rule, for he is the active partner in the 'schoolboy trick' (p. 277), as Talbot casually calls it, in the fo'c's'le. But this notion of defiling calls attention to the guilt of those (virtually everyone on board) who took part in or enjoyed or consented to Colley's humiliation. That obscenity is proleptic of the later one in one regard:

> ... as I opened my mouth to protest, it was at once filled with such nauseous stuff I gag and am like to vomit remembering it. For some time, I cannot tell how long, this operation was repeated; and when I would not open my mouth the stuff was smeared over my face. (p. 237)

He is eventually tipped into the tarpaulin in which some of the crew, Billy Rogers among them, have 'relieved nature' (p. 231). The misdemeanour with Billy Rogers may be regarded as a degradation or even a defilement, but in that case both parties were willing so to degrade themselves, for

Talbot is clear in his mind that Rogers consented, however jeeringly. In the case of the 'badger-bag' an entirely innocent man is defiled, degraded and brutalised *against his will* (is *raped*, might one say?) for the entertainment and with the consent of almost the whole community. Colley's conscience has him die of shame for what he willed upon himself, but the rest seem by and large to be untouched by remorse over their entertainment. It is hard not to feel that the wretched Colley, poor scapegoat, is more sinned against than sinning.

The one person on board who misses the spectacle of the badger-bag is Talbot, who is engaged in another obscenity, his 'passage' (p. 90) with Zenobia Brocklebank. Talbot recounts this episode very jovially to his godfather; but his 'seduction' of La Brocklebank, whose name is rather suggestive of the badger-bag, is not far short of being a rape. We are told of their brief struggle from Talbot's point-of-view, thus: 'We wrestled for a moment by the bunk, she with a nicely calculated exertion of strength that only just failed to resist me' (p. 86). Though Miss Brocklebank's virtue is not of the nicest, we have only Talbot's word for it that her resistance was *carefully calculated* to be of no avail. Talbot describes their encounter in terms of naval warfare ('My sword was in my hand and I boarded her!' (p. 86)), perhaps not in the best of taste but showing clearly enough that in this battle of the sexes Talbot is determined to emerge as victor and put Zenobia in the position of the subjugated. He seems to imagine that he shows a good deal of commendable care for her well-being, but this is perhaps mere selfishness in that he too would wish to avoid the embarrassment of a pregnancy. His attitude, however, shows the most extraordinary insensitivity and carelessness with regard to the woman's feelings: 'This with a great deal of heaving and — glowing, as it is called. Really, she was in a quite distasteful condition' (p. 88). The woman is to be merely a convenience, a source of welcome relief in that prickly equatorial heat, but the sight of her manifesting any human passion herself — showing that she too is a breathing and sweating self — is a source of distaste. Talbot shoos her off back to her own cabin, but records that he knew how a gentleman should show his gratitude to a woman in her position: 'I favoured her with a light salute' (p. 89). Talbot, that decent but limited soul, does not feel he has behaved at all badly in this matter, but he too has carelessly forced himself upon a person in a vulnerable position and used her, whether she will or no, as a mere convenience, to relieve the tension, *'pour passer le temps'* (p. 61), for a bit of a lark. The badger-bag and the victory over Miss Brocklebank are 'normal' and socially acceptable however, whereas Colley's actions are considered outrageous, but this is a commentary on the perverse nature of our notions of normality and outrage. 'We are a sporting nation.'

The public cause of Colley's disgrace is his drunkenness and urination in front of everyone aboard. It would seem, however, that the open performance of this eminently natural act is allowed to the common sailors. The line of decorum which Colley has crossed is a line of class. '"Class is the British language"' (p. 125), Summers ruefully remarks and that British obsession with class is obvious in the world of the ship. Talbot's language and attitude to the world are largely coloured by an awareness of position or rank and his rather sunny view of things may well be attributable to his sense of being at the top of the pile. He wastes no time in establishing his place on the ship by outfacing the captain on his own quarterdeck. He produces his godfather's name as a weapon and the captain realises he is outgunned: as Talbot writes with evident relish: 'what a silver-mounted and murdering piece of ordinance a noble name was proving to be among persons of a middle station!' (p. 31). Talbot is a defender of the *status quo*, makes reference in this very paragraph to the horrors of the Revolution in France, but his metaphors indicate that that state of affairs is a permanent civil war in which one side always has very much the upper hand.

This 'murdering' weapon is accidentally discharged by Talbot at Colley, for the irate Captain Anderson takes out his frustration on the feckless parson who is thus set upon the road to eventual oblivion, for the enmity of the captain, who cannot vent his ire upon Talbot, is a major factor in his destruction. Colley is not assured in his social position and it is his *parvenu* character which makes him loathsome to

Talbot. He certainly does show some nauseating traits of this nature, boasting to his sister that he is treated as one of the 'gentry' (p. 188), quoting Sophocles at her then explaining that he is a Greek tragedian, using Latin phrases then translating them for her benefit, fawning at Talbot's feet. He does, indeed, call to mind Jane Austen's despicable Mr Collins, that 'mixture of servility and self-importance' as Mr Bennet calls him.[17] Collins brags of his having been *twice* to dine with his adored patronness, Lady Catherine de Bourgh, just as Colley boasts of his having been '*twice* at my Lord Bishop's table' (p. 199). Collins makes a great issue of the dignity of his office, which, he wrongly imagines, entitles him to introduce himself to Mr Darcy: Elizabeth Bennet tries to stop him but he pooh-poohs her: 'for give me leave to observe that I consider the clerical office as equal in point of dignity with the highest rank in the kingdom — provided that a proper humility of behaviour is at the same time maintained.'[18] This model of self-vaunting humility is not to be gainsaid and Elizabeth is embarrassed 'to see him expose himself to' Mr Darcy.[19] Austen is, of course, blind to the *double entendre* here (and there are quite a number of similar cases in her novels) and this blindness is suggestive of the fact that vast areas of human experience are dark to her, those lavatorial areas which interest Golding. Colley exposes himself in a rather more serious sense, but in general the comparison with Austen's Collins tends to show Colley in a good light. Colley has a genuine spiritual life and is committed to his ministry: Collins' letter explaining that Lady Catherine has given him a 'valuable rectory', 'where it shall be my earnest endeavour to demean myself with grateful respect towards her Ladyship, and be ever ready to perform those rites and ceremonies which are instituted by the Church of England' makes his order of priorities very clear.[20] The perfunctory nature of his interest in religion is common among Austen's clergymen: perhaps such serious devotion as Colley displays was somewhat rare. Colley, though much put upon, is ever ready to forgive his persecutors, to love his enemies. This is in marked contrast to the attitude of Collins in his letter to the Bennett family regarding their reception of Lydia and Wickham, who have lived in sin: 'You ought certainly to forgive them as Christians, but never to admit them in your sight, or allow their names to be mentioned in your hearing.'[21] To Collins Christian forgiveness is a meaningless tag. What is important is that the decencies, the rites and ceremonies, of society be preserved: beside this wretch Colley appears almost saintly.

Talbot's own behaviour with regard to rank is in some ways as objectionable as Colley's. If Colley shows off his learning to his ignorant sister, Talbot parades his Greek and Italian before an uncomprehending midshipman and is just as keen as Colley to gild his letter home with classical allusions. His demeanour instantly upsets Captain Anderson, who feels cheated of place and preferment in society because of his background as the illegitimate son of a lord with a parson as stand-in father. This is Deverel's explanation of his hatred of parsons. 'It would surely be more reasonable in him to detest a lord!' (p. 268) writes Talbot, but he fails to see that Anderson *does* detest a lord and that his own lordly behaviour has been a dreadful provocation to the man. Because of his lack of deference Talbot makes Anderson out to be a tyrant, but both Colley and he record the fact that in the course of the voyage the captain does not order a single flogging. Like Captain Bligh he keeps plants aboard ship, but unlike Bligh he is prepared to accept the loss of every plant rather than deprive his crew of water. Captain Anderson in the 'private paradise' (p. 160) of his plant collection is an agreeable fellow who laughs happily and has a bluff forthrightness of which Austen's Mr Knightley would have approved. It is only when this Adam is unparadised and must rejoin society that his class bitterness overcomes his good nature and 'the expelled Adam' (p. 162) becomes sullen and stormy. Class is the serpent in his Eden.

The chief agent in the persecution of Colley is Lieutenant Deverel, whose haughty mien initially persuades Talbot that he is 'an ornament to the service' (p. 53). Deverel's name, however, suggests that he is something of a devil, and so he and Cumbershum appear to Colley as they come 'with heads of nightmare, great eyes and mouths, black mouths full of a mass of fangs' (p. 236) to drag him off to his ordeal. Deverel is known among the crew as 'Gentleman Jack', recalling perhaps the devilish Jack Merridew and the haunting line in *King Lear*: 'The Prince of Darkness is a gentleman.'[22]

The business of class certainly seems to further the ends of that potentate in *Rites of Passage*. At bottom of the class-system are property and money, which create privilege and confer power over others. Thus in *Pride and Prejudice* we are told how Mr Darcy drew everyone's attention at a ball by his height, good looks and 'noble mien', and 'the report which was in general circulation within five minutes after his entrance, of his having ten thousand a year'.[23] The values are those of *Dallas* or *Dynasty*: only the manners are slightly less vulgar. Thus Talbot recounts Captain Anderson's reaction to his production of the weapon of his godfather's name: 'Our captain squinted first ... down your lordship's muzzle, decided you were loaded ... and reined back with his yellow teeth showing!' (p. 31). Talbot's god-father is, indeed, 'loaded', is possessed of a great deal of money, and that gives him the power to cow the formidable Anderson. Talbot has great difficulty in locating the ship's Purser and eventually discovers that the rest of the crew are in fear of him because they owe him money. The Purser lives down in the rather foul-smelling underworld below decks, amidst all the ship's wealth of cargo, goods and tools, like Mammon in his cave, that particular manifestation of the Devil whom Spenser calls 'God of the world and world-lings'.[24]

Colley's sousing in the tarpaulin is reminiscent of one of the humiliations visited upon a novelistic clergyman very different to Mr Collins, the ducking by a debauched squire and his cohorts of Parson Adams in *Joseph Andrews*, the creation of 'lively old Fielding' (p. 3) as Talbot calls him.[25] Adams' protests at his mistreatment have at one point a very marked similarity to Colley's self-defence: 'He hath pleased to treat me with disrespect as a parson; I apprehend my order is not the object of scorn, nor that I can become so, unless by being a disgrace to it'.[26] Colley does go on to disgrace his order in ways probably unimaginable to Adams,

but he resembles Adams in being an innocent abroad, a man
of genuine Christian feeling in a world given over to worldliness and inclined to scorn the Christian as a holy fool.

With the exception of Summers, that 'GOOD MAN' (p.
136), Colley seems to be alone in the ship in having a
spiritual life or any real regard for religion. Talbot wishes to
support the Established Church but his view of religion is
that it should be used as a buttress to the *status quo*:
'"... in a state the supreme argument for the continuance of
a national church is the whip it holds in one hand and the
— dare I say — illusory prize in the other ..."' (p. 22), he
explains to Cumbershum. For the lower orders the prize is
illusory but the whip is real enough: Christianity is cynically
employed to preserve the illusion, is put to disgracefully un-
Christian ends. Colley at one point recalls the advice given
him at his ordination: '— words I must ever hold sacred
because of the occasion and the saintly divine who spake
them — "Avoid scrupulosity, Colley, and always present a
decent appearance"' (p. 226). It is a touching testimony
to Colley's naive trust in his church that he regards this
rather worldly exhortation, with its emphasis on keeping up
appearances and not thinking too hard about religion, as
sacred and its speaker, a cleric no doubt pickled in port and
prejudice, as saintly. Colley, the natural butt, in his persecution by a sinful world, in his role as holy fool, as scapegoat
and ritual victim in the guilt for whose death all have a
share, is another of Golding's strange Christ-like figures.
Our attention is drawn to this improbable likeness by a little
joke of Talbot's as Summers tells him of Colley's condition
after his disgrace: '"Phillips swears he has not moved for
three days." I made a perhaps unnecessarily blasphemous
rejoinder' (p. 148).

Colley draws a comparison between himself and Christ
which reminds us of Christ's role as holy fool:

> It is true I had been foolish and was perhaps an object of scorn
> and amusement to the officers and the other gentlemen with the
> exception of Mr Talbot. But then — and I said this in all
> humility — so would my Master have been! (p. 208)

So indeed, he would. The world of the ship despises, rejects and victimises Colley and in so doing re-crucifies Christ: 'Verily I say unto you, Inasmuch as ye have done it unto one of the least of these my brethren, ye have done it unto me.'[27] Colley might well be regarded as one of the least among Christ's brethren, but like Christ he has the spiritual strength to forgive and pray for those who persecute him.

Though Colley is thus very forgiving of others, he is, like Matty, extremely hard on himself. He cannot forgive himself for his Dionysiac excesses. E.R. Dodds remarks of participants in Dionysiac rites of tearing and eating the raw flesh of an animal:

> ... those who practise such a rite in our time seem to experience in it a mixture of supreme exultation and supreme repulsion: it is at once holy and horrible, fulfilment and uncleanness, a sacrament and a pollution — the same violent conflict of emotional attitudes that runs all through the *Bacchae* and lies at the root of all religion of the Dionysian type.[28]

Colley experiences this violent conflict of emotions, but discretely, one after the other. He is driven to despair — his real betrayal of Christianity, as Summers suggests — by supreme repulsion at the horror and uncleanness of his self-pollution, but his initial reaction is one of supreme exultation and fulfilment. Kinkead-Weekes and Gregor detect a likeness in general among Coleridge, his Ancient Mariner, and Colley:

> ... when Colley exclaims 'Joy!', or gazes into the water and blesses 'the blue, the green, the purple, the snowy, sliding foam' we feel the presence of 'The Dejection Ode' and 'The Ancient Mariner', not as discrete poems, but as extensions to Colley's sensibility, giving it precision and utterance.[29]

Again and again, we feel Coleridge's presence in Colley's voyage. Like the Mariner, able to bless the water snakes, Colley looks over the side of the ship and, no longer terrified by the unplumbed depths, sees the foam and the green weed, and is consumed 'by a great love of all things, the sea, the ship, the sky, the gentlemen and the people and of course *Our Redeemer* above all!'[30]

These are among Colley's last words before his disastrous visit to the fo'c's'le. When he emerges again he is shouting '"Joy! Joy! Joy!"', an important word to Coleridge (and, indeed, to Wordsworth), as Kinkead-Weekes and Gregor point out: 'For Colley, as for Coleridge in "The Dejection Ode", "Joy" was the power to make the universe anew, and when that was desecrated, then the universe turned into something monstrous.'[31]

There can be no doubt that we are asked to think of Coleridge and his poems as providing part of the Romantic background of Colley's sensibility, but it is not clear in what sense they may be said to give it 'precision'. Kinkead-Weekes and Gregor would map 'Dejection: An Ode' precisely onto Colley's experience: Coleridge therein speaks of joy as the emotion attendant upon an intense sense of union with the living and ever-changing world of Nature:

> Joy, virtuous Lady! Joy that ne'er was given,
> Save to the pure, and in their purest hour,
> Life, and Life's effluence, cloud at once and shower,
> Joy, Lady! is the spirit and the power,
> Which, wedding Nature to us, gives in dower
>   A new Earth and new Heaven ...[32]

Colley has felt a certain love for nature all around him, but in a moment of spectacular impurity, in his impurest hour, has desecrated that holy love and turned the world into a monstrous nightmare. This interpretation of Colley's fate *via* Coleridge *may* be valid, but it is certainly not the only possible interpretation, based as it is on a certain reading, a certain interpretation, of Coleridge. Such interpretation or judgement, we have learnt, is not an easy thing.

This particular judgement would also seem to offer no hope to the despairing Colley, to agree with Coleridge that joy is only for the pure and with Colley that his act was simply a desecration. Coleridge, however, does not always seem to be so piously on the side of the angels and the pure. In 'Kubla Khan' he seems to celebrate, albeit rather fearfully, a self-projection as a Dionysiac breaker of taboo:

Weave a circle round him thrice,
And close your eyes with holy dread,
For he on honey-dew hath fed,
And drunk the milk of Paradise.[33]

For Nietzsche, joy is certainly not the preserve of the pure, but is the Dionysiac emotion *par excellence*:

... the *Dionysian*, which is brought within closest ken perhaps by the analogy of *drunkenness*. It is either under the influence of the narcotic draught, of which the hymns of all primitive men and peoples tell us, or by the powerful approach of spring penetrating all nature with joy, that those Dionysian emotions awake, in the augmentation of which the subjective vanishes to complete self-forgetfulness.[34]

The drunken Colley forgot himself, but by so doing found himself, found the way of expressing his love and joy that was natural to him. It is a harsh judgement on his life to consider that Dionysiac gift a desecration. The reaction of most people may well be distaste but one of the gifts of Lusios, the Liberator, is to make holy and acceptable those facets of life which our everyday selves find repugnant or distasteful. Leopold Bloom in *Ulysses* remembers with relish a passionate kiss of years gone by:

Ravished over her I lay, full lips full open, kissed her mouth. Yum. Softly she gave me in my mouth the seedcake warm and chewed. Mawkish pulp her mouth had mumbled sweetsour of her spittle. Joy: I ate it: joy.[35]

One would not normally or naturally say 'Yum' to the offer of some cake which someone else had been chewing, but the power of ecstatic love is to turn everything which belongs to the other to a source of appetency and joy. It is this Dionysiac joy which Colley celebrates on his re-emergence from the fo'c's'le.

That Colley's foible was not a desecration but an expression and celebration of himself is another interpretation and one not wholly out of keeping with the self-exploratory spirit of Romanticism. Colley dies of shame, however, because he feels he has disgraced the spirit and example of his Master, Jesus Christ. Colley would no doubt see the Gospels as embodying a pretty plain set of moral guidelines for life, guidelines over which he has clearly strayed. He lives, however, in the early years of a century which was to demonstrate that the Gospels themselves are *interpretations* of the life of Jesus, which was 'a real life and a real death and no more to be fitted into a given book than a misshapen foot into a given boot', as Talbot writes of Colley. The Gospels and that life and death are susceptible of an infinite number of interpretations. To Hazlitt and Shelley, for example, Jesus is a radical and subversive moralist, an example to moral and political revolutionaries. In *The Marriage of Heaven and Hell* Blake, through the voice of his friendly Devil, asserts that Jesus, far from being an example of the importance of obeying rules and keeping within bounds, was a champion of rule-breaking in the cause of self-expression and self-discovery, the freeing of the self from moral and psychological repression:

> ... if Jesus Christ is the greatest man, you ought to love him in the greatest degree; now hear how he has given his sanction to the law of ten commandments: did he not mock at the sabbath, and so mock the sabbath's God? ... I tell you, no virtue can exist without breaking these ten commandments. Jesus was all virtue, and acted from impulse, not from rules.[36]

The Jesus who is the product of Blake's creative interpretation would not merely forgive Colley's folly, but would positively approve of his action as a triumph of self-expression in love and a bold attempt to break through society's selfish, repressive and absurd rules and guidelines concerning what is natural and decent. For Blake the Commandments, the rules themselves, are the true evil and not the breaking of them. They have stifled Colley's true nature and, when it suddenly and shockingly manifests itself, they kill him outright. Colley's voyage to a new world turns out to be a journey away from an orthodoxy which seems quite to have lost its command upon people's credence into the deep and dangerous seas of existential morality.

Oscar Wilde, victimised for crimes not dissimilar to those of Colley, speaks in 'The Soul of Man under Socialism' of a 'new world' of self-expression and self-realisation and, like Blake, produces a radical re-interpretation of the example of Christ to support his case for new and revolutionary morality:

> To live is the rarest thing in the world. Most people exist, that is all ...
> ... 'Know thyself!' was written over the portal of the antique world. Over the portal of the new world 'Be thyself' shall be written. And the message of Christ to man was simply 'Be thyself.' That is the secret of Christ.
> ... he who would lead a Christlike life is he who is perfectly and absolutely himself.[37]

Though he is but a little man, Colley *is* the book's tragic hero and his tragedy lies in his failure to reach the new world: having succeeded for a few minutes in *living*, in being himself, in expressing his nature and his love, he cannot live with the shame he feels at his joy.

· 9 ·
SALTWATER SOAP
·CLOSE QUARTERS (1987) and FIRE DOWN BELOW (1989)·

No man is a hero to his valet.
> Madame Anne Bigot de Cornuel (*et al.*)

I had in fact wondered whether or no I should entitle my three volumes nothing less than *Saltwater Soap* . . .
> *Fire Down Below*

Fire Down Below opens with a hint that the reader might regard the work as in some way operatic: Captain Anderson ' "sang out" ' and Lieutenant Benét replies in 'a tenor to his bass' (p. 3). Although the two novels which bring to a conclusion the trilogy of Edmund Talbot's sea-voyage may be said to be operatic in that they are, at least in some aspects, examples of extravagant and absurd entertainment, *Close Quarters* and *Fire Down Below* might rather more appropriately be characterised, to take the hint which Golding so disarmingly allows Talbot to drop towards the end of the final novel, as soap-operatic. They are soap-operatic in that they seem to go on forever, piling episode relentlessly upon episode. Lieutenant Summers remarks that the voyage ' "bids fair to be the longest in history" ' (FDB p. 119) and the trilogy which records that passage is, indeed, of challenging proportions (about half as long again as *Nostromo*, for example), yet is somewhat lacking thematic freight and intellectual ballast to sustain it through such vast verbal distances. The allegorical or symbolic density of *Rites of Passage* is much diluted in the later volumes of the trilogy. Mrs Prettiman (née Granham) warns Talbot against interpretation, against reading too much into his own story:

Do not refine upon its nature . . . it was not an Odyssey. It is no
type, emblem, metaphor of the human condition. It is, or rather
it *was*, what it was. A series of events.

(FDB p. 275)

This warning, indeed, echoes that given to significance-
spotting critics by Wilf Barclay in another late Golding novel
(see PM p. 121). The problem, in the case of the trilogy at
least, is that the reader is left with precious little but the
interest of finding out what is going to happen next to characters with whom he has become familiar — the essential pleasure of soap-opera — and the fascination of the minutiae of
how to take a sailing-ship to the other side of the world, the
Hornblowerism of the trilogy which provoked one critic to
describe it as a product of 'the Captain Birds Eye school' of
fiction.[1]

Another unflattering but, alas, irresistible comparison is
called to mind by the trilogy's pervasive interest in and notice
of *dress*. 'Some little flavours, but much spoils' was the sage
advice of G.M. Hopkins with regard to the use of archaisms,[2]
and it is in the latter two-thirds of the voyage that the sheer
weight of costume-dialogue begins to grate and to suggest
that Talbot's script might have come from the pen of Talbot
Rothwell:

"Wheeler! Curse it, you was drowned!" (CQ p. 52)

"Be easy again! You cannot go at this as if you was boarding an
enemy. Haste will ruin all." (CQ p. 80)

Indeed, the very humour of the novels descends at times to
the level of a 'Carry On' film, as in the riddle of Talbot's
barrel which Tommy Taylor finds so funny: the answer to the
question of why the ship rolls so much is ' "Lord Talbot's
firkin!" ' (CQ p. 278). The voyage turns away from the heart
of darkness in *Rites of Passage* towards romance and
comedy, and in this it may be said to resemble the course of
Golding's fiction. However, though the ending may be happy
for Talbot, the change of direction for Golding is a great deal
less happy. The whole episode of the firkin, for example, is so

dismally unfunny that its hilarious reception by the passengers and crew can only sensibly be regarded as an illustration of the commonplace that people in mortal danger find hysterical humour in almost anything.

The name of Byron is one that occurs several times in the latter stages of Talbot's voyage: Lady Somerset, wife of the captain of the frigate *Alcyone* which our voyagers bump into in mid-Atlantic, is a devotee of the poet and has been conducting some sort of *amour* with Lieutenant Bénét, the versifying Adonis who, apart from nimbleness of foot and a plentiful lack of talent as a poet, might almost be a type of Byron himself. It is almost as if the second-generation Romantic, Byron, has pushed gloomy old Coleridge into the background. There are, as we shall see, hints that we should compare the adventures of Talbot with the world of Byron's *Don Juan*. *Close Quarters* and *Fire Down Below* are abject failures if compared to *Don Juan* in terms of the quality of their comedy. (Most books are.) But the story of the fag-end of Talbot's voyage does resemble Byron's masterpiece in being something of a baggy monster, a story that is as copious and shapeless as life itself. Golding once again anticipates criticism by having Talbot himself complain of this aspect of his second journal: 'But this one lacked the accidental shape of narration which Colley and fate had forced on the other volume' (CQ p. 235). This baggy monsterism might equally well, of course, bear comparison, once again, with soap-opera.

These qualities make critical navigation through the waters of the two novels a tricky matter, but it is to be feared that a remark of Lieutenant Summers's may well serve as an epitaph on *Close Quarters* and *Fire Down Below* ' ". . . We were rather too long for comfort in the doldrums" ' (CQ p. 13).

The science of navigation is heard of a good deal in the course of the trilogy. It is much concerned with establishing the position or point of view of the person who is taking or making the observations, but it is a difficult and inexact science, as the story of Summers's first lesson in it makes clear (FDB pp. 86–7). As the navigator takes observations of the sun and stars, so Edmund Talbot observes the bodies around him and his observations tell us as much of his own position or point of view as they do of the people — and indeed the world — he is observing. As Talbot voyages on, his angle on things constantly changes and so too, apparently, does everyone around him.

The final words of *Rites of Passage* look foward to the novel's sequel:

> With lack of sleep and too much understanding I grow a little crazy, I think, like all men at sea who live too close to each other and too close thereby to all that is monstrous under the sun and moon.

In *Close Quarters* Talbot is further pained by the proximity of his fellow human beings. Seen 'too close', humanity can appear a pretty lousy lot, as Lemuel Gulliver finds in the second book of his travels, where he is forced to examine the physical nature of humans as if through a powerful magnifying glass and is thoroughly revolted. The fetor of *Rites of Passage* pervades the little ship throughout the voyage, but closer inspection of his fellows does not in the end drive Talbot crazy. The insights gained from close quarters are not all horrifying or nauseating. It is not the case that further acquaintance reveals everyone aboard to be mad or bad or both. Rather, the characters are shown to be *different* in nature from what Talbot had led us to believe of them in the first novel of the trilogy. Or, at least, they *appear* different to the developing Talbot. It is difficult to be entirely sure of one's ground, for the interpretation of narrative is, like navigation, a difficult and inexact science. Once the equator is passed the world of the ship is turned gradually upside down, as is Talbot's view of certain of his fellow passengers.

Thus the stiff and severe governess Miss Granham unbends a good deal and comes to have considerable attraction as a woman in Talbot's eyes, a development that would scarcely have been foreseen in the early part of the voyage. At one point the wildly rolling ship forces intimacy of a kind upon Talbot and Miss Granham. They wrestle for balance in the lobby and are thrown together through the door of someone's cabin: 'We were in it just long enough to see that an old lady lay there, her grey hair matted with sweat, her mouth open, her eyes in their sunken and discoloured sockets staring at us with terror'. It is as great a surprise to us as to Talbot to realise that this ghastly figure is 'none other than my onetime inamorata Zenobia Brocklebank' (CQ pp. 202–3). To this favour is come the beautiful Zenobia, the darling of our crew. Talbot is consistent with regard to Zenobia in that he sees no more in her than a sudoriferous body, though perhaps we can glimpse a little more in her than that. *Fire Down Below* records how the dying Zenobia sent a message to Talbot, suggesting that she had felt deeply for him. The message itself hints at a spiritual life in her of which Talbot was wholly oblivious: his interpretation of the message is a notable piece of literal-minded obtuseness (see FDB p. 295). Talbot also finds that one of Zenobia's admirers, Jack Deverel, is by no means so fine or handsome a fellow as he had thought. 'Gentleman Jack, the honourable Dashing Jack' is found to have 'a weak and slightly receding chin': Talbot concludes that he might have been 'an ostler, a footman, a gentleman's gentleman' (CQ p. 78). He is neither gentlemanly nor honourable (in any worthwhile sense of the terms) however, since he is a drunkard and a degenerate. If we are to take Mr Askew at his word (' ". . . it's any port in a storm with him from a lord's lady to a little girl what still bowls her hoop" ' (CQ p. 163)), Dashing Jack Deverel, the persecutor of the aberrant Colley, is himself a child-molester. Mr Brocklebank, who appeared wholly given over to drunken debauchery, searches for dignity (and by seeking finds it) in the face of death: ' "How does a man drown when he sees it coming? It is a question of dignity, Mr Talbot. I must have my dignity" ' (CQ p. 241). This nascency of stoicism in Mr Brocklebank is stifled, however, by resurgent epicureanism in *Fire Down Below* where, faced with a still more immediate prospect of extinction, Mr Brocklebank answers his own question by demanding some last-minute coupling from his poor wife.

In *Rites of Passage* Talbot portrays Captain Anderson as an ill-bred tyrant, but as the voyage progresses Anderson comes to seem less tyrannical and more admirable. Far from being a tyrant, he is willing to risk compromising his own dignity in order to save the unworthy Deverel. He puts his crew and passengers before himself, ordering that his own fire be put out to save fuel for the ship's galley. Wheeler bluntly tells Talbot: ' "Captain Anderson is a good captain, sir, nobody denies it." ' (CQ p. 187). Anderson is a fearsome figure and an uncommunicative one, but at one point in the narrative we catch perhaps a glimpse of an inner man who is a great deal softer and more appealing. At the lunch party aboard *Alcyone* Sir Henry Somerset casually delivers a shockingly unkind remark to his wife's dependant, Janet, telling her that she ' "was only brought in to make up the numbers" '. A little after this, Talbot observes Anderson 'staring glumly and silently at Janet whose eyes were deep in her plate' (CQ pp. 92–3). A glum silence is difficult to interpret, but we may perhaps guess that Anderson's glumness arises from sympathy for this poor belittled creature.

Perhaps the most spectacular changes, however, are to be seen in Talbot himself. The calculating careerist, the 'scurvy politician' (CQ p. 91), is transformed, by concussion and the appearance (aboard the chance-encountered *Alcyone*) of one Miss Chumley, into a lovesick fool, into a figure who recalls the unfortunate Colley. As Colley had made a demi-god of the rough-and-ready Billy Rogers, so Talbot imagines divinity into the bland Miss Chumley. Become ' "an advocate of impropriety" ' (CQ p. 103), Talbot behaves in an 'impossibly familiar' (CQ p. 92) fashion towards Miss Chumley in public, though in contrast to Colley his familiarity does not go much beyond holding hands. He does, however, attempt to organise the transfer of Miss Chumley from *Alcyone* to Captain Anderson's ship, giving up his own cabin in the mad hope of facilitating this ludicrous scheme and moving himself into the hutch where the wretched Colley breathed his last. He tries to take passage to India aboard *Alcyone*, thus bidding fair to ruin his career and disgrace his precious family. It seems Talbot too has come to a dangerous shadow line between youth and maturity. He is saved from himself by the care of Summers, who has him conveyed to his new cabin where 'in Colley's bunk' he is forced to endure 'the humiliations of delirium' (CQ pp. 133–4). Realising that *Alcyone* is gone, he sets 'a positive fool's cap' on his behaviour by emerging on deck, 'his thin body plainly to be discerned beneath the night-shirt', and climbing the rigging to implore his beloved to return (CQ pp. 134–5). Love exposes the fool in Talbot as it had done in Colley. As he begins to recover, Talbot examines himself in the mirror:

> . . . my face was so thin as to be positively bony. I passed a finger over the prominent ridges of my cheeks, touched my high, but now thin nose, pushed the hair off my forehead. It is surely impossible that a skull should shrink! (CQ p. 138)

He sees someone who looks like Colley.

Excuses are made, naturally enough, for Talbot, however, and his folly in love leads to a happy ending of marriage to Miss Chumley. More generally, Talbot learns not merely folly but a little wisdom too. At the outset of *Close Quarters* Talbot is still as 'Gothic' (RP p. 276) as ever in his political views. He makes an impassioned defence of privilege to Charles Summers, insisting that a 'civilised community' will always 'healthfully' limit the electorate to 'highly born, highly educated, sophisticated professional' people (CQ p. 11). It is difficult to say whether he cynically ignores or is simply blind to the problems with this argument in its practical application suggested by the fact, which Talbot has already revealed, that in the 'rotten borough' controlled by his godfather the entire electorate consists of 'a drunken shepherd and a cottager who spends the weeks after an election in a state of indescribable debauchery' (CQ p. 9). That is scarcely a 'healthful' state of affairs. Talbot, however, at this stage can scarcely see beyond self-interest: ' "Rotten boroughs for ever! But in the right hands, of course" ' (CQ p. 11). The right hands, *of course*, are those of Talbot and his class. It is all very convenient. Not long after this speech of Talbot's however, an event occurs aboard ship which it is tempting, *pace* Mrs Prettiman (née Granham), to interpret allegorically. Lieutenant Jack Deverel, the less than gentlemanly gentleman, proves to be a less than worthy officer of the watch. Deverel leaves the quarterdeck for a drink just when the wind veers freakishly so that the ship is 'taken aback' (CQ p. 25) and all but crippled. Deverel owes his position as one of the officers of the ship simply to birth: he was, to borrow Talbot's own terms, 'born to govern' (CQ p. 11). But, like the electors in the rotten borough, he is anything but deserving of the privilege by reason of character or habit. The common sailors at the wheel 'look for authority and find none' (CQ p. 26), their hereditary ruler having abandoned his responsibilities to pursue his own vicious pleasures. It is not difficult to see the relevance of this incident to Talbot's specious theorising.

Talbot himself does not seem to make any connection of this kind, however. It is only much later that he is himself taken aback by his close encounters with the egalitarian philosopher Aloysius Prettiman. In *Fire Down Below* Prettiman himself is transformed in our eyes (through being transformed in Talbot's) from a figure of fun to an impressive figure, an irascible and impatient old man but also a figure of moral grandeur. Talbot's personal voyage culminates in his encounters with this remarkable and charismatic man. Talbot comes to recognise even as early as the opening page of *Close Quarters* that his behaviour has been haughty and snobbish and, even if he is unable or unwilling wholly to correct this, he at least questions his own attitudes and habits. He literally changes his habit, his dress, to that of a common sailor in *Fire Down Below* and indeed, accepts Summers's gifts of clean sailors' 'slops' as 'gold armour' (FDB p. 29), an attitude it would have been difficult to foresee in the arrogant young man of *Rites of Passage*, who would not willingly have appeared arm-in-arm with a common sailor. Now he dons the garb of one, a change of apparel made also by the progressive-minded Mrs Prettiman. This change is brought about largely through necessity's sharp pinch: while Talbot remained in his class-uniform on shipboard he came gradually to 'stink' (FDB p. 42), though he could not detect the stench in his own nostrils. But the sea that makes dirty is also a cleaner. Towards the end of *Close Quarters* Talbot finds that the line on deck at the mainmast has been 'washed clean away' and on this occasion Talbot himself insists that this should be seen as 'more than a simple fact'. It is 'a metaphor of our condition' (CQ p. 277). Stephen Medcalf in a review of *Fire Down Below* suggests that there is a certain resemblance between Golding's trilogy and the three parts of the *Divina Commedia*, 'Inferno', 'Purgatorio' and 'Paradiso'.[3] While it would be equally true to say that there is a certain resemblance between Arthur's Seat and Mt Everest, it is the case that the effect of the sea-voyage on Talbot is *purgative*, albeit initially in a rather low comic sense. '*Saltwater Soap*' does its work on the stinking Talbot. Barriers of class give way, to some extent, in the emergency. Talbot, with great reluctance, allows Mr Pike to address him on first-name terms, though it is perhaps a comment on the extraordinary power of class in this society that it should require conditions of the most extreme emotional stress, the constant threat of drowning, to bring two men trapped together for months on an incommodious ship to first-name terms. Talbot is slowly and partially cleansed by the voyage and his encounters with Mr Prettiman, is stripped (to switch metaphors) of some of his gothic armour of prejudice: '— indeed there were times when it seemed to me that I threw off my upbringing as a man might let armour drop around him and stand naked, defenceless, but free!' (FDB p. 209). Talbot and Summers swap armour, in Talbot's own metaphor and simile, like Glaucus and Diomede (FDB p. 29), but the context of that story, though it is an emblem of friendship, is still war and both Talbot and Summers, in his less grasping way, are keen to win further promotion and favour in society, in which struggle some armour is necessary. Prettiman's idealistic rejection of conventional society, his attempt to found a new kind of community in the wilderness, offers the possibility to throw off the armour of class, prejudice, selfish ambition, once and for all. Talbot is, in the end, too much a product of his upbringing to follow Prettiman on such a risky pilgrimage, but he is a decent enough soul to find the prospect thrilling.

Although he comes to see that rotten boroughs and the like are indefensible, Talbot is still prepared to accept one as his means of entry into Parliament, a meal-ticket which enables him to win the golden fleece of domestic bliss with his adored Miss Chumley. It is all very convenient, once again. This is the happy or fairy-tale ending which Golding allows (for once) his hero and it is evident, since the final pages of the trilogy are written from a distance of many years, that the marriage has been happy and fruitful. Medcalf suggests that, in his Dantean scheme of things, Miss Chumley plays the role of Beatrice,[4] but it needs to be said that, although we see her chiefly through the eyes of the besotted Talbot, she is a somewhat sub-standard Beatrice. Talbot certainly places her on a pedestal, as does Dante his beloved, and his gallant courting of her is undoubtedly in marked contrast to his double-quick 'seduction' and dismissal of Zenobia (a contrast which echoes Oliver's attitude to Imogen and Evie in *The Pyramid*), but the reader who is not in love with her must be aware that Talbot's idol has feet of clay. The ultimate reality of Miss Chumley (*even* of a Miss Chumley) is unknowable: there are just different points of view on her. Talbot's lovesick, impassioned, 'poetic' view is one, but Lieutenant Benét's view that she is a mere schoolgirl with no character at all (CQ pp. 207–8) is a 'prosaic' (for once from him) view which ought to be taken into account. The misbehaviour of Benét and Lady Somerset seems, from the testimony of Benét in *Fire Down Below* (p. 170), to have gone a great deal less far than had appeared from *Close Quarters*, but Miss Chumley's role in it is still less than entirely honourable and undoubtedly out of keeping with the Dantean Beatrice. Indeed, the mystery of the scraps of verse and prose Talbot finds on her missive to him (CQ pp. 212–18) is never quite solved, so that a question-mark remains over Miss Chumley's feelings toward and relationship with both her guardian, Lady Somerset, and the handsome Benét.

Talbot speaks of the *coup de foudre*, of his desperate and undying love for the thoroughly perfect Miss Chumley. Perhaps we may entertain some doubts as to that perfection and, indeed, perhaps we may see that Talbot's love is a little less exclusive than he seems to think. There is the matter, for example, of his dream of reunion with his distant beloved:

She came towards me! We merged —
It was Miss Granham. She had no stays — I wrestled with her but could not get away. No wonder the two ships were laughing and I was unclothed — (CQ p. 222)

Once again the metaphor is one of *stripping*. Beneath the

civilised vesture of Talbot's belief in romantic love, exclusive and undying, there is the naked truth of desire, which is capricious and lawless, a Dionysian energy. (That it is proper to think of Dionysus in the context of this voyage is proved by Talbot's mention of the sprouting ship (CQ p. 152), a myth of Dionysus.)[5] The ideology of romantic love, however ill it may accord with the raw material of human nature, is perhaps a necessary (or at least emollient) delusion, one of those many lies we tell ourselves to make life bearable, because the truth is 'too dark altogether'.[6] The trilogy as a whole forces upon us truths straight from the very heart of darkness and yet acknowledges our need to delude ourselves, to run away from the truth, to make the best of a bad job and get on with life, and as the trilogy progresses it is the latter tendency that is in the ascendant. In *Rites of Passage* Talbot refuses, like Marlow in *Heart of Darkness*, to communicate home the details of the dishonour and death of an unfortunate and remarkable man. However, in the case of the Golding novel *we* are told, or think we are told, the full story. It seems that we are mistaken, since in *Close Quarters* Talbot manages to extract 'the true story of what had happened to Colley' from the servant Wheeler, who (in one of a number of 'Tell that to the Marines!' incidents in the trilogy) has been rescued from the sea. Talbot closes the book on the Colley affair with these words: 'The information was of such a nature that I do not propose to commit it to this journal' (CQ p. 211). So we are to be protected from the full horror, but this is a very dubious re-darkening of the story's heart since it is really rather difficult to conceive how Wheeler's information could be any more outrageous than what has been revealed to us already.

Colley and his tragedy gradually fade out of the story, out of Talbot's concerns, out of his consciousness. In *Fire Down Below* another eccentric figure whom Talbot had at first despised suddenly looms large and impressive. Mr Prettiman reveals in a more conscious and explicitly political fashion what the story of Colley had implied, that our civilisation (to put it crudely) *stinks*. Prettiman also offers, as Colley momentarily had done, the possibility of a joyous new start, the founding of a just society in the *tabula rasa* of the Australian

desert, the invention of a New World. Talbot accepts, to
some extent, the validity of Prettiman's critique of civilisation, but he refuses his invitation to go with the Prettimans on
their savage pilgrimage. He renounces the new world offered
by Prettiman in favour of the conventional world and marriage to Miss Chumley. Prettiman plans to build a new
Jerusalem in Australia's red and desert land, but Talbot's
Beatrice, unlike Dante's, leads him away from the celestial
city. Perhaps this is wise, certainly it is worldly wise, but it is
difficult not to feel that the marriage of Talbot and Miss
Chumley at the close of the trilogy is a case of the bland
leading the bland.[7] The trilogy's final point of view is that of
the aged Talbot, evidently a very eminent statesman, who in
the rosy twilight of his years is full of mellow happiness and
generous forgiveness. It is, indeed, moving to find, after all
the battles and bitternesses of the voyage, Talbot 'remembering all those old acquaintances — enemies who in retrospect
now seem to be friends' (FDB p. 312). This has all the
appearances of being a thoroughly happy ending, but it is
perhaps worth pointing out that it is too late for Talbot to be
friends with Zenobia or little Pike or Colley, whose names
figure in the list of his former companions, whom he remembers 'without much emotion' (FDB p. 312). He seems not to
see or not to care that it is *he* who is in need of *their* forgiveness. In other words he is metaphorically as well as literally
back where he started, back in dear old England, a dyed-in-
the-wool reactionary and a self-flattering and self-congratulatory monster of complacency. Talbot's dream, which
he records on the book's very last pages, indicates that he is
haunted by the vision of new horizons of joy and brother-
hood held out to him by Prettiman. In the dream Prettiman's
pilgrims pass Talbot by on their way, he supposes, 'to some
great festival of joy'. The laughter, the singing, the 'honey
light' recall Wilf Barclay's final beatific vision in *The Paper
Men* (pp. 160–1). It is a vision of the Kingdom of God on
earth. The pilgrims have 'faces glowing as in a successful hunt
for treasure': they have found the 'treasure hid in a field'
which is the Kingdom of Heaven.[8] Talbot observes all this
from below because he is himself 'buried quite comfortably'
up to his neck 'in the earth of Australia'. His position in life

is, indeed, comfortable and his response to the thrilling idealism of Prettiman is thoroughly conservative and stick-in-the-
mud: 'The world must be served, must it not?'. Not rejected,
not changed, but served. This comes close to putting Mammon before God. The last words of the novel, the final sentence of the entire trilogy, 'Still, there it is', ensure that the
work ends not with a bang but a whimper, since they are, for
all Golding's wily word-play where 'Still' signals lack of
movement on Talbot's part and anticipates the silence which
follows hard upon it, an expression of notable blandness and
complacency (FDB pp. 312–3).

One's final judgement on Talbot depends, of course, on
one's own position, for readers of novels are also like voyagers or navigators. Perhaps it is not difficult from the angle
on Talbot in the above paragraph for the reader to work out
roughly where the author of this text stands. The experience
of reading literature, however, would be less enriching if we
did not attempt to stand outside of ourselves, as it were, try
to judge works or characters from positions which are not
our own, try to achieve a kind of parallax view. With this in
mind then, it might be said that the trilogy, despite its elaborate fancy dress, is very much a work of its time, of the
nineteen-eighties, of the Thatcher era. Thus, the promises and
ideals of egalitarianism and socialism, however inspiring and
fine-sounding they may be, lead only into a wilderness. The
world (which in this context connotes human nature) inevitably defeats such enthusiasms, such dreams. The surest
route to happiness is to 'serve' the world and the best form of
service to the world (in the sense of the community or one's
nation) is to conform to the norms of human nature and
pursue one's own happiness and to seek to ensure that the
freedom to pursue one's own happiness (at least in the sense
of making money) is defended against all other rights and
claims. This is a realistic world-view; socialistic world-views
are dreamy, 'poetic', romantic. All competing theories have
now been disproven and we may proceed with certainty. It
would be very difficult to deny that a reading of the trilogy
could easily be constructed which was in broad conformity
with the spirit of the age.

Prettiman's projected journey into the outback, his attempt

to build an ideal community with the assistance of the criminal rejects of a very imperfect one, may be romantic in the sense of fabulous or lacking any foundation in reality, but it is also Romantic in its turning away from corrupt civilisation towards undefiled nature and in its idealistic optimism about human nature, perhaps calling to mind specifically the schemes of the young Wordsworth and Coleridge to found a 'Pantisocratic' community in the wilds of America. The theme of Romantic *versus* Augustan, easily detectable in *Rites of Passage*, is continued through the rest of the trilogy. One of the most notable changes which Talbot undergoes in the course of the voyage is that he comes to admire Colley, at least with regard to his gifts as a writer. Indeed, though Talbot himself could hardly be expected to think in these terms, his insight into the sources of power in Colley's writing portray the poor man as an archetypal Romantic artist: his 'very innocence, his suffering and his need for a friend if only a piece of paper, gave his writing a force which I can admire but not imitate' (CQ p. 69). Artistic achievement comes through pain, through the sorrows of a man alienated from his fellow men, and it does not come through imitation. The Wordsworthian valorising of innocence appears also in the incident of Mrs East's song. Talbot is moved to public tears by the artless rendition of a song 'simple as a hedge rose' by a woman of the lower orders, 'clad in the simplest of dresses' and 'childlike' in appearance. This humble folk-art has a profound effect on Talbot, an effect of which a Romantic artist would certainly approve; it widens his horizons of feeling: 'it admitted *me* to halls, caverns, open spaces, new palaces of feeling' (CQ p. 116). It is worthy of note in this regard that Miss Chumley criticises Mrs East's song on the basis of established notions of how things should be done: ' "Our singing master . . . would have wished more tremolo and of course a more practised presentation" ' (CQ p. 117). She would prefer less innocence, more convention, more artifice. Her objections appear footling, however, in the context of the powerful, indeed revelatory, effect which Mrs East's singing has upon Talbot. She openly declares her preference for Art over Nature, since as an orphan she sees that 'orphans are the victims of Nature and that Art is their resource and hope'

(CQ p. 118). Despite her own suggestion that this is an 'adult' view of the matter, it is possible to turn this remark against her, since she uses a fair degree of artfulness to ensnare Talbot, a man of considerable resources. They are, in the last analysis, a well-matched pair.

Miss Chumley asks Talbot not to tell Lady Somerset that she has spoken a word against nature ' "for it is fashionable nowadays to believe in Nature" ' (CQ p. 118) and Lady Somerset is a leading votary of that deity or, it would perhaps be more accurate to say, a dedicated follower of fashion, since her enthusiasm for nature seems to be as much an affectation as that of Dickens's Mrs Skewton in *Dombey and Son*, from which model of artificiality posing as nature it is tempting to believe she may have been drawn. Lady Somerset, as was noted above, is specifically a devotee of the poetry (and, one might well imagine, of the *persona*) of Byron. This may in itself be evidence of the faddish quality of Lady Somerset's nature-worship since that found in Byron's own poetry has often been thought to convey a strong sense of insincerity and affectation. Byron is, indeed, a most interesting and beguiling figure to ask us to think of in the context of Talbot's voyage, since he embodies in himself the struggle of Romantic against Augustan. In some ways the quintessential Romantic artist, he was nonetheless the mocker of Wordsworth and the admirer of Pope. His gushy apostrophe to Ocean quoted (anachronistically) by Lady Somerset (CQ p. 98)[9] may ignore, as Golding does not, the emetic qualities of the oceanic roll, but Byron himself, in a later and ironic phase, will have Juan's declaration of eternal love for Donna Julia cut short by the appalling retching of a bout of seasickness.[10] The Byron of *Childe Harold's Pilgrimage* may have helped to popularise nature-worship, but the Byron of *Don Juan* brilliantly undermines faith in the benevolence of all things natural. So that when Talbot wittily describes himself as 'relieving nature into Lord Byron's "dark blue ocean" ' (CQ p. 102) he pokes fun at the author of *Don Juan* in a highly Juanesque fashion.

In the opening pages of the second volume of the trilogy Talbot casts about to find a suitable hero for his journal: 'I need a hero' and again 'Wanted! A hero' (CQ pp. 7–8). This too has a Byronic ring to it. The first words of *Don Juan*, after the dedicatory verses, are 'I WANT a hero'.[11] Byron playfully varies the old saw about the hero and his valet in *Beppo*: 'In short, he was a perfect cavaliero,/And to his very valet seem'd a hero'.[12] *Don Juan* tends to force upon one the view that heroism, in love, in war, in shipwreck, does not stand much looking into. The examination of heroism in Golding's trilogy has something of this Juanesque quality.

When *Alcyone* is first sighted through the mist she is wrongly identified as an enemy ship: this gives Talbot the chance to observe the heroism of war (literally) at close quarters and to try his own heroism. He gains great credit for bravery by volunteering to join Jack Deverel in the boarding party, but as the unidentified vessel comes toward them through night and fog his feet, unbeknownst to anyone else aboard, are rooted to the spot with fear. Deverel is prepared to face anything, it seems, but his advice to Talbot on the finer points of naval warfare shows that such heroism has its grotesque aspects:

> 'Kick 'em in the balls, it's as good as anything. Mind your own . . . But it'll be all over in seconds one way or another. Nobody goes on fighting — that's only in books and the gazette.'
> 'The devil.'
> 'If you're alive after one minute you'll be a hero.' (CQ p. 46)

The heroism of naval warfare is not as represented from a safe distance in books and newspapers. It resembles a playground fight. Deverel, moreover, is emboldened by rum: Talbot is almost knocked over by a whiff of the man's breath. 'Heroics and rum!' writes Talbot (CQ p. 47). The noble courage of the warrior has a somewhat base support in stupefying liquor. Summers suggests to Captain Anderson that some heartening message be passed to the men before the engagement and Anderson agrees to remind them of 'the unforgettable signal' given by Nelson at Trafalgar, but perhaps fearing that talk of England and duty may cut no ice with his own motley crew he adds a message of his own: ' "Remind them of prize money" ' (CQ p. 47).

Deverel is willing to play the hero when self-advancement is at the stake, when a moment of Dutch courage will suffice, but is found sorely lacking when it comes to the everyday heroism of standing and waiting, of maintaining a constant vigilance over the ship and against the sea. Indeed, it is his inability to stand the wait for his next drink which puts the ship in such mortal danger. The flashy heroism of a Dashing Jack Deverel is shown to be worth little beside the unfailing care in the face of grave and unremitting danger shown by Charles Summers or, indeed, the unquenchable vivacity and remarkable ingenuity shown by the officer who replaces Jack Deverel, Lieutenant Benét. Benét is, of course, another flashy figure and Talbot tries to present this ambitious, handsome and gifted young man in as bad a light as possible. Benét's successes in ship-management make him the favourite of Captain Anderson and even the good Charles Summers is moved to bitter envy of his rival. In the rivalry of the two lieutenants an old theme of Golding's appears yet again, the struggle between the religious and scientific world-views.

Benét is positively brim-full of ingenious and innovative scientific ideas to improve the lot of the ship's people and rescue them from their predicament. Summers, on the other hand, is a devout Methodist who, although an entirely dutiful officer and admirable man, is much more old-fashioned than Benét. Benét's ingenuity and dash gain the favour of Captain Anderson, who is convinced that the young officer will go far, much farther than the plodding Summers, whom he slights. Indeed, it is interesting to compare Benét and Summers with the original types of science and spirituality in Golding, Simon and Piggy. In *Lord of the Flies* it is the scientific Piggy who is the slow-moving and unattractive one, while Simon has a certain glamour. But in the trilogy it is as if Benét, the scientist, had stolen all the glamour from the religious side, a not inappropriate emblem of how things stand between the two world-views in the modern world. One might, indeed, argue that Benét finally destroys his rival altogether, for it is surely the fire employed by Benét in repairing the mast which ultimately breaks out and immolates Summers, who goes down (or is it up?), dutiful to the end, with his ship. This ultimate triumph for Benét is, of course, a tainted one, since it involves the killing, however accidental, of a good man, a death which recalls, as Stephen Medcalf points out, that of

Matty in *Darkness Visible*.[13] Summers is killed by the 'fire
down below' kindled by Benét and this title-phrase of the
third volume is anticipated in *Close Quarters* by Anderson as
he is giving his opinion of steam-powered vessels: ' "There is
too much fire below . . . I cannot like the things. If they
should explode they might touch off a fleet like tinder" '
(CQ p. 99). Benét's scheme is thus associated with a scientific
or technological development which *will* prove successful,
despite Anderson's misgivings. And yet those misgivings have
their force, because such a development will lead to greater
power in *destructiveness* as well as to improved communications. Science may come as a boon and a blessing to men but
it also threatens us all with destruction: Anderson is, after all,
thinking of a chain-reaction. Similar reflections are provoked
by another of Benét's ideas. There is talk at one stage of
attempting to kill a whale, but the crew, Talbot records, were
not keen 'particularly after they had heard [Benét's] mad idea
for a harpoon with an explosive charge of gunpowder
attached to it' (FDB p. 185). This mad idea will, we know,
prove immensely successful, but will also threaten the anni-
hilation of the whales, an evolutionary disaster the full mag-
nitude of which we are only now beginning to realise.

The wholesale slaughter of the whales is attributable quite
simply to human greed, the desire to satisfy selfish appetites.
Benét is by no means an unpleasant young man, but he is
fired with ambition for himself and the 'fire down below' of
which he is possessed is the fire of lust, for Benét is a would-
be womaniser and does not care for little matters such as the
sanctity of marriage. (There is something of the young
Romantic poet again here.) When the phrase 'fire down
below' is used in the trilogy with regard to love, it is to
describe a love which is not selfishness or lust but loving-
kindness. It is Mr Prettiman who speaks of his caravan as 'a
fire down below here — sparks of the Absolute — matching
the fire up there', the fire up there in the heavens being 'that
love, that χάρις' (FDB p. 219). Of the two officers it is, of
course, Summers, who may be said to exemplify best the
imitation of divine love of which Prettiman is speaking. Even
Summers's finest piece of nautical ingenuity may be seen to
exemplify this. Where Benét's scheme kindles fire down

below, Charles Summers's stratagem involves pouring oil on troubled waters (FDB p. 135). Summers's self-sacrificing devotion to duty, which is devotion to the care of others, shows the spark of divine love that he carries unostentatiously within him.

From Mr Prettiman's point of view, however, Summers would not be the perfect example of his notion of 'fire down below'. For Summers, although as a Methodist he is a Non-Conformist, is far too much of a conformist in political terms to satisfy the radical Prettiman, whom Summers regards as dangerous, one whose ideas might stir up mutiny (FDB p. 223). To one so steeped in the ways of the Navy, the idea of mutiny is to be regarded with the utmost horror. Seen from Prettiman's point of view, then, the thoroughly good Summers is the devoted servant and defender of a thoroughly corrupt and unjust polity, a society which is simply ' "sick" ' (FDB p. 203). Under the philosophical influence of Prettiman, Talbot finds Summers 'diminished', a man whose 'devotion to the *customs of the sea service*' would not allow him to criticise his superior even when his superior was wrong (FDB p. 211). Prettiman does not hesitate to criticise authority and does so passionately. He has at least as much passion as Benét, he has 'fire' within him (FDB p. 219), but this fire is not selfish but idealistic, a burning love for others, a passion for social justice (which must, inevitably, involve social change). Prettiman is also, like Benét and unlike the prosaic Summers, an enthusiast for poetry and in his fulminations against the *status quo* he is reminiscent of the political voice of Shelley or of Blake, who wrote that 'the voice of honest indignation is the voice of God'.[14] Talbot remarks that Miss Chumley would 'always suggest, imply more than state — like the greatest of poets' (CQ p. 90) and this is rather the case with Prettiman. We do not find out in any detail his political or religious views. We have to piece them together from hints and fragments and there remains an essential vagueness about them. In politics he is some sort of Utopian egalitarian, but it is difficult to be much more specific. In religious terms it is fairly clear that he shares the *caritas* of Summers, but there are hints that his religious view is a great deal less conventional than that of Summers. He is dismissive of organised religion, as is shown by his enthusiasm for a quotation from Voltaire: ' "We don't pray to God . . . we do not need priests, we are all priests!" ' (FDB p. 205). But he also seems keen, on this evidence, on the idea that each of us should perform a sacerdotal role, transforming *this* world into the Kingdom of God, so that, like the inhabitants of Pindar's Fortunate Isles, we can ' "rejoice in the *presence* of the gods" ' (FDB p. 206). Those present gods will be our fellow men. For Prettiman ' "*that* is what this voyage is about" ' (FDB p. 207). The point of man's life, so often likened to a voyage over perilous seas, is not that it is a preparation for a post-mortal heaven but rather that we must try to create that paradise here on earth. It is through our own love that we fill the heavens with beauty, music and the fire of love.

That is a somewhat speculative account of Prettiman's views, but necessarily so. If it is correct, then Prettiman is a highly progressive religious and social thinker who would no doubt have got on very well with Blake or Shelley. His association with the poetic, however, though it has connotations of inspiration or sublimity (Talbot speaks to Prettiman of poetry as ' "a loftiness — man at full stretch" ' (FDB p. 218)), contributes to his association with dream and fantasy. When Prettiman suggests to Talbot that he should come with him on the great adventure, the quest for the true Eldorado, Talbot hears a wordless voice: 'It was the cold, plain awareness which we call common sense' (FDB p. 219). It is a Johnsonian warning of the dangers of imagination or fantastic idealism. Fire can prove deadly to such decent, ordinary souls as Summers. Prettiman's quest is for an ideal community and this will involve abandoning civilisation in the primitive surroundings of a howling wilderness, which sounds more than a little like the plot of *Lord of the Flies*. It is not certain, however, that Prettiman's pilgrims will end as badly as Ralph's tribe, but it is difficult to avoid the reflection that there is no such ideal community in Australia (or, if there is, it has been kept well-hidden). There is, of course, a *possible* world in which Utopia is built in the Australian desert or, to put it another way, one can construct for oneself a *fictive* world in which this is the case, but the fact that we are clearly called upon to think of what has happened in the actual world since the time of the voyage (in the matter of the explosive harpoon, for example) militates against the deployment of any such argument.

Prettiman the holy fool disappears into a wilderness where surely his community will fail, except in so far as such noble sentiments and such selfless courage as inspire his project represent *in themselves* a glorious triumph over that shoddy thing, human nature. If we use the real world to judge the success of Prettiman's venture, perhaps it is allowable also to suggest that it may provide a memorial to such nobility: in the very heart of the Australian desert there is to be found a Mount Aloysius. If the trilogy leans toward the view that common sense insists that Talbot is right to stick with Miss Chumley and the City of London rather than following Mr Prettiman to the New Jerusalem, it does so with deep regret and with a keen sense of the limitations as well as the power of common sense. In Talbot's final dream we may sense that, for all his success and happiness, he has, to borrow two fine lines from Seamus Heaney missed 'The once-in-a-lifetime portent,/The comet's pulsing rose.'[15]

· 10 ·

ESCHATOLOGICAL
·THE PAPER MEN (1984)·

> Do not let me hear
> Of the wisdom of old men, but rather of their folly,
> Their fear of fear and frenzy, their fear of possession,
> Of belonging to another, or to others, or to God.
> *Four Quartets*

> For what is a man profited, if he shall gain the whole
> world, and lose his own soul?
> St Matthew 16. 26

The Paper Men, published in 1984 after Golding had been awarded the Nobel Prize for Literature, is narrated by Wilfred Barclay, an ageing and highly successful English novelist, and its orientation is eschatological: it is concerned with those four last things, death, judgement, heaven and hell. Heaven is rather less in evidence than the other three, however, and the novel is anything but serene or autumnally rosy. Wilfred Barclay and his novel are horribly bitter and sour, ashes to the taste.

Wilfred Barclay's account of his declining years and his attempts at escaping the indefatigable academic biographer Rick L. Tucker is written in a style that might be designed to set the reader's teeth on edge. It is weary and wearisome, cynical and cynically unconcerned at its own clumsy and cliché-ridden nature. This is from the opening page:

I could also have pleaded that it had been my fiftieth birthday and that we had been having, quote, one of those long, continental meals that are at the heart of European civilization, unquote. (Come to think of it I don't know if that's a quote or not. Call it a clitch.) (p. 7)

This tired, couldn't-care-less style is reminiscent in its extreme awfulness of the 'Eumaeus' episode of *Ulysses*, in which Joyce places his weary and disshevelled characters in a narrative medium suitably washed-out, clumsy and inept.

> *En Route* to his taciturn and, not to put too fine a point on it, not yet perfectly sober companion Mr Bloom who at all events was in complete possession of his faculties, never more so, in fact disgustingly sober, spoke a word of caution *re* the dangers of nighttown, women of ill fame ...[1]

and so on, and on, and on, in this dreadful, jaded, would-be clever-clever manner. Barclay at times, as here where he is determined to establish the extent of his drunken excess, is a stylist of comparable gifts: 'If it proved necessary, I must sneak out of the back door — no, the conservatory was quieter — get to the dustbin, ashcan, *poubelle*, whatever one chose to call it and, not to elaborate, count the empties' (p. 9). Golding does not seem to want us to think well of Wilfred Barclay as a novelist, but the overall effect is to make the book pretty unpalatable: in this regard *The Paper Men* recalls *The Pyramid* and its unprepossessing central character and narrator.

Joyce in 'Eumaeus' creates marvellous comedy from the sheer variety and extravagance of his narrator's stylistic and syntactical gaucheries, Ollie in *The Pyramid* recounts some tales which might conceivably raise the ghost of a smile on the countenance of a person of a markedly risible disposition, but Wilfred Barclay, though he regards himself as one of nature's clowns, is a desperately unfunny writer of comedy. Barclay himself provides the appropriate response to the book's humour with the ubiquitous 'Ha etc.' with which he marks any near-miss at a witticism or comic turn of phrase on his own part. 'Ha etc.' is both an apology for a laugh and an apology for the absence of a laugh: there is certainly need of apology. Peter Green, who must be gifted with a preternaturally low threshold of hilarity, approves of the novel's lampooning of academia: 'Something of Bill's attitude to Eng. Crit. professionals, a mixture of high amusement and even higher exasperation, comes out in that hilariously funny squib *The Paper Men* (a predictably damp squib for those it satirizes with such lethal accuracy).'[2] *De humeris non est disputandum*, but this professional begs to differ. Rick L. Tucker, the young American academic desperate to become Barclay's official biographer, and his blandly sweet or saccharine wife Mary Lou are made fools of by Barclay in brutal and profoundly unfunny ways. Barclay complains that the Rick Tucker he meets is, as a novelistic character, 'quite spectacularly unbelievable' and that he will have to 'tone down' the original to 'produce a comically loathsome figure, recognizable and tolerable' (pp. 78–9). The Rick Tucker in the novel *is*, however, quite spectacularly unbelievable and is not so much comically loathsome as the object of loathsome comedy. Rick and his wife are, indeed, recognisable: they are walking, talking clichés, embodiments of a certain *de haut en bas* English view of the backwoods of American academia (Rick's university is Astrakhan, i.e. the middle of nowhere), boringly earnest, plodding, obtuse, humourless, flat and dull even in speech: '"Was there any sun, hon?" "Sun, hon?" "In our room this afternoon, hon." "Why none, hon, I guess not."' (p. 72). Ha etc. It is a cliché that American academics in the field of literature spend their time researching into ludicrously obscure and worthless areas and topics, but Rick, speaking to Barclay about his meeting with Barclay's ex-wife Liz, outdoes all: '"... You both laugh a lot. I'd like to research that"' (p. 45). Undergraduates at American universities or colleges, we all know, read for degrees in subjects that are grotesquely unacademic: hence the following exchange between Barclay and Mary Lou, referring to Halliday the billionaire who sponsors Rick's research:

> 'He's rich. Real rich I mean. He's read your books. He likes them.'
> 'It's nice when rich men can read.'
> 'Yes. It's nice for them, isn't it? He liked your second book best, that's *All We Like Sheep*.'
> 'How do you know the names of my books when you haven't read them?'
> 'I majored in flower arranging and bibliography ...' (p. 65)

Ha etc.

Barclay's treatment and presentation of Rick and Mary Lou reflects rather badly on himself as man and as writer. He dislikes and fears critics and academics generally, the sort of people who award prizes and invite distinguished authors to junket and be lionised at their conferences. At one such conference Barclay reflects contemptuously on the principles in the light of which academic critics operate: 'One was that you can understand wholeness by tearing it into separate pieces. Another was that there is nothing new. The question to be asked when reading one book is, what other books does it come from?' (p. 25). It is unsurprising that Barclay should feel uneasy at this latter principle, for we later discover that he has been guilty (accidentally, he assures us) of what would appear to be rather shameful plagiarism in the composition of one of his novels. Barclay feels that he has plenty to hide and that critics and the biographer Rick will pluck out the heart of his mystery, will discover the filthy truth: they'll publish and he'll be damned. It is perhaps also worthy of mention that Golding himself discarded three novels before *Lord of the Flies* because they were derivative and that much of his work can be shown to 'come from' other books. Rick and Mary Lou, for example, seem to be near relations of Nick and Honey in Edward Albee's *Who's Afraid of Virginia Woolf*. Barclay, at any rate, is very much against interpretation and against criticism, taking time out to warn the reader against finding any arcane significances or mythological sub-strata in his text:

> There was an ancient lady sitting outside the central door of three on a rush chair and spinning a fine thread. *No*, she wasn't one of the Fates, she was an ancient lady put there to see that none of the tourists who visited the place every ten years or so had a camera with him. (p. 121)

Despite this and despite his open mockery to Rick of the 'proper parlour game' (p. 59) of spotting quotations, Barclay peppers his narrative with references and allusions which send the critic scurrying to dictionaries of quotations.

Thus on a visit to Rome Barclay adapts J.W. Burgon's well-known line on the 'rose-red' city of Petra with a variation which aptly reflects the tone of his own novel: 'There I would be on the balcony, facing the dung-coloured city half as old as time' (p. 163).[3]

Golding creates through Barclay a dung-coloured narrative of unfunny farce and paper-thin characters. The ending, for which Barclay can scarcely be blamed, is of the sort that earns schoolboy essayists low marks and scornful comments. Barclay is still being spied on by Rick: 'Now he is leaning against a tree and peering at me through some instrument or other. How the devil did Rick L. Tucker manage to get hold of a gu' (p. 191). And so, we are to imagine, Wilf Barclay slumps over the typewriter, killed off in the process of asking a not very interesting question. Barclay deserves to be slaughtered by a critic, has this dreadful ending awarded to him by Golding because it is a fittingly rotten ending for a rotten novelist. The apparent awfulness of the novel is a commentary on the awfulness of Barclay, a damning commentary upon him as a novelist. On an alpine stroll, Rick produces a quotation which rather impresses Barclay '"... 'Two voices are there, one is of the deep —'"' (p. 83). This refers to some lines by J.K. Stephen that admirably pastiche and comment upon Wordsworth:

> Two voices are there: one is of the deep ...
> ... And one is of an old half-witted sheep
> Which bleats articulate monotony ...
> ... And, Wordsworth, both are thine.[4]

The same might be said of *The Paper Men*. The surface voice, as it were, is that of the old half-witted Barclay (author of *All We Like Sheep*) bleating insufferably on, but there is also a voice of the deep, the presence of Golding, allowing Barclay to damn himself out of his own mouth as an artist but meditating on the perhaps more serious question of his damnation or salvation as a man. Barclay, whose theology seems to be as execrable as his style, comes to think of himself as one of the predestinate damned, but whether Golding would wish us to be convinced by this is open to question. On the face of it, Barclay is a thoroughly bad number in a thoroughly bad novel, but perhaps both have some redeeming features.

The darkness of revelation, the knowledge that he is heading inexorably toward damnation after death, comes to Barclay on an island, one of the Lipari Islands, to which he has fled in his mad fugue from Rick Tucker and his own past. That this cataclysmic event should occur on an island is perhaps not without significance. The novel chronicles the progressive islanding or isolation of its narrator, opening with Barclay's feckless attempt, thwarted by Tucker, at destroying the evidence of past sins and the consequent beginning of divorce proceedings. Throughout, Barclay attempts to isolate or divorce himself from his own past and from relationships with his fellow human beings. His off-putting style even has the effect of alienating the reader. His anxiety-ridden isolation causes Barclay to see other human beings, who might conceivably offer friendship or love, simply as threats. So he runs from them and from himself, his own past, using the considerable weapons made available to him by his wealth to cover his trail, to hide the evidence even from himself. On the viewless wings of credit-cards he flies all round the world to escape his pursuers and himself, forgetting where he has been, at times unable to establish to his own satisfaction the name of the country in which he happens to be staying. His principle weapon in this willed amnesia, this deliberate devastation of his own identity, is drink: he is charioted by Bacchus and his pards away from the fever and the fret of his corrosive worries, but those very pards are devouring him, tearing to pieces the continuity and coherence of his sole self. The novel opens with Barclay, already a confirmed drunkard, waking with a hangover and coming to awareness of a 'black hole' (p. 8) in his consciousness, an absence where there should be a memory of the previous evening's proceedings, a sheer gap in the fabric of time or memory blasted by the dynamite of alcohol. This 'black hole', like the black holes in the fabric of space which seem to hold a fascination for Golding, draws more and more of the matter and light that surrounds it into its abyss: Barclay's memory becomes a mess of disparate reels of film, its main substance gone into some great blankness. Virtually all that remains are memories of those things he wished to forget in the first place.

Drink and advancing age island Barclay in a kind of no-time, a shifting phantasmagoria without sequence or coherence. His nomadic, rootless, footloose lifestyle lands him also in an everchanging, neverchanging no-place, an uncountry of indistinguishable motorway, *autobahn*, *autoroute*, *autostrada*:

> The relatively cheap but also efficient milieu of the motorway in every country, its spiritual emptiness, its pretence of shifting you to another place while all the time keeping you motionless on the same concrete waste — that kind of internationalism became my way of life, my homeland if you like. (p. 26)

This concrete waste land, like the forecourt of Henry Williams' garage in *The Pyramid* spread over whole continents, embodies the spirit or lack of spirit of the modern world, yet it is also an image of the state of Barclay's own soul, his personal hell. Christopher Martin on his minute island is deprived of all the pleasures and comforts of the world: Wilfred Barclay need only wave his magical credit-card to be given the whole world, yet this profits him nothing because he has wilfully lost himself, has lost his own soul. Though framed in prose as bland as the furnishings of a motorway cafeteria, Barclay presents a touching and pitiful figure, a man whose most intimate human contact is with Swiss hoteliers and assorted other hirelings, who finds himself 'always' sitting at the same 'round metal tables' (p. 41). The iron of this dispirited emblem seems to have entered his soul: 'had I developed the chameleon's power? Had I looked like an iron chair or a stretch of stone wall?' (p. 97).

The title of one of Barclay's novels quotes from Isaiah: 'All we like sheep have gone astray; we have turned every one to his own way'.[5] Barclay has certainly gone astray, but his drunkenly aberrant state is perhaps more aptly expressed in some related but blaringly vulgarised lines of Kipling:

> We're poor little lambs who've lost our way,
>   Baa! Baa! Baa!
> We're little black sheep who've gone astray,
>   Baa — aa — aa!
> Gentleman-rankers out on the spree,
> Damned from here to Eternity,
> God ha' mercy on such as we,
>   Baa! Yah! Bah![6]

On his morose intercontinental spree Barclay the black sheep runs up against a statue of what may be the good shepherd, but a Jesus who has turned his visage to terror:

> It was crowned and its eyes were rubies or garnets or carbuncles or plain red glass that flared like the heat in my chest. Perhaps it was Christ. Perhaps they had inherited it in these parts and just changed the name and it was Pluto, the god of the Underworld, Hades, striding forward ... I knew in one destroying instant that all my adult life I had believed in God and this knowledge was a vision of God. (p. 123)

This visionary experience, later explained by an Italian doctor as a 'leedle estrook' (p. 124), is far from being a vision of bliss or heavenly light however: Barclay's spiritual emptiness is replaced by an entirely negative or dark spirituality: 'I saw I was one of the, or perhaps the only, predestinate damned. I saw this hotly and clearly. In hell there are no eyelids' (p. 124).

Barclay has found his maker but not his saviour or redeemer, rather his judge, executioner and torturer. If we accept Barclay's reading of his own life, we have a novel which endorses a theology in which God arbitrarily chooses souls who will be damned for all eternity and who cannot redeem or save themselves by virtuous action. Many people seem to be content with such theology, despite the plain fact that the God it posits is a devil, the supreme embodiment of evil. The image of that God which so terrifies Barclay has the blazing red eyes traditionally associated with demons and is indeed, as Barclay suspects, 'the god of the Underworld' (p. 123). The encounter reveals to Barclay something of the truth about his own unhappy condition, that he has made a dreadful mess of himself, is 'bepissed and beshitten', but his theological interpretation of his state seems to be highly questionable. Don Crompton perceptively points out that 'the God he finds is formed in his own image, encased in a rigid structure, its eyes burning; it shares his intolerance and regards him as its chosen comic victim'.[7] The statue on the island is an image not of his maker, but of himself, the state of his soul, what he has made of himself.

The statue's eyes are a burning red, like those of the colossal boozer that Barclay is. The church and the statue, possibly a gift from the Mafia we are told, seem to be in pretty execrable taste, an analogue to Barclay's own style and a commentary, perhaps, on his sin of squandering the talent given him on increasingly banal and sloppy pot-boilers. The God imaged by the statue is described by Barclay himself, using Blake's phrase, as 'old nobodaddy' (p. 126), nobody's daddy, not a loving father at all but a crucifier of his own son and a torturer of his many human children. Barclay is a negligent failure as a father to his daughter and refers to Rick Tucker as 'son' as he puts him through a 'rite of passage' (p. 147) which is actually a kind of psychological crucifixion. At bottom, Barclay punishes Rick for Barclay's sins and then proceeds to cheat him of his inheritance. Barclay too is old nobodaddy, violently intolerant of Rick, of homosexuals (he is generous to Johnny St John John just to get him out of sight), even of himself.

It is the central paradox of Barclay's nature that he is both self-centred and extremely hard on himself, that he evades responsibility and yet condemns himself to eternal perdition. On his second visit to the Weisswald he borrows an abandoned t-shirt bearing the motto 'TRY ME' (p. 134) and it is characteristic of him to put himself on trial and find himself guilty. Faced with the certainty of guilt and condemnation there is nothing to do but run away into the uncountry of the motorway and the black holes of drunkenness, though these actions tend in the long run to make things worse, to exacerbate the guilt. Barclay's God reflects this paradoxical nature: he is justice without mercy, but he provides an excuse for Barclay. Barclay's God predestined him to sin and hell, so Barclay's personal guilt is very much extenuated. Barclay in some pickle or other claims 'it was all the fault of Halliday' (p. 103), the billionaire who at times seems to represent the vengeful God who will not let him go. Barclay's sense of justice forces him to see that in various ways he has done wrong, has gone astray, but he seems to have very little capacity for mercy and forgiveness and exaggerates his guilt, takes the blame out of all sense and reason. He simply cannot bear or cure the terrible guilt which his own wrongdoing has brought upon him and fears an increase in that guilt and shame should an inquisitive world come to know of his sins: like Macbeth, he cannot bear to think what he has done and dares not look upon it, but the tragic fact is that he *is* what he has done and in the end cannot avoid seeing that: 'in hell there are no eyelids'.

Running away has always been Barclay's way of coping with life, even in his youthful rugby-playing days: 'Running. Always running, a wing three running in panic lest I should be grabbed by some enormous oaf from the scrum — ' (p. 54). He is a habitual worrier, suffers from chronic anxiety, a dreadful gnawing fear of some imagined worst, being caught, being exposed, being damned. His anxiety-ridden view of the world is capable of interpreting or twisting events and circumstances in ways that are madly suspicious and intensify the all-pervasive worry, as here where he is wondering how Rick could have traced him to Rome: 'Customs had been indifferent, a young man who opened the passport and shut it again without looking — or had that been deliberate, to lull me into a *sense* of his indifference?' (p. 98). He has just 'seen' Rick in Rome where, common-sense should tell him, Rick could not have been: there is no comfort to be had from reality, reality is becoming the creation or embodiment of Barclay's fears. So too the three-times-real reality of spiritual things, in which realm Barclay conjures up a God who is certain to deliver the worst imaginable. The hypochondriac fears that some terrible disease is about to take him over, torture him and kill him, but fails to see that his fear is itself the disease. So Barclay fears heights, his own novelistic gifts, critics, human relationships in general (he admires a round-the-world solo yachtsman 'because his voyage was so like mine, an attempt to avoid everything' (p. 28)), life, death and a God who has decided from all eternity that Barclay's lot will be the everlasting fire, but cannot see that his state of fear and anxiety is itself a hell. His is a hell of intense loneliness, cut off from and desperately afraid of the touch of other human beings. The loneliness is hellish, yet an end to that loneliness and isolation is seen by Barclay as a hell desperately to be avoided. There seems to be no way of escaping this island. After the revelation or stroke Barclay's speech is for a time badly impaired and he speaks haltingly of '"My — sin."', but corrects himself '"Not. Sin. I. am. sin."' (p. 127). The self-condemnation is absolute, but the strange phrase perhaps recalls the heart-stopping line in which Milton has Satan realise the full horror of his situation: 'Which way I fly is Hell; myself am Hell'.[8] Barclay's life has become, quite simply, hell on earth.

It seems to Barclay that Rick L. Tucker is a great source of danger to him, a constant threat, an everlasting torture. Though scarcely a devil, this persecutor of the unhappy lost soul is a pretty horrible character. Limited in his critical gifts, he will do *anything* to make a little beetle-like progress up the great dunghill of literary academia. He lies, making out that he is a full professor when he is no more than a research student, pretending to a friendship with John Crowe Ransom, announcing to a conference of fellow academics that he has 'a deep personal relationship' (p. 23) with Barclay, whom he has met once, and that Barclay had given his verbal agreement to Tucker's view of his novels. This mendacity suggests that his determination to research Barclay to the last dregs is not born of any idealistic passion for the truth, but rather a desire to make a living out of someone else's creativity: he is a parasite, almost a Mosca to Barclay's wily Volpone. He is a pimp and ponce, willing to offer his own wife to Barclay in the hope that Barclay in exchange will make him his official biographer. In this respect he might recall Jonson's Corvino, who offers his wife to Volpone in order to gain the Fox's legacy. As Don Crompton observes, Rick plays Mephistopheles to Barclay's Faust, offering the beautiful Mary Lou, whom Barclay associates in his mind with Helen of Troy, in exchange for Barclay's soul. Rick is staked out for seven years in his quest for Barclay by the sinister billionaire Halliday, an incarnation of mammon whose wealth makes him the veritable Prince of this World, a collector of lovely women and of the souls or biographies of authors. Rick attempts to lead Barclay to a high mountain and in a dream or vision Barclay joins Halliday at the pinnacle of the temple. It really does seem as though Barclay's soul is in mortal peril and that he is being pursued by scheming devils.

Rick and Halliday seem bent on capturing Barclay's life and soul, but from the point of view Barclay gains after his experience on the island they can scarcely be regarded as a threat to his spiritual well-being since he is supposedly already irretrievably lost. On such a reading their devilry would at most be to give Barclay a taste of the horrors to come. But Barclay's loss of his soul in the here and now, his truly hellish condition in this life consists largely of his alienation from others and from himself in his refusal to face up to and admit to others the truth about his own past. The God Barclay finds is a cruel, sadistic devil who has nothing to offer but intolerance and eternal damnation: perhaps the devils he flees have something to offer that might be salvific, or at least might point in some more hopeful direction. Rick is determined to save Barclay for posterity, to ease his elevation into the Great Pageant of English Literature, a secularised version of the Communion of Saints. Rick offers Barclay devotion of a kind, is prepared to do anything, including laying down his wife, for the man he wishes to claim as a friend. Rick's motives may for the most part be very unworthy, but his offer of relationship does at least point towards the sort of salvation needed by Barclay, encased in exoskeletal armour against the rest of the world and rotting away inside. Rick threatens Barclay's Dôle-ful isolation by offering a productive relationship and threatens Barclay's secrecy and self-alienation by his project of digging up and publishing Barclay's past, his buried life. This Barclay fears above all else, of course, but only by that mortal wound to his pride can he be cured. Rick and Halliday will forgive him his sins because they believe that great writers are above the moral law and Don Crompton has shown how scornfully the book treats such aesthetic morality. But forgiveness and self-forgiveness are the only hope for Barclay: again Rick shows the way toward salvation. Barclay must face the past and find forgiveness or remain on the island of torture, rotting away within his armour.

Crompton points out that Barclay resembles Christopher Martin in that, 'clenched upon his own sinfulness and self-regard', he 'vainly attempts to escape from a ubiquitous God',[9] a God represented by Halliday, who seems to Barclay to be everywhere, to be all-powerful and to know everything, even Barclay's secret heart. Halliday, though far from ruined in the financial sense, seems to recall the paternal God outlined in 'East Coker' of Eliot's *Four Quartets*:

> The whole earth is our hospital
> Endowed by the ruined millionaire,
> Wherein, if we do well, we shall
> Die of the absolute paternal care
> That will not leave us, but prevents us everywhere.[10]

Halliday is preparing a book on Barclay *in quo totum continetur*, a book of judgement. Yet he seems an odd sort of deity or representative of deity with his propensity for collecting young and beautiful women ('"... The old devil!"' (p. 66)), a quality not among those traditionally associated with God. Some religious thinkers have been of the opinion that God is above having qualities and attributes and that would help explain the fact that the page of *Who's Who in America* which should contain a synopsis of his life and interests is a total blank, yet one might also interpret this strange fact as evidence that Halliday's accursed name has been stricken from the book of life.

Both of the representatives of divinity whom Barclay encounters on his *via dolorosa*, the statue on the lonely island and the worldly ubiquitous Halliday, seem an odd mixture of the heavenly and the hellish, of good and evil, perhaps because they are, at least in part, projections of Barclay's own soul, externalisations of drives, needs and desires which the befuddled old drunk can scarcely recognise within himself. The statue passes stern judgement upon him and metes out the most appalling punishment, a characteristic we observe earlier in Barclay as he punishes himself with the filthy cocktail that resembles diarrhoea. He forces his own filth upon himself and the encounter with the statue shows him how foul his state, 'bepissed and beshitten', really is. This *rex tremendae majestatis* administers harsh justice without mercy, offers not hope but despair to the sinner, a devilish trick. Halliday, a potentate of a rather more worldly and easy-going nature, holds out hope of acceptance and forgiveness, is Barclay's hope, though Barclay also fears the price, which is the resurrection of his past. Halliday, through his agent 'the resurrection man' (p. 52) Rick Tucker, who plays or mimes Edgar to Barclay's Gloucester or Chamois-hunter to Barclay's Manfred as he 'saves' him from the 'precipice' in the Weisswald, would resurrect the rotting corpse, would redeem the sinner from his hell on earth. In Rome after his savaging of Rick on their second meeting in the Weisswald, Barclay, who is in the grip of the statue's absolute despair, describes with a sourness understandable in a man certain of his own damnation, the human trash on the steps that lead to his hotel:

> They were littered with dropouts, hippies, junkies, drabs, punks, nancies and lesies and students, as usual, and all of them were wearing guitars or playing them very badly or trying to sell the tin shapes they'd cut out and spread round on the stairs as necklaces or rings or earrings or noserings, there were carpets of artificial flowers and so on. (p. 159)

This may well be the truth about these young people and their products, but it is a partial, superficial and deeply intolerant vision, utterly lacking in forgiveness or charity. In a delirium or vision Barclay sees from his hotel-room Halliday standing on the top of a neighbouring church and in a second such vision finds that he himself is on the church roof gazing down at the steps:

> There was sunlight everywhere, not the heavy light of Rome but a kind of radiance as if the sun were everywhere. I'd never

noticed before, but now I saw, looking down, that the steps had the symmetrical curve of a musical instrument, guitar, cello, violin. But this harmonious shape was now embellished and interrupted everywhere by the people and the flowers and the glitter of the jewels strewn among them on the steps. All the people were young and like flowers. I found that he was standing by me on the roof of his house after all and we went down together and stood among the people with the patterns of jewels and the heaps of flowers all blazing inside and out with the radiance. Then they made music of the steps. They held hands and moved and the movement was music. I saw they were neither male nor female or perhaps they were both and it was of no importance. What mattered was the music they made. Male and female was of no importance for me, he said, taking me by the hand and leading me to one side. There were steps going down, narrow steps to a door with a drum head. We went through. I think that there was a dark, calm sea beyond it, since I have nothing to speak with but with metaphor. Also there were creatures in the sea that sang. For the singing and the song I have no words at all. (pp. 160–1)

This vision, which recalls those of Sammy after his encounter with Halde and of Pedigree as Matty returns to attempt to save him, seems to be vouchsafed to Barclay by the spirit of forgiveness, who looks down into the world and transforms it from ugly nightmare to heavenly light and harmony. In language that again calls to mind Thomas Traherne, the young people are seen not in terms of those personal idiosyncracies which might be regarded as sinful but in the radiance of their *haecceitas* or *Istigkeit*, revealed in this epiphany as souls worthy of and offering love. Their proclivities and activities which had called forth scorn and indignation earlier in Barclay, are now seen as part of their dance and music, their harmonious and beautiful relationship. Sexuality, homosexuality and sexual misdemeanours are of no importance in this world of radiant tolerance and forgiveness. The passage ends with an acknowledgement by Barclay of his own artistic humility.

Halliday, the spirit of forgiveness, offers a heaven that inheres in the world around us, even as the condemnatory God of the statue embodied a hell on earth of despair. Barclay blunders on through the novel's final pages still torn between his two deities, those lords of comfort and despair. He tries to make some sort of amends to his ex-wife but he is too late. She dies and at her funeral he informs the young vicar that he suffers from the stigmata (though he has never considered this self-punishment as any token of sanctity), but the vicar has a fairly nasty put-down for him: '"After all. There were three crosses."' (p. 188). Barclay has the stigmata of a thief, but that token is itself highly ambivalent since, as Vladimir points out in *Waiting for Godot*: 'One of the thieves was saved. It's a reasonable percentage.'[11] Barclay organises a last supper attended by his friend St John, but his cruelty to Rick on this occasion leads to the breaking of his club's statue of Psyche, an emblem perhaps of the death of the soul. But perhaps a misleading one, since Barclay is intending to give Rick the substance of what he wanted when Rick puts a stop to Barclay and the novel. It would, as ever, be presumptuous to pass judgement on Barclay's salvation or damnation. The novel, though eschatological, does not encourage us to look well to that last end which we must all face but rather shows us that heaven and hell are states we can create here and now within ourselves. Barclay, through guilt for sin, has suffered hell on earth or rather in the no-time and no-place of his derangement, yet a spirit of forgiveness has also shown him the beauty of heaven, of blessed relief from that lonely bitterness, guilt and despair, has shown him the gates of Blake's paradise. Barclay by the mere fact of writing his novel has confessed his sins, faced his past and the world. Rick's adventitious bullet puts an end to Barclay's agony and seems to tell us, more positively than the full-stop it prevents, it is finished.

·NOTES·

1

1. *King Lear*, III. 7. 81
2. Ibid., V. 3. 197
3. Compare *King Lear*, IV. 6. 4.
4. *King Lear*, III. 7. 81.
5. Ibid., III. 6. 74.
6. More, p. 20.
7. Alastair Niven suggests that 'Ralph's words are an uncomprehending child's expression of what W.B. Yeats wrote in his poem "The Second Coming"'. Niven, *William Golding*, p. 21.
8. Huxley, *Do What You Will*, p. 113.
9. Ibid.
10. Kinkead-Weekes and Gregor, *William Golding*, p. 40.
11. Huxley op.cit., p. 114.
12. Hodson, *William Golding*, p. 38.
13. Swift, *Gullivers Travels*, p. 190 (Book IV, Chapter 3).
14. Swift op.cit., p. 212 (Book IV, Chapter 6).
15. Whitley, *Golding* p. 43.
16. Swift op.cit., p. 213 (Book IV, Chapter 6).
17. Hobbes, *The Leviathan*, p. 186 (Book II, Chapter 13).
18. The importance of Hobbes as background-reading for *Lord of the Flies* is stressed by Alastair Niven. See Niven op.cit. p. 38.
19. Joyce, *Finnegans Wake*, p. 4.
20. Ian McEwan, 'Schoolboys', in Carey, *William Golding*, p. 158.
21. Whitley op.cit., p. 28.
22. Tiger, *William Golding*, p. 51.
23. See 'Copernicus' in *The Hot Gates*.
24. Hodson op.cit., p. 29.
25. Erasmus, *Praise of Folly*, pp. 198–9.
26. *The Tempest*, V.1. 275.
27. Milton, *Paradise Lost*, XII. 644.

2

1. Quoted in Hodson op.cit., p. 40.
2. Blake, *Complete Writings*, p. 211.
3. I Corinthians 13. 4–8.
4. Hodson op.cit., p. 4. Other critics have commented on the poetic nature of Golding's fictions: see Carey, *William Golding*, p. 133; Kermode, *Puzzles and Epiphanies*, p. 207; Page, *William Golding*, pp. 44 and 84.
5. Quoted in Medcalf, *William Golding*, p. 5.
6. Kinkead-Weekes and Gregor op.cit., p. 72.
7. Wordsworth, *Poetical Works*, p. 164 ('Tintern Abbey', l.49).
8. Coleridge, *Poetical Works*, p. 101 ('The Eolian Harp', l.26).
9. Blake op.cit., p. 793 (to Trusler, 23 August 1799).
10. *Biographia Literaria*, p. 169 (Chapter 14).
11. Quoted in Tiger op.cit., p. 18.
12. Raine, *A Martian Sends a Postcard Home*, p. 1.
13. Carey op.cit., p. 161.
14. Clarke, *2001*, p. 35.
15. Swift op.cit., p. 107 (Book II, Chapter 6).
16. Swift op.cit., pp. 220–1 (Book IV, Chapter 9).

3

1. Josipovici, *The World and the Book*, pp. 252–3.
2. Kinkead-Weekes and Gregor op.cit., p. 126.
3. Conrad, *Nostromo*, p. 409 (Part III, Chapter 10).
4. Golding himself has explained the significance of the name. See Kermode op.cit., p. 208.
5. Conrad, *Victory*, p. 303 (Part IV, Chapter 11).
6. Ibid., p. 307.
7. Defoe, *Robinson Crusoe*, p. 75. The similarity to Crusoe in general is pointed out by Gabriel Josipovici. See Josipovici op.cit., p. 243.
8. Defoe op.cit., p. 15.
9. An observation made by Peter Green and Samuel Hynes. See Page op.cit., pp. 90 and 126.
10. Defoe op.cit., p. 13.
11. Ibid., p. 14
12. Quoted in Hodson op.cit., p. 66.
13. Crompton, *A View from the Spire*, p. 173.
14. Erasmus op.cit., pp. 201–2.
15. I Corinthians 3. 18–19.
16. This has been suggested by Craig Raine as a possible source. See Carey op.cit., p. 102.
17. Huxley, *Eyeless in Gaza*, p. 20 (Chapter 3).

18. Ibid., p. 156 (Chapter 17).
19. Ibid., p. 406 (Chapter 54).
20. Golding has spoken of his respect for Huxley's 'cleverness'. See Carey op.cit., p. 189.
21. Hopkins, *Poems and Prose*, p. 24 ('The Wreck of the Deutschland', st.35).

4

1. Hopkins op.cit., p. 27 ('God's Grandeur', l.5).
2. Dante, *La Vita Nuova*, p. 59 (Chapter 20).
3. Ibid., p. 29 (Chapter 2).
4. Tiger op.cit., p. 156.
5. Dante op.cit., p. 41 (Chapter 12).
6. Ibid., p. 42 (Chapter 12).
7. Ibid., p. 109.
8. Ibid., p. 79 (Chapter 28).
9. Ibid., p. 48 (Chapter 14).
10. Quoted in Erasmus op.cit., p. 23.
11. Huxley, *Eyeless in Gaza*, p. 14 (Chapter 2).
12. Kinkead-Weekes and Gregor op.cit., p. 183.
13. Joyce, *A Portrait of the Artist as a Young Man*, pp. 65, 39, 155 and 156.
14. Byron, *Poetical Works*, p. 397 (*Manfred*, II. 2. 117).
15. Auden, *Collected Shorter Poems*, p. 143 ('In Memory of W.B. Yeats', l.55).
16. Ibid., p. 168 ('In Memory of Sigmund Freud', l.55).
17. Quoted in Hodson op.cit., p. 18.

5

1. Yeats, *The Collected Poems*, p. 228 ('Meditations in Time of Civil War', III. 13).
2. Layamon, *Arthurian Chronicles*, p. 210.
3. Jonson, *Timber, or Discoveries*, p. 38.
4. Carlyle, *Past and Present*, p. 62 (Book II, Chapter 4).
5. Page op.cit., p. 146.
6. St Matthew 7. 3–5.
7. Genesis 11. 4.
8. St Matthew 4.7.
9. Chaucer, *Complete Works*, p. 148 ('The Pardoner's Prologue', l.6). The Pardoner is quoting I Timothy 6. 10.
10. Kinkead-Weekes and Gregor op.cit., p. 207.
11. Browning, *The Poems*, vol. I, p. 404 (ll.42–4).

12. *Shakespeare's Sonnets*, p. 108 (Sonnet 135, l.2).
13. St James 2. 20–1.
14. Donne, *The Sermons of John Donne*, vol. V, pp. 93–4 (On St Matthew 12.31).
15. Welsford, *The Fool*, pp. 73–4.
16. Crompton op.cit., p. 45.
17. Welsford op.cit., pp. 68–9.
18. Lawrence, *Phoenix*, p. 22 ('Pan in America').
19. *Letters of John Keats*, p. 93 (to J.H. Reynolds, 3 May 1818).
20. Hopkins op.cit., p. 82 ('(Ash-Boughs)', ll.10–11).
21. Carlyle op.cit., p. 39 (Book I, Chapter 6).
22. St Matthew 7.1.

6

1. Crompton op.cit., p. 52.
2. Hazlitt, *Selected Writings*, p. 262 ('On the Periodical Essayists' in *Lectures on the English Comic Writers*).
3. Page op.cit., p. 173.
4. Keats, *Poetical Works*, p. 54 ('Preface' to *Endymion*).
5. David Skilton makes similar observations on the significance of the motto. See Page op.cit., p. 179.
6. Austen, *Emma*, p. 355 (Chapter 42).
7. Crompton op.cit., p. 58.
8. Ibid., p. 72.
9. Quoted in ibid., pp. 61–2.
10. Medcalf op.cit., p. 38.
11. Crompton op.cit., p. 84.

7

1. Quoted in Hodson op.cit., p. 6.
2. Ezekiel 16. 14–15.
3. Ezekiel 16. 20–1.
4. Lamentations 1. 16.
5. St Matthew 3. 11.
6. Ezekiel 1. 4.
7. Kinkead-Weekes and Gregor op.cit., pp. 280–1.
8. St Matthew 8. 16–17.
9. Elliot, *Collected Poems*, p. 212 ('The Dry Salvages', V. ll. 1–12).
10. Jeremiah 20. 7.
11. Kinkead-Weekes and Gregor op.cit., p. 283.
12. Ezekiel 7. 24–25.
13. Bronowski, *The Ascent of Man*, p. 374.

14. Kinkead-Weekes and Gregor op.cit., p. 283.
15. St Mark 10. 45.
16. Cupitt, *The Sea of Faith*, p. 106.
17. St John 3. 19.
18. Gunn, *Poems*, p. 16' ('On the Move', l.30).
19. Crompton op.cit., p. 117.
20. Revelation 17. 4–6.
21. Revelation 3. 17.
22. Ezekiel 6. 9.
23. Arnold, *Poetical Works*, p. 182 ('To Marguerite — Continued', ll. 1–4).
24. Sartre, *No Exit*, p. 52.
25. Traherne, *The Centuries of Meditations*, p. 153 ('The Third Century', 3).
26. Huxley, *The Doors of Perception*, p. 16.
27. See *Timon of Athens*, V. 1. 187.
28. St Matthew 9. 11–12.
29. Arnold, *Culture and Anarchy*, p. 129 (Chapter 4, 'Hebraism and Hellenism').
30. St Matthew 23. 27–8.
31. Crompton op.cit., p. 119.
32. Romans 3. 23.
33. St John 8. 7.
34. St Matthew 5. 27–8.
35. *Hamlet*, II. 2. 524–5.
36. Huxley, *Eyeless in Gaza*, p. 98 (Chapter 11).
37. IV. 6. 162–5.
38. Nietzsche, *Thus Spoke Zarathustra*, p. 84 (Part I, 'Of the Thousand and One Goals').
39. Blake op.cit., p. 761 (*For the Sexes: The Gates of Paradise*, (Prologue)).

8

1. De Quincey, *The Collected Writings of Thomas De Quincey*, vol. XIII, p. 369 ('Levana and Our Ladies of Sorrow').
2. Kinkead-Weekes and Gregor op.cit., p. 270.
3. Austen, *Persuasion*, p.120 (Chapter 11).
4. Quoted in Crompton op.cit., p. 153.
5. Conrad, *Heart of Darkness*, p. 111.
6. Conrad, *The Shadow Line*, p. 98.
7. Ibid., p. 81.
8. Ibid., p. 124.
9. Conrad, *Heart of Darkness*, p. 101.
10. Dodds, *The Greeks and the Irrational*, pp. 76–7.
11. Nietzsche, *The Birth of Tragedy*, p. 26.
12. Ibid., p. 83.
13. Ibid., pp. 24–5.

14. *King Lear*, IV. 6. 57–9.
15. Conrad, *The Secret Agent*, p. 147 (Chapter 8).
16. Bergson, *Laughter*, pp. 18–21.
17. Austen, *Pride and Prejudice*, p. 108 (Chapter 13).
18. Ibid., p. 139 (Chapter 18).
19. Ibid., p. 140 (Chapter 18).
20. Ibid., p. 107 (Chapter 13).
21. Ibid., p. 372 (Chapter 57).
22. III. 4. 147.
23. Austen, *Pride and Prejudice*, p. 58 (Chapter 3).
24. Spenser, *Poetical Works*, p. 100 (*The Faerie Queene*, II. 7. 8).
25. This was suggested to me by my colleague Dr Neil Rhodes.
26. Fielding, *Joseph Andrews*, p. 235 (Book III, Chapter 7).
27. St Matthew 25. 40.
28. Dodds op.cit., p. 277.
29. Kinkead-Weekes and Gregor op.cit., p. 277.
30. Ibid., p. 276.
31. Ibid., p. 277.
32. Coleridge, *Poetical Works*, pp. 365–66 ('Dejection: an Ode', ll.64–9).
33. Ibid., p. 298 ('Kubla Khan', ll.51–4).
34. Nietzsche, *The Birth of Tragedy*, p. 26.
35. Joyce, *Ulysses*, p. 144.
36. Blake op.cit., p. 158.
37. Wilde, *De Profundis*, pp. 26–30.
38. Byron op.cit., p. 627 (*Beppo*, st.33).
39. Ibid., p. 637 (*Don Juan*, I.1).

9

1. Roger Lewis, 'The Bluffers Guide to Autumn Fiction', *Observer Magazine*, 8 October 1989, pp. 38–42, p. 42.
2. Hopkins op. cit., p. 204 (Letter to Robert Bridges, May 17, 1885).
3. Stephen Medcalf, 'Into the southern seas', *TLS* no. 4,485, March 17–23, 1989, p. 267–8.
4. Ibid., p. 268.
5. Graves, *Greek Myths*, p. 106.
6. Conrad, *Heart of Darkness*, p. 111.
7. I ought to acknowledge that I have borrowed this little *bon mot* from my friend Tony Hennessy.
8. St Matthew 13.44.
9. Byron op cit., p. 251 (*Childe Harold's Pilgrimage*, Canto IV, st. 179).
10. Ibid., p. 663 (*Don Juan*, Canto II, st. 18–23).
11. Ibid., p. 637 (*Don Juan*, Canto I, st. 1).
12. Ibid., p. 627 (*Beppo*, st. 33).
13. Medcalf, *TLS*, p. 268.
14. Blake op. cit., p. 153 (*The Marriage of Heaven and Hell*, Plates 12–13).
15. Heaney, *Selected Poems*, p. 136 ('Exposure', ll. 39–40).

10

1. Joyce, *Ulysses*, p. 502.
2. Carey op.cit. p. 54.
3. Burgon, *Poems*, p. 26 (*Petra*, l.132).
4. Stephen, *Lapsus Calami*, p. 83. ('A Sonnet', ll. 1–9).
5. Isaiah 53. 6.
6. Kipling, *The Complete Barrack-Room Ballads*, p. 46 ('Gentlemen-Rankers', ll. 9–16).
7. Crompton op.cit., p. 160.
8. Milton, *Paradise Lost*, IV. 75.
9. Crompton op.cit., p. 173.
10. Eliot op.cit., p. 202 ('East Coker', IV).
11. Beckett, *Waiting for Godot*, p. 11.

·BIBLIOGRAPHY·

Arnold, Matthew, *Poetical Works*, ed. C.B. Tinker and H.F. Lowry, Oxford Standard Authors (Oxford University Press, London, New York and Toronto, 1950)
———, *Culture and Anarchy*, ed. J. Dover Wilson (Cambridge University Press, Cambridge, 1963)
Auden,W.H., *Collected Shorter Poems 1927–1957* (Faber and Faber, London, 1966)
Austen, Jane, *Pride and Prejudice*, ed. Tony Tanner (Penguin, Harmondsworth, 1972)
———, *Emma*, ed. Ronald Blythe (Penguin, Harmondsworth, 1966)
———, *Persuasion*, ed. D.W. Harding (Penguin, Harmondsworth, 1965)
Beckett, Samuel, *Waiting for Godot*, second edition (Faber and Faber, London, 1965)
Bergson, Henri, *Laughter: An Essay on the Meaning of the Comic*, tr. Cloudesley Brereton and Fred Rothwell (Macmillan, London, 1921)
Blake, William, *Complete Writings*, ed. Geoffrey Keynes, Oxford Standard Authors paperback (Oxford University Press, London, Oxford and New York, 1974)
Bronowski, Jacob, *The Ascent of Man* (British Broadcasting Corporation, London, 1973)
Browning, Robert, *Robert Browning: The Poems*, ed. John Pettigrew, 2 vols (Yale University Press, New Haven and London, 1981)
Burgon, John William, *Poems* (Macmillan, London, 1885)
Byron, George Gordon, Lord, *Poetical Works*, ed. Frederick Page, new edition, corrected by John Jump, Oxford Standard Authors paperback (Oxford University Press, London, Oxford and New York, 1970)

Carey, John, ed., *William Golding: The Man and his Books* (Faber and Faber, London and Boston, 1986)

Carlyle, Thomas, *Past and Present*, The World's Classics (Oxford University Press, London, 1909)

Chaucer, Geoffrey, *Complete Works*, ed. F.N. Robinson, second edition, Oxford Standard Authors paperback (Oxford University Press, London, Oxford and New York, 1974)

Clarke, Arthur C., *2001: A Space Odyssey*, Arrow edition (Hutchinson, London, 1968)

Coleridge, Samuel Taylor, *Poetical Works*, ed. Ernest Hartley Coleridge, Oxford Standard Authors (Oxford University Press, London, Oxford and New York, 1967)

———, *Biographia Literaria*, ed. George Watson (Dent, London, Dutton, New York, 1965)

Conrad, Joseph, *Heart of Darkness* (Penguin, Harmondsworth, 1973)

———, *Nostromo* (Penguin, Harmondsworth, 1963)

———, *The Secret Agent* (Penguin, Harmondsworth, 1963)

———. *Victory* (Penguin, Harmondsworth, 1963)

———, *'Typhoon' and 'The Shadow Line'* (Dent, London, Melbourne and Toronto, 1978)

Crompton, Don, *A View from the Spire: William Golding's Later Novels*, ed. and completed Julia Briggs (Basil Blackwell, Oxford and New York, 1985)

Cupitt, Don, *The Sea of Faith* (British Broadcasting Corporation, London, 1984)

Dante (Alighieri), *La Vita Nuova*, tr. Barbara Reynolds (Penguin, Harmondsworth, 1969)

Defoe, Daniel, *Robinson Crusoe*, ed. Angus Ross (Penguin, Harmondsworth, 1965)

De Quincey, Thomas, *The Collected Writings of Thomas De Quincey*, ed. David Masson, 14 vols (Adam and Charles Black, Edinburgh, 1890)

Dodds, E.R., *The Greeks and the Irrational* (University of California Press, Berkeley and Loss Angeles, 1951)

Donne, John, *The Sermons of John Donne*, ed. George R. Potter and Evelyn M. Simpson, 10 vols (University of California Press, Berkeley and Los Angeles, 1953–62)

Eliot, T.S., *Collected Poems 1909–1962* (Faber and Faber, London, 1974)

Erasmus, Desiderius, *Praise of Folly*, ed. A.H.T. Levi (Penguin, Harmondsworth, 1971)

Fielding, Henry, *Joseph Andrews*, ed. R.F. Brissenden (Penguin, Harmondsworth, 1977)

Graves, Robert, *Greek Myths* (Cassell & Company, London, 1958)

Gunn, Thom, *Poems 1950–1966: A Selection* (Faber and Faber, London, 1969)

Hazlitt, William, *Selected Writings*, ed. Ronald Blythe (Penguin, Harmondsworth, 1970)

Heaney, Seamus, *Selected Poems 1965–1975* (Faber and Faber, London, 1980)

Hobbes, Thomas, *The Leviathan*, ed. C.B. Macpherson (Penguin, Harmondsworth, 1968)

Hodson, Leighton, *William Golding* (Oliver and Boyd, Edinburgh, 1969)

Hopkins, Gerard Manley, *Poems and Prose*, ed. W.H. Gardner (Penguin, Harmondsworth, 1953)

Huxley, Aldous, *Do What You Will* (Chatto and Windus, London, 1929)

———, *Eyeless in Gaza* (Granada, St Albans and London, 1977)

———, *'The Doors of Perception' and 'Heaven and Hell'* (Granada, St Albans and London, 1960)

Jonson, Ben, *Timber, or Discoveries*, ed. Ralph S. Walker (Syracuse University Press, Syracuse, 1953)

Josipovici, Gabriel, *The World and the Book: A Study of Modern Fiction* (Macmillan, Basingstoke and London, 1971)

Joyce, James, *A Portrait of the Artist as a Young Man* (Granada, St Albans and London, 1977)

———, *Ulysses*, Student's Edition, ed. Hans Walter Gabler with Wolfhard Steppe and Claus Melchior (Penguin, Harmondsworth, 1986)

———, *Finnegans Wake* (Faber and Faber, London, 1975)

Keats, John, *Poetical Works*, ed. H.W. Garrod, Oxford Standard Authors (Oxford University Press, London, Oxford and New York, 1956)

———, *Letters of John Keats*, selected and ed. Robert Gittings (Oxford University Press, London, Oxford and New York, 1970)

Kermode, Frank, *Puzzles and Epiphanies: Essays and Reviews 1958–1961* (Routledge and Kegan Paul, London, 1962)

Kinkead-Weekes, Mark, and Ian Gregor, *William Golding: A Critical Study*, revised edition (Faber and Faber, London, 1984)

Kipling, Rudyard, *The Complete Barrack-Room Ballads*, ed. Charles Carrington (Methuen, London, 1973)

Lawrence, D.H., *Phoenix* (Heinemann, London, 1936)

Layamon (and Wace), *Arthurian Chronicles*, tr. Eugene Mason, Everyman's Library (Dent, London, Dutton, New York, 1962)

Medcalf, Stephen, *William Golding* (Longman for the British Council, Harlow, 1975)

Milton, John, *Poetical Works*, ed. Douglas Bush, Oxford Standard Authors (Oxford University Press, London and Oxford, 1966)

More, Thomas, *Utopia*, ed. Paul Turner (Penguin, Harmondsworth, 1965)

Nietzsche, Friedrich, *The Birth of Tragedy*, vol 3 in *The Complete Works of Friedrich Nietzsche*, ed. Oscar Levy (T.N. Foulis, Edinburgh and London, 1909–13)

———, *Thus Spoke Zarathustra*, tr. R.J. Hollingdale (Penguin, Harmondsworth, 1969)

Niven, Alastair, *William Golding: Lord of the Flies*, York Notes (Longman York Press, Beirut and Harlow, 1980)

Page, Norman, ed., *William Golding: Novels 1954–67*, Casebook Series (Macmillan, Basingstoke and London, 1985)

Raine, Craig, *A Martian Sends a Postcard Home* (Oxford University Press, Oxford, 1979)

Sartre, Jean-Paul, *No Exit*, tr. Paul Bowles (French, New York, 1958)

Shakespeare, William, *Shakespeare's Sonnets*, ed. Martin Seymour-Smith (Heinemann, London, 1963)

———, *Hamlet*, ed. Harold Jenkins, Arden edition (Methuen, London and New York, 1982)

———, *King Lear*, ed. Kenneth Muir, Arden edition (Methuen, London, 1972)

———, *Timon of Athens*, ed. H.J. Oliver, Arden edition (Methuen, London, 1959)

———, *The Tempest*, ed. Frank Kermode, Arden edition (Methuen, London, 1961)

Spenser, Edmund, *Poetical Works*, ed. J.C. Smith and E. de Selincourt, Oxford Standard Authors paperback (Oxford University Press, London, Oxford and New York, 1970)

Stephen, J.K., *Lapsus Calami*, new edition (Macmillan and Bowes, Cambridge, 1891)

Swift, Jonathan, *Gulliver's Travels and Other Writings*, ed. Louis A. Landa (Oxford University Press, London and Oxford, 1976)

Tiger, Virginia, *William Golding: The Dark Fields of Discovery* (Calder and Boyars, London, 1974)

Traherne, Thomas, *The Centuries of Meditations*, ed. Bertram Dobell (P.J. and A.E. Dobell, London, 1908)

Welsford, Enid, *The Fool: His Social and Literary History* (Faber and Faber, London, 1935)

Whitley, John S., *Golding: Lord of the Flies*, Studies in English Literature, 42 (Edward Arnold, London, 1970)

Wilde, Oscar, *De Profundis and Other Writings* (Penguin, Harmondsworth, 1973)

Wordsworth, William, *Poetical Works*, ed. Thomas Hutchinson, revised by Ernest de Selincourt, Oxford Standard Authors paperback (Oxford University Press, London, Oxford and New York, 1969)

Yeats, W.B., *The Collected Poems of W.B. Yeats* (Macmillan, London, 1961)

·INDEX·

Note Golding's novels and other well-known novels and plays are listed by title, not author. Lesser known works are listed by author.

Adolescence, 109–10
Adultery, 94–5
Aeneid, 44–5
Aggression, 26–7, 33, 40
Albee, Edward
    Who's Afraid of Virginia Woolf?, 202
Allegory, 90
Apocalypse, 125, 129, 133, 136, 139, 142, 145
Arnold, Matthew, 144, 147
Art, 43–4, 75, 78–81, 92, 118
Auden, W.H., 80
Austen, Jane, 111, 155–7, 169–70, 171

Baptism, 131
Beckett, Samuel
    Waiting for Godot, 199
Blake, William, 25, 31, 33, 43, 153, 176, 196, 214
Blasphemy, 92
Bronowski, Jacob, 137–8
Browning, Robert
    'The Bishop Orders his Tomb at St Praxed's Church', 92
Byron, Lord, 155, 192–3

Caravaggio, 129–30
Carlyle, Thomas
    Past and Present, 88, 103–4
Castaways, 5, 48–53
    see also Islands
Chaucer, Geoffrey, 111
Chauvinism, 12
Chiaroscuro, 129
Childhood, 1–2
Children, 127

Christianity, 58, 126–7, 172
    and paganism, 100–1
    see also Jesus; Religion
Civilised values, 8–14
Clarke, Arthur C., 40
Class, 10–13, 59–60, 75, 108, 114–20, 122, 155–8, 168, 170–1, 184–6
Close Quarters, 178–198
Comedy, 86, 164–5, 200–1
    see also Humour
Coleridge, S.T., 30, 31, 173–5, 180, 191
Conrad, Joseph
    Heart of Darkness, 14, 159–60, 166, 188
    Nostromo, 48, 178
    The Secret Agent, 165
    The Shadow Line, 160–1
    Victory, 49–50
Copernicus, 15
Coral Island, The, 5, 14–15, 50
Creativity, 44
Crompton, Don, 57, 92, 99, 106, 107, 108, 111, 113, 119, 122, 128, 132, 133, 141–2, 145, 148, 151, 157, 159, 207, 209, 211
Cupitt, Don, 139

Dante, 79, 187, 189
    La Vita Nuova, 65–70, 78, 110
    Divina Commedia, 185–6
Darkness Visible, 18, 57, 73, 78, 105, 125–53, 157, 195
Death, 59, 69
Della Mirandola, Pico
    Oration on the Dignity of Man, 70
De Quincey, Thomas, 155

Dickens, Charles
  Bleak House, 109
  Dombey and Son, 192
  Great Expectations, 119
Dodds, E.R.
  The Greeks and the Irrational, 162,
    173
Donne, John, 97
Drunkenness, 36–7, 42, 162, 168, 175,
    204

Eating, 50, 53–4
Egyptians, 122
Eliot, T.S., 108, 120, 134, 199, 211
Erasmus, 18, 58
Evil, 1–3, 7–8, 20
Experience, 44, 92
Ezekiel, 127–8, 131, 137

Faith versus reason, 83–6, 90, 95–6
Fielding, Henry
  Joseph Andrews, 171
Fire, 40
Fire Down Below, 178–98
Folly and fools, 33, 93–6, 98–9, 101,
    122–3, 139, 183–4
  see also Holy fools
Forgiveness, 212–4
  see also Salvation
Fox, George, 135
Free Fall, 15, 59, 63–82, 121
Freedom, 142
  loss of, 68–9
Free will, 74
Freud, Sigmund, 80–1, 149

Genocide, 41
Ghoulishness, 120–1
Glaucus and Diomede, 186
God, 56–8, 62
  see also Religion
Golding, William
  his boyhood, 116, 117–18
  post-war pessimism, 77
  as prophet, 40, 125
  his prose style, 27–33, 87, 109
  his prose style, 27–33, 87, 109
Gospels, interpretations of, 176
Greed, 53
Green, Peter, 185–6
Gregor, Ian, 30, 43, 48, 76, 90, 106,
    131, 136, 138, 155–6, 163,
    173–4
Grief, 128

Guilt, 75–6, 78
Gulliver's Travels, 5, 7–8, 14–15, 42–3,
    44, 181
Gunn, Thom, 141

Hamlet, 80, 97, 150
Hazlitt, William, 108, 176
Hell, 55, 60–1, 68, 71–2, 204, 214
Herbert, George, 61
Heroism, 193–4
Hobbes, Thomas, 9, 21
Hodson, Leighton, 7, 16, 27
Holy fools, 17–18, 34, 58–9, 72,
    130–2, 172, 198
Hope and despair, 19–20, 23
Hopkins, Gerard Manley, 24, 61, 62,
    64, 98, 102, 179
Human Nature
  filthiness of, 7–8, 14, 112, 150
  optimism about, 2, 6
  pessimism about, 42
  wickedness of, 1–3, 7–8, 20, 25, 42,
    127
Humour, 108–9, 157, 164
  see also Comedy
Huxley, Aldous, 77, 145
  Eyeless in Gaza, 60–1, 63, 70, 150
  'Wordsworth in the Topics', 6

Identity, 48–9
Igdrasil, 103–4
Illusion, 155
Imagination, 47
Indifference, 108
Inheritors, The, 4, 24–45, 51, 87
Innocence, 24–7, 33–5, 38, 90
  loss of, 1, 86
Intolerance, 136
Irony, 36
Island (Huxley), 5
Islands, 4–8, 35, 47, 117, 144, 204,
    209
Isolation, 36, 144, 209–10
  see also Islands

Jesus, 3, 17–19, 34, 49, 95–6, 98, 103,
    139, 146–7, 148–9, 153, 173,
    176–7
  see also Christianity
Jonson, Ben
  Volpone, 209
Josipovici, Gabriel, 47
Joy, 173–5

Joyce, James
    'The Dead', 79
    Exiles, 79
    Finnegans Wake, 10
    *A Portrait of the Artist as a Young
        Man*, 79, 80
    Ulysses, 80, 81, 175, 200

Keats, John, 31, 102, 109
Kermode, Frank, 88
King Lear, 2–4, 48, 49, 150, 164–5, 171
Kinkead-Weekes, Mark, 30, 43, 48, 76,
    90, 106, 131, 136, 138, 155–6,
    163, 173–4
Kipling, Rudyard, 205–6

Language, 27–33, 87
Laughter, 165, 166
Leviathan (Hobbes), 9, 21
Lodge, David
    How Far Can You Go?, 105
Lord of the Flies, 1–23, 26, 30, 35, 40,
    42, 50, 57, 128, 149, 160, 194,
    197
Love, 25–6, 64–70, 110, 183–4, 195–6

Martian Poets, 32
Maxwell, Gavin, 27
McEwan, Ian, 10
Medcalf, Stephen, 116–17, 194
Metaphor men, 32
Money, 50
Moral rules, 176
Music, 109, 110
Mystery, 130–2, 152
Mysticism, 145–6

Narrative, 159
Nature, 6–9, 43–4, 192
    control of, 39–41
Navigation, 180–1, 190
Nietzsche, Friedrich, 151, 162, 175
Nuclear war, 10, 13, 22, 40, 137–8

Obscenity, 21, 166
Optimism and pessimism, 19–20, 23,
    57, 82
Orwell, George
    1984, 76
Othello, 97, 164

Pandora's box, 45
Paper Men, The, 4, 57, 179, 189, 199–
    214

Paradise Lost, 44, 209
Paranoia, 41
Pastiche, 158, 188
Pincher Martin, 4, 18, 46–62, 63–4,
    73, 76, 151, 205
Pindar, 197
Pride, 89
Primitivism, 14
Progress, 38–40
Prometheus, 53
Prophecy, 17, 127–31, 133, 135
Prose style, 27–33, 87, 109
Purgatory, 55, 77–8, 124
Punishment, 52–4, 76–8, 95
Pyramid, The, 10, 39, 59, 106–24, 187,
    200, 205

Racine, 164
Raine, Craig, 32
Rape, 167
    see also Sex
Reason, 8
Reification of people, 12–13, 115
Religion, 15, 34, 66, 74–5, 88, 122,
    137, 172
    pagan, 93, 98–103
    pseudo, 134–5
    se also Christianity
Resurrections, 78
Rites of Passage, 10, 15, 73, 109, 154–
    77, 178, 181, 182, 188, 191
Reynolds, Barbara, 69
Robinson Crusoe, 5, 50–3
Ross, Angus, 51, 52
Rothwell, Talbot, 179

St Paul, 59, 149
Salvation, 21–2, 55–8, 97–8, 152–3,
    203–4
Savagery, 14, 160
Scapegoats, 99, 123, 147–8, 165, 167,
    172
Schweitzer, Albert, 139
Science versus mysticism, 15–16, 66,
    72–5, 194–7
'Scorpion God, The', 121–2
Sex and sexuality, 67, 70–1, 76–7, 113,
    133–4, 141–2, 167, 213
    energy of, 85, 92
Sexual sin, 54, 64, 90
Shame, 43, 45, 81
Shelley, P.B., 31, 176, 196
Silence, 144

Sin, 52–7, 71, 97
    externalisation of, 91
    inconsistency of, 151
    responsibility for, 64, 70
    sexual, 54, 64, 90
    see also Wickedness
Sleep, 56
Spire, The, 4, 15, 57, 73, 79, 83–105, 165
Stephen, J.K., 203
Survival, 51–2
Swallows and Amazons, 5

Taboos, 122, 162–3
Tempest, The, 5
Tiger, Virginia, 13, 67
Torture, 72, 76–7
Tower of Babel, 89, 90
Tragedy, 86, 164–5
Traherne, Thomas, 77, 145, 213
    Centuries of Meditations, 67

Treasure Island, 5
Trees, 31, 40–1, 102–3
Turner, Paul, 5

Uncertainty, 72, 98, 105, 129
Utopia, 5, 196

Violence, 111, 127, 142
Voltaire, 197

Wells, H.G., 25, 41
Welsford, Enid, 98–100
Whitley John S., 8, 12
Wickedness, 1–3, 7–8, 20, 25, 42, 127
Wilde, Oscar, 177
Will, 94–5
Wordsworth, William, 30, 31, 164,
    191, 203

Yeats, W.B., 83